Ancient Wisdom Explored

Part 1

PRABHU R

DEDICATED

To my parents

P. N. RENGASWAMY

&

R. PARVATHAVARTHINI

.

CONTENTS

CONTENTS

FOREWORD

Dhivakar Venkataraman,
Novelist and Writer.

"India's future lies in the past. Not in the recent past but remote past." said Sadhguru Sivanandamurthy. So, the Tamil's future too relies on past when Nayanmars, Azhwars, Great Sidhdhas and Tiruvalluvar who gave us for everything we need till the end of world. While people in the present age talking more on glory of Tamil language actually do not understand the real meaning of what they say. The glory is always there for every language. Every race has got their glorious past. But just saying those past without clarifying what the elders told in their verses is just utter waste. You should understand the meaning of Tirukkural; understand the meaning of Thirumurai, Dhivyaprabhandams; and many classical works they have written and sang for the sake of future generations of years to come. If we do not understand the minimum basic on these Tamil classical works, according to me, the life offered to us by God as human beings, is just waste.

Prabhu has clearly understood the way of life offered to human being by our elders and he has explored the same with meanings to our present generation through "AWE! – Ancient Wisdom Explored". A well explored and beautiful work which is surely to attract the readers as he gave in simple English and Tamil translations.

Prabhu has started the book with Thirumandiram written by Thirumoolar. It was told that Thirumoolar released his 3000 songs, one for each year, for 3000 years. Whether it is acceptable or not, the each and every song in Thirumandiram has high validity especially for human being. The purpose of this human birth is not only to enjoy or suffer according to our karma, but definitely to evolve our status. Thirumandiram, exactly helps the people to make themselves to evolve their status in other worlds or even making us towards without any further birth. Prabhu gave us very selected poems with meanings that gives every reader the essence of divine status. And his explanations through mathematical solutions to some songs surprise everyone. Yes, the true meaning is always to be explored. That is what he did.

On April 14th, during Tamil New Year Puja, I always open the new panchaangam where they calculate the timings of stars and thithi's were given for whole year. They also used to give a four line 'poem of prediction' of that New Year which is always fascinating me and mostly it happens as if what was said. This year too I read the poem first. Why I am writing this here, these poems are written by 'Edaikkadu Sidhdhar' long long time ago. Surprisingly, Prabhu has given in this book very elaborately on Edaikkadar and his work. Very good presentation and Prabhu must have worked hard to collect all these songs. His exploration is highly appreciated. It is a very worthful presentation too.

Tamil language is not only sweet and old, it has got a technical superb and this was well explored by many saints and poets in very early times. The grammar of Tamil was done by Tholkappier happened to be disciple of Saint Agasthya, who learnt Tamil language from Lord Muruga, it is said. Even Iraiyanar means the God, who happened to be a top poet during Inaugural Tamil Sangham belongs to unknown old period. Tholkappier who wrote grammar for Tamil language is even now followed by scholars with letter and spirit. In Tamil there were several new systems were derived and one such is Maalai Maatru padhigam, and first it was handled by Thirugnana Sambandhar during 7th Century CE on Shiva. Now Prabhu has given some sample of such songs written by Sambandhar. Mahakavi Kalamegham also wrote Maalai Maatru and in recent past Vallalar of 19th century wrote. Prabhu aptly gave us this exceptionally sweet treasure to make us enjoyable. We understand how difficultly the elders constructed the Tamil Language but at the same time how easily they themselves explored the same language for the future generations.

When we read Naga Bhandana classical works, we will come know how Prabhu worked hard to explore these difficult works by giving us illustrated explanations. I simply admire him not only on his knowledge on various parts of technology in Tamil but what is important is that he gives to others what he has gathered. This is a great quality.

There is plenty of sweet honey available for us to enjoy in this book. I wanted to write on everything Prabhu wrote erudite in this but it will become as another book. This is also a book for the children and students who look out for various information on our past glory. Ancient Wisdom of Tamils should be known to every one spread across the world. As I mentioned initially, by just shouting Tamil is oldest language and its glory was topmost among the world languages, will not work out with the youth generation of current and future. We should give a proper structure and that should be attractive one, to be presented to present and future generation. Prabhu has done this job. I wish him all success and expect more such works from him in future too.

Mahakavi Bharathi said the biggest donor, is the one, who donates his enlightened knowledge to others. "AWE! – Ancient Wisdom Explored" I can simply put into this title without any hesitation.

Bowing to the greatest language Tamil.

Dhivakar
Novelist and Writer.
April 2019

PREFACE

I got drawn towards Tamil Literature when my father told an analogy of a good deed done without expecting a return in favour will definitely provide a benefit in the future – (தாளுண்ட நீரை தலையாலே தான் தருதலால் – Thaalunda Neerai Thalaiyaalae Thaan Tharuthalaal) – Like the coconut tree that returns the benefit, holding on its head, for the water that is poured on its feet. It is a verse from Avvaiyar's Moodhurai. It fascinated me on how a noble thought of deed can be explained in such a succinct, yet, effective way. I started exploring the works of Avvaiyar and I am proud that Tamil people were forerunners in educating women and respecting them for their knowledge way before the rest of the world did.

As I delved deeper, it opened up doors to more enlightenment and knowledge. I was very much fascinated and amazed at the amount of wisdom that our forefathers had and how they used Tamil to pass it on for thousands of years through many hundreds of generations, the same way as they had realised during their time. The efforts to propagate the wisdom are huge, undaunted and persistent. They used palm leaves (olai chuvadi), sculptures, copper plates to record their knowledge that still serves a beacon of guidance.

They were masters in literature, agriculture, architecture, sculpture, medicine, water management, astronomy, morals and values, education, administration and more. The legacy they have left behind is a hallmark of their way of life. It is a pride to showcase to the entire world. As I started to read more and more, I thought that all this wisdom of our forefathers should reach even a wider audience, and that I should do my small part in letting the world know about our exemplary culture, language and the people who paved a great way of life for others to follow. So, I started writing a blog. I did not think at that time that I would be writing a book, though some of the readers of my blog encouraged me to publish the articles I posted in the blog as a book. And now, it has become a reality.

This book is, though, a collection of the blog articles; many of the chapters have been expanded, modified and added with the new information. The writer-reader ecosystem shapes the way a writer writes. At the time of writing the blog articles, I was naïve and did not have the extensive knowledge I gathered as the years passed by. So, I thought it would be right to revise and augment the chapters wherever it was appropriate.

I hope that the readers would support me as always and shape up my writing as an author. I believe with their help I would evolve to a better author in my writing career.

Prabhu R
Coimbatore
April 2019

ACKNOWLEDGMENTS

Writing is book is a herculean task and editing and proofreading them is even a daunting task. First, one needs the time to compose the chapters which will pretty much make the author sacrifice a lot of things. That could be the reason, where many such good writers have stuck to blogging alone. I too was of that kind, until now. I must thank many who helped this happen, that includes the blog readers who shaped my writing over the years.

I would like to mention the people who really put in a lot of effort and helped me throughout the process. First and foremost are my parents – P. N. Rengaswamy and R. Parvathavarthini. With their blessings I was able to complete this great task.

I must thank my elder brother Dr. R. Rajesh, who gave this fantastic title for the book, which is simply AWEsome, while I was settling for some dull, common title for the book. Next, I would like to thank my younger brother R. Pradeep; he was the guy who pushed me into writing this book. He proofread multiple times, which is a painstaking task and gave great ideas to add more content at the appropriate places. My wife P. Rajeswari and my daughter P. Vijaya were tolerant enough of my absence and being immersed into this authoring.

I would like to thank my sister S. Supriya, my brother-in-law K. Sivakumar, and my niece S. Tanishka for their support. I would also like to thank my family members – the in-laws R. Ambika, P. Meenadevi – who thoroughly went through the book catching a lot of corrections that inadvertently slipped my eyes. My lovely nieces R. Priyanka, P. Akshaya and R. Jayani who along with my daughter add spice to everybody's life in our home. The kids' welcome distractions forced me to take a break from the serious writing involved. I would like to sincerely thank my friends, particularly, M. Kannadhasan for designing the fantastic and vibrant book cover; K. Vijayendran for his wonderful insights and suggestions to rephrase and modify the content to make it more interesting and B. Krishna in reviewing this book.

I wholeheartedly thank and appreciate the help of S. Vijay Kumar, the author of the highly acclaimed book – The Idol Thief, who helped and supported inspite of being tied to his busy work. He is also the one who introduced me to Dhivakar Sir.

Dhivakar Sir is a very learned person and a notable author, novelist and writer. He readily agreed to read through the book and also write the wonderful foreword within a short span of time. His foreword itself shows the depth of his knowledge. I feel very honoured for the acknowledgement, encouragement and support he has given. Just the words of thanks would not be enough for what he did within such a short time.

I would also like to thank all those names whom I might have missed and all those people who work behind the scenes to bring the book to its form.

PROLOGUE

What is a language? Is it a tool to communicate with others? Is it just a vehicle to carry one's thoughts? Is it something man invented to express himself? Is it just a sound with design and method? Is it something discovered by accident? Is it given by God or is it mankind's greatest invention?

To me, it is more than that. It is an identity, an expression and it is what makes me who I am. It carries the wisdom of thousands of years. It carries the breath of my forefathers. It carries the music of the Kuzhal (குழல்), Yaazh (யாழ்) and the Muzhavu (முழவு) – all three types of instruments (wind, string and percussion) expressed using the "ழ". It carries the breeze of the Pothigai. It enables me see the The Periya Kovil of Thanjavur, the Gangai Konda Cholapuram being built. It makes me sit beside Kambar. It makes me argue with Nakeeran. It lets me converse with my granny, Avvaiyar.

It will make my grandchildren understand that there is love, there is hope and there is the world to embrace with affection when I say "Yaadhum Oorae, Yaavarum Kaelir" (யாதும் ஊரே, யாவரும் கேளிர்). It is the one link that binds the past, present and future. It has guided my forefathers for generations and will be a beacon for the generations to come.

The Tamil Language and the Tamil Civilization have wisdom, legacy, and invaluable treasures that could.be cherished and felt proud of. The Tamil ancestors were thoughtful, pioneers in many aspects; they taught the world a lot of things. They were masters in various fields – Agriculture, Medicine, Architecture, Sculpture, Alchemy, Literature, Philosophy, Astronomy and many others. The language they used is equally versatile, flexible and rich, that it has helped them convey the most complex, subtle and interesting forms of ideas, philosophies.

Only a few languages have the continuity with their past. Tamil is one such language, where the literature that was written thousands of years ago has been propagated as it is without modification for many generations and its pristine quality is still being preserved. People still enrich their knowledge with the wealth of wisdom that their forefathers left behind.

This book is an attempt to bring forth such glorious treasures to the people of the world. Some readers of my blog have already asked me the question of why I chose to write in English rather than in Tamil. My answer is that if I write this in Tamil, it will be localized to people who can read Tamil; however, I wanted to take this wealth of information to the world so that they will understand the legacy of the Tamil language and its people; about what it has had within it for a very long time – the rich, beautiful and vibrant language and the people who thrived under its umbrella.

With that, we will begin our exploration starting with a Sivavaakiyar's song

*****

கரியதோர் முகத்தையொத்த கற்பகத்தைக் கைதொழக்
கலைகள்நூல்கள் ஞானமும் கருத்தில் வந்துதிக்கவே
பெரியபேர்கள் சிறியபேர்கள் கற்றுணர்ந்த பேரெலாம்
பேயனாகி ஓதிடும் பிழைபொறுக்க வேண்டுமே.

*****

Kariyadhor Mugaththaiyoththa Karpagaththai Kaithozha
Kalaigalnoolgal Gnanamum Karuththil Vandhu Udhikkavae
Periapergal Siriyapergal Kattrunardha Perellam
Peyanaagi Odhidum Pizhai Porukka Vendumae

*****

Meaning – Worshipping the God that resembles the face of an Elephant; the ever-gifting tree of wishes – The Karpagam, The knowledge of art, books and wisdom will rise in our minds. I am starting to write this like a ghost. Therefore, to all the high, low and the learned people, I request to forgive and bear with the mistakes in my work.

1. Fascinating Thirumandhiram

Thirumandhiram, the name seems to sound like something that is involved with some magic, etc. But it is a great work that describes various parts of the human life – Birth, Living, Death. The book describes a great deal of Science, that really makes me wonder – how was it possible to ponder about such things at that time, having no modern tools or technological advancements as we have now. Thirumandhiram is written by a Siddhar (loosely a saint, rather a disciplined one), Thirumoolar, whose real name was Sundarar and then later due to reason that he had to transfuse his soul into to the body of a sheperd named Moolan, he got the name Thirumoolar. But what he has given to the world is an extraordinary piece of work, that even if he is reborn, it is a doubt that he could produce such a work. It is vast and cannot be explained in just one chapter. His work consists of medical information, human virtue, scientific terminologies and many others that one has to delve deep into it to understand and realise the truth he has described. For example, he states that human's have 10 senses, contrary to what the world believes – six. The song that says this is

*****

உற்றறி வைந்தும் உணர்ந்தறி வாறேழுங்
கற்றறி வெட்டுங் கலந்தறி வொன்பதும்
பற்றிய பத்தும் பலவகை நாழிகை
அற்ற தறியா தழிகின்ற வாறே

*****

21

Uttrarivu Ainthum Unarntha Arivu Arum Ezhum
Kattrarivu Yettum, Kalantha Arivu Onbadhum
Pattriya Pathum Pala Vagai Naazhigai
Attrathu Ariyathu Azhigindra Vaaray

*****

The five senses, Vision, Hearing, Touch, Taste, and Hearing are built-in. The sixth is "Common Sense". The seventh is the knowledge obtained by experimenting. The eighth one is the one you get by learning. The ninth one being wisdom of experience obtain using the other eight. The tenth one being attachment to the Supreme Being. And it takes a long time to attain all these. So don't let bad things disturb you in the process of attaining these senses.

Not only this, he gives the size of atom in the human cell, the position of the pitutary gland, the Higgs-Boson particle (The God Particle) the components of the gene (A, C, T, and G) and much more. The following songs illustrate such concepts he was able to visualize.

*****

மேவிய சீவன் வடிவது சொல்லிடில்
கோவின் மயிரொன்று நூறுடன் கூறிட்டு
மேவிய கூறது ஆயிர மாயினால்
ஆவியின் கூறுநூ றாயிரத் தொன்றாமே

*****

Meviya Seevan Vadivadhu Sollidil
Kovin Mayirondru Noorudam Koorittu
Meviya Kooradhu Aayiram Aayinaal
Aaviyin Kooradhu Noorayirathu Ondrae

*****

Meaning – To mention the size of the soul (the power that drives the human body), take a cow's hair split it into 100 parts and from that take one part and split it again into a 1000 parts, now the size of the soul is one of the one-hundred thousand parts split up.

In all, Thirumoolar's visualization of the power that drives the human body is so miniscule that it is just one-hundred thousandth of a cow's hair, which pretty much is the size of an atom in the human cell.

In the following songs he hints about the God particle

*****

அணுவில் அணுவினை ஆதிப் பிராணை
அணுவில் அணுவினை ஆயிரங் கூறிட்டு
அணுவில் அணுவை அணுகவல் லார்கட்கு
அணுவில் அணுவை அணுகலு மாமே

*****

Anuvil Anuvinai Aadhi Piraanai
Anuvil Anuvinai Aayiram Koorittu
Anuvil Anuvai Anuga Vallarkku
Anuvil Anuvai Anugalumaamae

*****

Meaning – The Supreme Being exists as an atom within an atom. Those who are able to split the atom of the atom into one-thousand parts and are able to see/reach one of the thousand parts, they will be able to see the Supreme Being in there.

*****

அணுவுள் அவனும் அவனுள் அணுவுங்
கணுவற நின்ற கலப்ப துணரார்
இணையிலி யீச னவனெங்கு மாகித்
தணிவற நின்றான் சராசரந் 2தானே

*****

Anuvul Avanum Avanul Anuvum
Kanuvara Nindra Kalappadhu Unaraar
Inaiyili Eesan Avan Engumaagi
Thanivara Nindraan Sara Asaram Thaanae

*****

Meaning – He within an atom and an atom within Him, seamlessly blending together is not realized by people. The incomparable Lord Shiva has permeated across everything in the Universe – the animate and the inanimate; the expanse and the void

In the following song he discusses about the DNA molecule and the gene composition

*****

நாலான கீழது உருவம் நடுநிற்க
மேலான நான்கும் அருவம் மிகுநாப்பண்
நாலான ஒன்றும் அருவுரு நண்ணலால்
பாலாம் இவையாம் பரசிவன் தானே

*****

Naalaana Keeladhu Uruvam Nadunirkka
Melaana Naangum Aruvam Migunaappan
Naalaana Ondrum Aruvuru Nannalaal
Paalal Ivaiyaam Parasivan Thaanae

*****

24

Meaning – The one at the top has four parts, the one below has four parts and the one in the center is common. All these form a single unit – Lord Paramasivan – who is composed of these nine components – The top four are envisioned as "Sivam, Sakthi, Nadham, Vindhu", the bottom four are envisioned as "Maheswaran, Rudran, Thirumal, Brahman", the uniting one is Sadasivam.

Though he envisions the genetic composition as the manifestations of Lord Shiva, it is comparable to the two nucleotides of the DNA strand which is the common Sadasivam. The four bases in each nucleotide – Adenine (A), Cytosine (C), Thymine (T), and Guanine (G) – bond with each other and form the DNA molecule. The A on one nucleotide chain bonds with the T on the other, likewise C with the G

His visualization of such microscopic details are amazing though he envisions them as forms of Lord Shiva, in a time where the technology to even see those weren't invented yet. He and his works stand as a proof that the human mind is all too powerful if harnessed properly to realize a vast amount of knowledge beyond the normal human comprehension. Apart from the physiological aspects of humans, he also describes about the practices of Yoga and how that would have a positive impact on the life of humans. He also discusses a lot of moral philosophy, righteousness and more. We will see more of Thirumoolar's Thirumandhiram in subsequent chapters.

2. Pythagoras Theorem – A Linear Perspective

Pythagoras Theorem, as every one would have studied in their high school mathematics or in their geometry classes, is defined as follows

"In any right triangle, the area of the square whose side is the hypotenuse (the side of the triangle opposite the right angle) is equal to the sum of the areas of the squares of the other two sides."

So, the hypotenuse can be calculated as h = $(a^2 + b^2)^{1/2}$, that is square root of $(a^2 + b^2)$. But there is an amazing theorem in Tamil, rather a statement to find out the hypotenuse without the use of square-roots. This was stated, by Bodhayanar or Buddhayana, even before the time of Pythagoras. The statement goes like this

*****

ஓடுந் நீளந்தனை ஒர் எட்டு
கூற தாக்கி கூரிலே ஒன்றைத்
தள்ளி குன்றத்தில் பாதியைச் சேர்த்தால்
வருவது கரணந் தானே

*****

Odum Neelam Thanai Ore Ettu
Kooru thaaki Koorilae Ondrai
Thalli Kundrathil Paadhiyai Saerthal
Varuvathu Karnam Thane

*****

Which means split the base (Neelam) into 8 equal parts (Kooru) and subtract 1 part from it and add half the height (Kundru) which gives the hypotenuse (Karnam). So let's work this out with an example. Consider a right triangle, of dimensions base 8 units and height 6 units so according to the Pythagoras theorem the hypotenuse is square root of (64 + 36) which is 10. Now let's try the same with the above theorem

*****

Divide the base into 8 equal parts so in this case each part is 1 unit

Subtract 1 part from the 8 parts so the remaining is 7 units →(1)

Add half the height which is 1/2 of 6 = 3 units →(2)

Now, adding (1) and (2) gives the total 10 units which is the hypotenuse of the triangle.

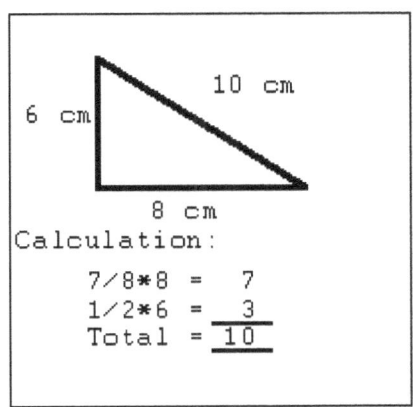

Right Angle Triangle and the Pythagoras

*****

Amazing isn't it? Also if you notice there is no use of any square roots, but simple basic arithmetic addition, subtraction, multiplication and division. The only condition for this to work is that the base has to be greater than the height. So we can summarize the above as follows. If x, y are the base and height of a right triangle respectively then the hypotenuse

$$z = 7/8*x + 1/2*y \text{ where } x > y$$

This works 100% accurately for all integral pythagorean triplets (i.e, the right triangles with dimensions that are round numbers like [3, 4, 5], [8, 6, 10], [5, 12, 13] etc) for the others it works with a reasonable accuracy

There isn't any rigorous mathematical proof defined for it, but it seems to work reasonably well!

3. Interesting use of Pun in Tamil Literature

Pun, called Silaydai or Iratura Mozhidhal – in Tamil, is one of the interesting things that could be often found in Tamil Literature. One poet famous for composing songs and poems with pun is the famous Kaalamega Pulavar (We will see more about him in the upcoming chapters). His style and elegance in the usage of pun is quite remarkable. He is even attributed with the name "Silaydai Pulavar". His songs contain the liberal use of pun. Let us see one example for it, the song goes like this

*****

முக்காலுக் கேகாமுன் முன்னரையில் வீழாமுன்
அக்கா லரைக்கால்கண்(டு) அஞ்சாமுன் - விக்கி
இருமா முன் மாகாணிக் கேகாமுன் கச்சி
ஒருமாவின் கீழரைஇன் றோது

*****

Mukkaaluk Kegamun Munnaraiyil Veezhamun
Akkaalarai Kandu Anjamun Vikki
Irumamun Maakaanikku Yegamun Kachi
Orumaavin Keezharaiyin Rodhu

*****

At the first reading of this song, the meaning might reveal that he has used all the unit of measurements in Tamil – Mukkaal – three-quarters; Arai – Half; Kaalarai – one-eighth; Iruma – one-tenth; Maakaani – one-sixteenth; Oruma – one-twentieth; Keezharai – 1/640

But the actual meaning of the song is that –

*****

Before you need a third leg (your walking stick).

Before your hair grows white due to age.

Before you fear the Lord of death (The yama).

Before you hiccup and cough to your death at the end.

Before the great earth to give you a place.

Go and Worship the Lord Shiva in the name Kachiappar residing under a mango tree in the place called Keezharai"

*****

Now, let me paraphrase the song. Mukkaal is a word formed by merging syllables of Moondru (Three) + Kaal (Leg). Yega means reaching, attaining, getting; so Mukkaalukku Yegamun - Before you yearn for three legs. Narai means whitening of hair due to old age. Mun – means front, before, Veezhamun mean before falling into, so Munnaraiyil Veezhamun – Before your hair falls into whitening phase due to old age. Kaalar – means The lord of death (Yama), kandu means found, see. Anja means fearing; so Akkaalarai kandu anjamun – Before you see/find Yama and fear. Vikki verb form of Vikkal – Hiccup, Iruma verb form of Irumal – Cough, so Vikki Irumamun – Before you hiccup and cough before death. Maakaani mean vast or big earth where kaani means earth, Yega means reaching, attaining, getting; So Maakaanikku Yegamun – Before you get a place for you on earth after death. Kachi Orumavin Keezharaiyin Rodhu – this requires quite an explanation Kachi means – Lord Shiva with the name Kachiappar,

30

Oruma is a combination of Oru (One) + Ma (Mango Tree), Keezharai – a place in Tamil Nadu. Odhu means praise, enchant, worship. As a whole the combined meaning is as above.

It is quite amazing to see such eloquence and adeptness of Kaalamega Pulavar with many of his songs involving pun. But he is not the only one; there are other poets who have mastered using the pun. There was an interesting event that happened between Kambar and Avaiyar.

Once, when there was a gathering of all great poets during the Sangam age. On that occasion, the two famous poets, Avaiyar and Kambar met. During such events, normally there will be question/answer sessions, debates, and song compositions held. Being such an event, Kambar used that opportunity to denigrate Avaiyar, and asked a question

*****

ஓர் காலடி நாளிலை பந்தலடி

*****

Ore Kaaladi, Naalilai Pandhaladi

*****

Normally, "Adi" is used to address females in derogatory tone or among friends or elderly people calling women. So Kambar felt happy that he addressed the elderly poet Avaiyar, the then great female poet, as Adi though not directly. But what Kambar meant to ask as a question in the song was to identify a plant, called Aarai that has one foot but four leaves. For those know about the Vallarai (Indian Pennywort – Biological name Centella asiatica), that is now used as a natural memory power enhancer and rejuvenator, is a relative of the Aarai family.

Let's see the paraphrase below,

31

Ore Kaaladi – Ore – One; Kaal – Foot; Adi – base, the lowest part, the surface beneath something. So, it means – Thing having One Foot at the base.

Naalilai Pandhal Adi – Naal – four; Ilai – Leaf, Pandhal – Tent having only the roof. So, it would mean – The four leaves forming a tent beneath.

So Avaiyar on hearing Kambar calling her derogatorily, fumed into fury and repeated with a similar pun answering his question

*****

எட்டேகால் லட்சணமே எமனே றும்பரியே
மட்டில் பெரியம்மை வாகனமே முட்ட மேற்
கூரையில்லா வீடே குலராமன் தூதுவனே
ஆரையடா சொன்னா யடா

*****

Ettaekaal Latchanamae Yemenerum Pariyae
Mattil Periyammai Vaaganamae Mutta Mael
Koorai Illa Veedae Kula Raaman Thoodhuvanae
Aaraiyada Sonnai Ada

*****

Meaning – You disfigured beauty, You buffalo – the mount of Yemen (The Diety who is believed to take the lives when someone dies), You donkey – The mount of Moodhevi (The elder sister of Goddess Lakshmi who is believed to bring bad luck), a roofless wall/home (Kutti Suvar in Tamil), You monkey – the messenger for Lord Rama. How dare you address me like that?. The last line is interpreted as a pun. With the second meaning indicating the answer to Kambar's question, "You mentioned the Aarai Keerai".

Ettaekaal Latchanamae – Eight and a quarter beauty – In Tamil, 8 is written as அ and quarter as வ, put together it would be அவலட்சணமே, meaning ugliness or disfigured.

Yemen – The deity of death

Erum Pariyae – Buffalo, the mount of Yemen

Periyammai – Moodhevi, who is believed to bring bad luck is the elder sister of Goddess of wealth, Lakshmi.

Vaaganam – Mount of Moodhevi – The donkey

Koorai – Roof

Veedu – Home

Kula Raman Thoodhuvan – Hanuman, the monkey God, here refers Kambar as a monkey

Aarai – Refers to the pronoun "who" and the plant "Aarai"

Sonnai – Tell, Told

Ada – Derogatory addressing of a man

Also **"Ada"**, **"Dei"** is a colloquial or a friendly commonplace expression used among friends or by elders to address men. However, in formal situations it would imply disrespect or a derogatory reference.

Aarai is also used as an interrogative pronoun – Who. And this formed an interesting incident, where Kambar got paid back through the same coin (The Pun) by Avaiyar.

Similarly there was another gathering of poets for a grand feast with the King, where one poet named Vemburaar (Person from the land of Neem) rushed in late to only find that he had no place in the feast. And the King remarked humorously at the poet with a pun.

*****

வேம்புக்கு இங்கு இடமில்லை

*****

Vembukku Ingu Idam Illai

*****

The first meaning, Vembu means Neem tree which is an indication of bitterness, has no place in this happy and august gathering.

And the other meaning, Vemburar does not have a seat in the feast as he arrived late.

Then the poet's eloquence and brilliance showed up, he went straight to the King's seat and just pushed the King a bit and sat in that place saying

*****

வேம்பு என்றும் அரசுடனே இருக்கும்

*****

Vembu endrum Arasudanae Irukkum

*****

The first meaning, Vemburar will always be beside the King.

And the other meaning, Vembu – Neem, Arasu – Peepul tree. In Hindu tradition it is considered as auspicious and sacred to have the Peepul and Neem grow beside each other. Implicitly means that Vemburar being beside the King is sacred.

There is another similar story with another poet and the head of a monastery. The poet was from a place called Kadaimadai that means the last sluice. The poet went to meet the head of the monastery and the head of the monastery jovially insulted the poet with a pun for which the poet repaid through the same coin

*****

வாருங்கள் கடைமடையரே, வணக்கம்!

*****

Vaarungal Kadaimadaiyarae, Vanakkam!

*****

Meaning – The head of the monastery said "Welcome! The poet from Kadaimadai– Kadaimadaiyar". In a straightforward way it means the person who belongs to the place Kadaimadai. The pun here is that Kadai Madaiyar would also refer to the last of the idiots. So, the pun would be "Welcome! Last of the idiots"

The poet's reply was

*****

வணக்கம் மடத்தலைவரே!

*****

Vanakkam Madaththalaivarae

*****

Meaning – The poet replied "Greetings! Monastery's Head", however the pun would mean, "Greetings! Leader of the idiots".

Pun used by poets not only reveals their literary eloquence but also exhibits their presence of mind along with the language bending skills to make the most out of the situation

4. Pattinathaar: The Tycoon turned Sanyasi – Part 1

Tamil Nadu has a lot of poets, siddhars, sages and many wise men, who, have left behind their experiences as the great wealth that future generations to learn and follow. However, Pattinathar is unique to list of great people that Tamil has as its pride. It would be surprising that Pattinathar was a tycoon who has business all over the world. He was born in an affluent family and yet he turned to be a Sanyasi. Thiruvenkadar/Thiruvenkaattu Adigal were his names when he became a Sanyasi. This series of chapters narrate the life of Pattinathar and the incidents that lead him to become a Sanyasi. Pattinathar has given us his experience and wisdom in the form of songs that we will see in this series of chapters. His works include Koyinaan Manimaalai (கோயினான் மணிமாலை), Thirukazhumala Mummanikkovai (திருக்கழுமல மும்மணிக்கோவை), Thiruvidai Marudhur Mummanikkovai (திருவிடைமருதூர் மும்மணிக்கோவை), Thiruvegambam Udaiyar Thiruvandhaadhi (திருவேகம்பமுடையார் திருவந்தாதி), and Thiruvottriyur Orupa Orupadhu (திருவொற்றியூர் ஒருபாவொருபது). Now, let us see how a legendary tycoon of Kaveripoompattinam (Poompuhar) turned into Sanyasi.

Pattinathar, also called Pattinathu Chetty, was born in an affluent tycoon family. His parents were Sivanesan Chettiar and Gnanakalai Aachi. They were so affluent, that in those days it was a customary that kings of the various dynasties and empires who rose to the throne will be crowned by the wealthiest in the country. And for three generations or more, Pattinathar's ancestors have crowned the kings in the Chera, Chola, Pandya and the Pallava Kingdoms. That would give us an understanding of how wealthy their family should have been. They had a lot of ships that sailed across to various countries in the globe for trade purposes. Pattinathar was born and he was named Swetharanyan. He had an elder sister.

Swetharanyan grew up as kid with lots of love, affection and lenience. He spent most of his time playing and studies were a far distant thing to him. Pattinathar's father was worried that his son does not study well, but his mother convinced him that they had wealth that would feed more than 10 generations, so why worry about their son not studying. A few years later, Pattinathar's father died and his mother had to take care of business. Though she was able to manage that, her brother – Pattinathar's maternal uncle – gave her a helping hand and looked after the business.

Swetharanyan, born in the lineage of traders, instinctively had the skills for trade. He picked up the nuances quickly and wanted to venture into the seas to get more hands-on experience about trade across the oceans. He became well-versed and later he was married to a girl named Sivakalai at the age of 16. In those days, marrying at a young age was practised. Over the years, he grew to be a man who can handle businesses himself and became the wealthiest trader in Kaveripoompattinam. Thereafter he was referred to as Pattinathu Chetty or Pattinathar.

For a long time, the couple did not have a child as the heir to their wealth. They went to a lot of temples but they were still not blessed with a child. They were worried, and Pattinathar's mother even suggested that he marry another woman. Though polygamy was common in those days, Pattinathar was not willing to marry another woman, as his mother had suggested. People in those days respected their mother's words and obeyed them usually. But Pattinathar expressed clearly, his unwillingness to think of any other girl as his wife other than his wife - Sivakalai. His mother honoured his wish and did not talk about that later.

Pattinathar had a dream one night. In the dream, he saw an elderly couple near Thiruvidai Marudhur, who had a young infant and were worried as they were not able to feed for themselves, and feeding and bringing up that infant was worrying them more. Pattinathar heard a divine voice asking him to travel to Thiruvidai Marudhur. He woke up from his dream and the next day Pattinathar and Sivakalai headed to Thiruvidai Marudhur. And when he reached Thiruvidai Marudhur, he saw the same elderly couple that he saw his in dreams. The elderly couple also heard the divine voice that instructed them to give the child for adoption and get gold and money in return to spend their lives in comfort without poverty. When the elderly couple explained about the divine instructions, Pattinathar and Sivakalai eyes were in tears and they thought that Lord Shiva and Parvathi themselves came as the elderly couple and blessed them with the child.

Then Pattinathar and Sivakalai took the elderly couple to Kaveripoompattinam and said that they will adopt the child and gave the elderly couple a good amount of wealth for them to survive through their age. Then they planned for the adoption ceremony of the child. Now, Pattinathar's sister, who thought that the wealth of Pattinathar will automatically be for her family as Pattinathar had no heir, had her dreams shattered by the adoption of this child. She argued and quarrelled with his brother. But Pattinathar made a firm decision that he is going to adopt that child and that child will be his heir. The adoption ceremony went very well in all its grandeur and they name the baby boy – Marudhavanan, in relation to the place where they adopted him – Thiruvidai Marudhur. They considered Marudhavanan as their own child and showed him a great love and affection.

5. Pattinathaar: The Tycoon turned Sanyasi – Part 2

Marudhavanan grew like a prince and enjoyed his life like a calf capering in the lush green fields. As Pattinathaar, Marudhavanan, like his father, did not show interest in his studies. Pattinathaar was worried that education is his lineage seems to be a curse. As far as he can remember, nobody fared well in education in his ancestral lineage. However, he consoled that his son will get to learn the nuances of the business and will learn to manage the property over time, as he gets older. Time went on, and one day Marudhavanan expressed his interest to set sails across the oceans to where Pattinathaar's business ships travelled.

Pattinathaar got excited that Marudhavanan is growing up to become a tycoon like him. And that, he can slowly educate him on the nuances of the trade, made preparations for his travel. He gave instructions to the sailors of the boat that Marudhavanan went aboard. And Marudhavanan set sails on the ocean to far off countries where his father had business contacts. Before leaving he promised his father that he will bring the most valuable wealth that his father has ever seen. In all the places Marudhavanan went, he was invited with a lot of respect and grandeur.

Days went on and one fine day, the ship that Marudhavanan went, returned back to Kaveripoompattinam. Pattinathaar was excited to hear the news that his son is back. He went to receive his son back home. Marudhavanan hugged Pattinathaar and happily exclaimed that he has brought all the treasures he promised. He asked his father to order the workers to unload the treasures he brought with him and ran out saying that he is going to meet Grandmother. Pattinathaar ordered his men to unload the treasure. The men unloaded many sacks that arised a doubt in Pattinathaar mind, because, usually precious gems and gold will never be tied up in sacks rather they will be safely kept in boxes. Then, he opened one of the sacks and all he found was dried cow dung and husks.

Pattinathaar grew furious and asked one of his men to carry a sack, went home angrily and shouted where Marudhavanan was. His mother came out and was surprised to see her son angry, asked why he was angry. Pattinathaar told irritatedly "See what you grandson has got?" and kicked the sack down. The sack fell open and to his surprise the dried cow dung that contains precious gems shattered on the floor spreading the gems all through the room and the husk was nothing but golden husk. Pattinathaar's joy knew no bounds and was very happy that his son Marudhavanan has brought in an enormous amount of wealth in a way he did not even imagine.

By then, his mother came near him, gave him a box and told that Marudhavanan asked her to give Pattinathaar this box. She also told Marudhavanan is a very playful kid that he gave this box and ran away saying not to search for him. Pattinathaar opened the box and found an eyeless needle and a small palm leaf with something written on it. It read,

*****

"காதற்ற ஊசியும் வாராது காணும் கடைவழிக்கே"
*****

"Kaadhatra Oosiyum Vaaraadhu Kaanum Kadaivazhikkae"
*****

40

Meaning, This eyeless needle is useless and will not see the market. Even the eyeless and useless needle will not accompany you in your final destiny (after death).

Pattinathaar felt dizzy and felt as if everything was spinning around him. He understood that everything in this world is an illusion and realised that he was actively searching for wealth that is unstable in life. His mother appeared to him as Goddess Shakti (Lord Shiva's consort) and Marudhavanan as Lord Kandhan (Lord Murugan). He realised that everything in life is just a hoax or an illusion and that we all are trapped in such an inescapable illusion. Now, he had his first wisdom realised.

*****

நாபிளக்க பொய்யுரைத்து நவநிதியம் தேடி
நலனொன்றும் அறியாத நாரியரைக் கூடி
பூப்பிளக்க வருகின்ற புற்றீசல் போல
புலபுலென கலகலெனப் புதல்வர்களை பெறுவீர்
காப்பதற்கும் வகையறியீர் கைவிடவு மாட்டீர்
கவர்பிளந்த மரத்துளையிற் கால்நுழைத்துக் கொண்டே
ஆப்பதனை அசைத்துவிட்ட குரங்கதனை போல
அகப்பட்டேரே கிடந்துழல அகப்பட்டேரே

*****

Naapilakka Poiuraiththu Navanidhiyam Thaedi
Nalanondrum Ariyadha Naariyarai Koodi
Poopilakka Varugindra Puttreesal Pola
Pulapulena Kalakalavena Pudhalvargalai Peruveer
Kaapadharkkum Vagai Ariyeer Kaividavum Maateer
Kavarpilandha Maraththulaiyil Kaalnuzhaithu Kondae
Aapadhanai Asaithuvitta Kurangadhanai Pola
Agappatteerae Kidanthuzhala Agapatteerae

*****

Meaning – You gather all the nine kinds of wealth by uttering lies until your tongue gets split. You get together with women who don't even know what is good and what is bad. And like the termites that fly out cracking up the earth, you beget a lot of children. You don't know how to save them; you won't leave them and go away. This act is like the monkey that inserts its leg in the gap of a tree branch split up by a wedge and trying to shake that wedge.

Pattinathaar sang the song above, as he realised that he too was in the same position, got caught in the whirl of bonding and affection. There he decided to become a sanyasi.

6. Pattinathaar: The Tycoon turned Sanyasi – Part 3

Pattinathaar made his decision to become a sanyasi and expressed his decision to his wife Sivakalai. She cried heavily on hearing that her husband is leaving her alone and becoming a sanyasi. But later, she consoled herself and she too decided that she will live the life of a sanyasi by being at home. Then Pattinathaar got from Sivakalai, a box that had the dress of his ancestor, who became a sanyasi. Pattinathaar's family had been worshipping that box considering that dress to be divine.

Pattinathaar first renounced his wife and then renounced his chariot, so he walked across the streets to meet his mother. When he informed his decision about becoming a sanyasi to his mother, his mother said that she was not surprised, but she expected this. Pattinathaar told his mother that he is going to wear the saffron cloth of his ancestor. His mother insisted that he opens up that box and sees that.

When Pattinathaar opened the box, all he found was six loin cloths. Now, Pattinathaar's mother told that this was the property of her father-in-law and that he would say that full clothing is itself a big burden for a sanyasi. Pattinathaar went inside one of the rooms in the house and came out dressed in the loin cloth. Then his mother instructed that he should get the blessings and word from the guru from whom his grandfather got sanyasam. Before he left, his mother tied some small cloth packet to his hip and told that he should meet her if the pack unties, because that will happen when it is the end of her life.

Pattinathaar went to the Gurukulam for the first time in his life, though it was the Gurukulam started off by one of his ancestors and their lineage were the patrons of that Gurukulam, yet Pattinathaar never ventured into the Gurukulam before. He went in and got the blessings and word from the Guru. When he came out of the Gurukulam, he was given the beggar's shell (Thiruvodu). He got the thiruvodu. As sanyasi's are expected to beg and eat their daily meal as they have renounced everything in life and nothing belongs to them. Hence even the food for their living has to be given by others, symbolising that everything in this world, including one's soul is the alms given by God.

Pattinathaar, with his Thiruvodu, went to meet his mother as the first alms for a sanyasi should be from his mother. That's when he thought

*****

வீடிருக்க தாயிருக்க வேண்டுமனை யாளிருக்க
பீடிருக்க ஊணிருக்க பிள்ளைகளுந் தாமிருக்க
மாடிருக்க கன்றிருக்க வைத்த பொருளிருக்க
கூடிருக்க நீ போன கோலமென்ன கோலமே

*****

Veedirukka Thaayirukka Vendu Manayaal Irukka
Peedu Irukka Oon Irukka Pillaigalum Thaanirukka
Maadirukka Kandrirukka Vaitha Porulirukka
Koodirukka Nee Pona Kolamenna Kolamae

*****

Meaning – Pattinathaar thinks to himself "You have your home; you have your mother; you have a wife. You have the fame; you have good healthy body; you even have children. You have the cow; the cow has its calf; you even have the wealth for generations. While body is still alive, look what you have been – a Sanyasi"

Then he walks straight to his home to get the first alms from his mother. He called his mother from the gates. His mother came out with an empty hand and asked "My dear son, are you still rich?". Pattinathaar was puzzled at his mother's question. He thought he had renounced everything and is begging for alms before his mother and his mother is asking such a question. He asked his mother in a puzzled tone "Why do you ask that way mother?". His mother replied

*****

"வீடு உனக்கு அந்நியம் ஆகிவிட்டது ஆனால் ஓடு உனக்கு சொந்தம் ஆகிவிட்டதே அப்பா"

*****

Meaning – "The home is now alien to you, but now you own a thiruvodu that makes you richer than other sanyasis".

Pattinathaar had a much better realisation now, he was about to throw away his thiruvodu, but his mother stopped him and said. "Use it my son, but if you lose it don't search as if you have lost your property". Then she gave the first alms to Pattinathaar, he moved on. Then he came across his elder sister's house, she saw him and invited him into her home and provided him a feast. When Pattinathaar obliged and sat for the meal, his sister asked about transferring the right to Pattinathaar's property in writing. Pattinathaar immediately left the house without eating and made up his mind never to come to that house.

But his sister went behind him always, she sent spies to look where he was going. Finally one day, she sent her children to meet their maternal uncle. She asked the children to give their uncle the Appam (pancake) she had prepared. The children sprang up in love on Pattinathaar when they saw him. He had a lot of affection for those kids, so he picked them up in his arms and talked to them. They gave him the Appam that their mother had asked to give it to him and they left. When Pattinathaar was about to eat to he saw that the appam had some phosphoric poison in it. He realised that it was his sister who tried to kill him. He went straight to his sister's house and threw the appam on roof top and went away singing these two lines

*****

தன் வினை தன்னை சுடும்
ஓட்டப்பம் வீட்டை சுடும்

*****

Thann vinai thannai Sudum
Ottappam Veetai Sudum

*****

Meaning – like one's sins burns them up, the appam in the roof top will burn the house. The next day the entire house was engulfed in flames.

From then on Pattinathaar went on to the temples in the nearby towns and sang in praise of Lord Shiva in those temples. One day when he was in Thiruvidaimarudhur, the small pack that his mother tied to his hips untied itself indicating that his mother was her deathbed. He rushed to see his mother and as he was praying while he rushed, his mother held her life in her hands until Pattinathaar reached. Then his mother passed away in his hands. Pattinathaar wept uncontrollably remembering how his mother had brought him up from a baby to a man. After that, he set fire to his mother's body and then sang the following song

46

*****

முன்னை யிட்டதீ முப்பு ரத்திலே
பின்னை யிட்டதீ தென்னி லங்கையிலே
அன்னை யிட்டதீ அடிவ யிற்றிலே
யானு மிட்டதீ மூள்க மூள்கவே

*****

Munnai Itta Thee Muppurathilae
Pinnai Itta Thee Then Ilangaiyilae
Annai Itta Thee Adi Vayitrilae
Yaanum Itta Thee Moolga Moolgavae

*****

Meaning – The Fire in the front from the third eye of Lord Shiva charred the country of Thirupura Asuras. The fire, that was behind in the tail of Lord Hanuman set fire to Sri Lanka. There is another interpretation for the second line, where Pinnai refers to Nappinnai which is Goddess Sita it was her power that set Srilanka ablaze. The fire that the mother holds is the womb. And let the fire that I hold shall grow and grow to char the mother's body"

Then he thought that being born is a big sin and that is what puts everybody in the inescapable loop of affection and bonding. So, he sang another song after that realising that he grew tired going from one womb to another in every birth.

*****

மாதா வுடல் சலித்தால் வல்வினையேன்
கால்சலித்தேன்
வேதாவும் கைசலித்து விட்டானே நாதா
இருப்பையூர் வாழ்சிவனே இன்னுமோ ரன்னை
கருப்பையூர் வாராமல் கா

*****

Maadha Udal Salithaal, Vall Vinaiyaen Kaal Salithaen
Vedhavum Kaisalithu Vittaanae Naadha
Iruppaiyur Vaazh Sivanae Innumore Annai
Karuppaiyur Vaaramal Kaa

*****

Meaning – Mother got tired by giving birth in every life taken; my legs grew tired by going from one womb to another in every birth. Lord Bramha's hands got tired by creating life again and again. Oh! Lord Shiva of Iruppaiyur, bless me that I shall not go into the womb of another mother"

Then he wandered in the same place for sometime, when again his sister started to give troubles in connection with the property. Pattinathaar transferred all the rights to the property to the temple. And he decided to go to Ujjain to worship the Goddess Kali and left his hometown for good.

7. Pattinathaar: The Tycoon turned Sanyasi – Part 4

Pattinathaar reached Ujjain and worshipped the Kali and decided to stay there for a while. He was getting acquainted with the place and walked along the streets of Ujjain. There was a sudden excitement in the crowd and the reason was that the King of Ujjain Badhragiri (Bharudhahiri) visited that place with his soldiers escorting him. The people there respectfully bowed to the King when he went past them. But Pattinathaar did not bow to the King. The King grew a bit disturbed and asked Pattinathaar why he did not bow. Pattinathaar said he does not bow to anyone other than Lord Shiva himself.

The king roared, "It is the King who is talking to you". Pattinathaar replied "So is the **ONE** replying to you". He referred to Lord Shiva as "the One" who is talking from within him. The King was surprised by that answer and went quietly ahead. The town settled down for the day at dusk and Pattinathaar along with a few sanyasis settled down in the nearby Sathiram

When Pattinathaar was telling about his life history to the other sanyasis, a stranger who claimed that he was a merchant joined the group of people in the sathiram. The merchant was listening to the conversation between Pattinathaar and other sanyasis. Pattinathaar was explaining about the realisation he had in his life and that the meaning of life is to get rid of the materialistic pleasures of this world and realising the Supreme Being. The merchant interrupted, telling his views. He argued explaining that the purpose of life is to enjoy every moment of it. To get rid of materialistic pleasures are the words of the weak and the impotent. The merchant added, "In addition to the pleasures of wealth, the company of a woman you marry adds more value to your life. You should not miss the comfort, love and compassion. The wife has only one mind and that mind thinks only about you."

But Pattinathaar differed saying that, women are like men do have multiple minds, you can never say that their minds are set on only one man – the husband. Before marriage they could have admired other men too. The merchant grew a bit disturbed by the answer asked if it was true for noble women. Pattinathaar replied that it was true for all women in this world. The merchant, who was none other than the King himself in disguise, came out of his disguise, grew more viscious and told Pattinathaar "My Queen is nobler and she has only one mind thinking about me"

Pattinathaar laughed and told "She has many minds!". This made the King very angry and he shouted at Pattinathaar to get his word back. Pattinathaar was determined that he told that he spoke only the truth. The King intimidated Pattinathaar that he would be killed if did not apologize and take his word back. Pattinathaar did not budge. The King went out of the Sathiram asking Pattinathaar to be ready for his sentence in the morning. Pattinathaar told he is a sanyasi who sacrificed everything in life and life itself is no matter to him. The King ordered his men to put Pattinathaar in the prison.

The next day the King issued an order to his men to put Pattinathaar to sentence in a Kazhumaram. (Kazhumaram, a conical shaped mast made of tree or iron fully lubricated with oil, where criminals are mounted on it on the sitting position with their hands tied to their back. The criminals will have painful death). Pattinathaar was brought before the Kazhumaram where he was about to be sentenced. He realised that it is the will of Lord Shiva and sang the following Aram (Truth) song

*****

என்செய லாவதியாதொன்று மில்லை
இனித்தெய்வமே
உன்செய லேயென் றுணரப் பெற்றேன் இந்த ஊன்
எடுத்து
பின்செய்த தீவினையாதொன்று மில்லை பிறப்பதற்கு
முன்செய்த தீவினை யோலிங்ங னேவந்து
மூண்டதுவே

*****

Enn Seyal Aavadhu Yaadhondrum Illa Ini Dheivamae
Unn Seyal Endru Unarappetraen Indha Oon Eduthu
Pin Seidha Theevinai Yaadhondrum Illai Pirappadharkku
Munn Seidha Theevinaiyo Innaganae Vandhu
Moondadhuvae

*****

Meaning – There is nothing I did or can do to this. I now realize that it is your will my God. I haven't committed any sin after being born into this body. But the sins that accumulated over my previous births is now standing before me to end this life

As soon as he finished singing this Aram, he fainted and fell to the ground. The Kazhumaram started burning in flames. This incident was reported to the King; the King was amazed and went to meet his queen. She thought the King was disturbed by the incident and requested him to relax, gave him wine and ordered her servants to keep the King this way. The King enjoyed the wine and literally forgot his kingdom and the world. In the meanwhile, the queen went to meet Pattinathaar herself and ordered him to apologize and tell the world that she was noble to get himself released from prison. Pattinathaar said that he would rather die. She went away saying that she will make sure that the miracle like the one that happened before does not happen the next time.

The King was inebriated and never cared about his kingdom for a few days. After he came to his senses, he went in search of his queen. Suddenly, he heard her talking to someone and discovered that she was intimate with one his horse chariots drivers. He also heard her telling the plans to execute the sanyasi (Pattinathaar) and once that is done, then the King. As a result, her secret lover would become the next King.

The King was shocked to hear that from the woman who he believed to be noble. He was much disoriented to see the queen betraying him and having an affair with an ugly servant of his. Now he remembered Pattinathaar, and the truth he said. He immediately ordered his men to behead the chariot driver and to humiliate the queen by a practice called Karum Pulli Sem Pulli Kuthudhal (A practice where the person punished was tonsured, applied black and white spots all over the body, mounted on a donkey and make them go around the city/town). He did that to set them as examples of what would happen if someone betrays the King. The order was executed, and his former queen went around the city, people pelted her with stones and she died.

King Badhragiri decided to become a sanyasi and a disciple of Pattinathaar. He handed over his kingdom to his chief minister and went in search of Pattinathaar.

8. Pattinathaar: The Tycoon turned Sanyasi – Part 5

King Badhragiri who went in search of Pattinathaar and found him. The King fell at Pattinathaar's feet and apologized for ordering his men to execute Pattinathaar. He then requested Pattinathaar to accept him as a disciple. Pattinathaar denied saying that Badhragiri was a king, who has lived a posh life and being a Sanyasi means relinquishing everything in life; as nothing belongs to a sanyasi. Even the air he breathes does not belong to him. But Badhragiri was determined; he expressed his determination of becoming a disciple and that he was no longer a King, as he had already handed over the kingdom to the chief minister. Pattinathaar finally agreed to take Badhragiri as his disciple.

Then, they started out on their journey south. They followed the rule of the Sanyasi, relinquishing everything. For food, they just get some alms from the homes that provided food. During some days they get food in plenty, well enough to feed thrice a day or even more, and on some days they don't get food at all.

One day, Badhragiri found a Thiruvodu and he took it. Pattinathaar told him that a Sanyasi has no property, so he told Badhragiri to leave that Thiruvodu where he found. Badhragiri justified saying that they don't get food quite often and the Thiruvodu is the vessel used by Sanyasis, even Lord Shiva used it. Pattinathaar said, "It's your wish". Then they proceeded, later Badhragiri found a small bag, he took and looked at Pattinathaar, and again Pattinathaar told "See you are starting to gather your assets". Badhragiri argued, "it's of no use to others, why not we using it". Pattinathaar said, "It's your wish" and proceeded.

On another day, he found a puppy stranded in the road. It was very weak and appeared starved for a few days without food. Badhragiri took pity on the puppy, fed it well and took it with him. Pattinathaar reminded Badhragiri that he was a Sanyasi and he is going back into his family bonding by taking the puppy with him. Again, Badhragiri argued that being a sanyasi does not mean that we should ignore the poor and hapless creatures. As usual, Pattinathaar said, "It's your wish" and proceeded.

A few days passed, then one day, both of them did not get any food for the day and they decided to rest for the night in the Thinnai – a small area in front of the house, usually where people sit. Pattinathaar lay down to rest in one end of the lobby and Badhragiri in the other end keeping all the possessions and the puppy nearby. Sometime later in the night, a beggar came near Pattinathaar and begged for food. Pattinathaar and Badhragiri woke up on hearing the beggar. Pattinathaar told the beggar that he is a Sanyasi however the man on the other end of the lobby is a family man and he might have something.

Badhragiri realised that Pattinathaar was mentioning about the the various things he had collected in due course has made him attached to those things. At the same time, he got angry because he renounced the luxurious king's life to become a Sanyasi, yet his own Guru told that he is still a family man. Immediately, he threw away his possessions and threw the puppy against the wall that it died after having a last gaze at Badhragiri. Badhragiri could not understand the meaning of that gaze the puppy gave him. Then the beggar showed who He was, He was lord Shiva incarnate. Lord Shiva gave enlightenment to Badhragiriyar and vanished

However, Pattinathaar had to wait for some more time, until he reached Thiruvottriyur where he was playing with the kids there and that was when, he attained enlightenment and turned into a Shiva lingam.

That was the life history of the legendary Pattinathaar who was born as a wealthy man, but renounced everything on realisation that nothing in this world is permanent. He has left us his life experiences and his realisations as songs that will serve as a reminder that one should not be attached to the materialistic possessions in this world.

9.An unsolved conundrum about a bullion

The world would have been aware of the famous bullion mystery Yamashita's Gold and many around the world are digging even today to search it. But there is one in Tamil Nadu, in a place called Marungapallam, within the Peravurani jurisdiction of Thanjavur District (Thanjavur, also called Tanjore – The place of the great Brahadeeshwara temple). The inscriptions on the rock carvings in the temple of Lord Shiva at Marungapallam have one similar unsolved conundrum about a bullion. The puzzle is unsolved to this day. It has a story behind it, but first the inscription in the form of a song. It goes like this,

*****

எழுவானுக்கும் தொழுவானுக்கும் இடையிலே
காக்கை மூக்கின் நிழலிலே
கள்வர் போகும் வழியிலே
கண்டாலும் கம்மாளன் கண்ணிலே
எழுபது கொடி பசும்பொன்

*****

Ezhuvaanukkum Thozuvaanukkum Edaiyilay
Kaakai Mookin Nizhalilay
Kalvar Pogum Vazhiyilay
Kandaalum Kammaalan Kannilay
Ezhubadhu Kodi Pasumpon
– Inscription at Lord Shiva Temple in Marungapallam

*****

Meaning –

Between the one who rises and the one who worships,

In the shadow of a crow's beak,

In the path used by thieves,

Even if seen only recognisable by the goldsmith,

There is Seventy Crores pure gold

Ezhuvaan – The person who rises, probably the Sun

Thozhuvaan – The person who worships, probably the human

Edaiyilay – in between

Kaakai – Crow

Mookin – possessive case of Mooku – beak, nose

Nizhalilay – possessive case of Nizhalal – shadow

Kalvar – Plural of Kalvan – Thief

Pogum – Going

Vazhi – Path or route

Kandalum – Seeing, in this case, even if seen

Kammaalan – Goldsmith

Kannil – in the Eyes (Kann)

Ezhubadhu – Seventy

Kodi – Crore

Pasumpon – Pasumai (fertile, pure, rich) + Pon (Gold)

Well, now the story behind it. There once lived a goldsmith who had somehow acquired huge bullion of gold. He kept that information as a secret and he began the purifying process of the gold. So while purifying the gold, he collected the wastes which were like impure iron and threw it away as it had no use or value. This aroused suspicion among the spies of the then king of the region and the secret was delivered to the king and the king ordered his men to get that gold. The goldsmith on knowing that the secret is not a secret anymore hastily went to hide the gold. And he hid that bullion in some place and to safeguard that place, he sacrificed his own daughter to the Gods (a cruel practice that was believed in those days), called Kaavu Koduthal in Tamil meaning sacrificing life for some purpose, and wrote the above song in an inscription and committed suicide. The waste product that the goldsmith dumped was collected by people and used as a cure to Anaemia. It was named as Nagur Raththa Sogai Marundhu (Nagur – a place in Tamil Nadu near Thanjavur; Raththa (Blood) Sogai (non-vitality) – Anaemia; Marundhu – Medicine). And it is said that people actual got cured of anaemia. Whatsoever be it, the place where he hid that gold is still a mystery to this day as Yamashita's Gold.

10. The 16 and The 10

Well, what's the big deal about 16 and 10? These numbers have a special significance among the Tamil people. Go ahead read about interesting fact about the 16 and the 10.

You could hear the Tamil people telling these two phrases

*****

பதினாறும் பெற்று பெருவாழ்வு வாழ்க

Pathinaarum Petru Peruvaazhvu Vaalga

*****

பசி வந்தால் பத்தும் பறந்து போகும்

Pasi Vandhal Paththum Paranthu Pogum

*****

"Pathinaarum Petru Peruvaazhvu Vaalga" means attain all the 16 kinds of wealth and prosperity and live a long life. This phrase is used when the elderly people bless the young people, when the younger people fall at the elders' feet or during some auspicious events.

"Pasi Vandhal Paththum Paranthu Pogum" means when you are hungry all your 10 characters/characteristics would go away from you. This is a song sung by Avaiyar in one of her works, Moodhurai. The phrase usually is used in times of penury.

But, what are those 16 kinds of wealth and the 10 things/characters. Here they go.

The following song enlists the 16 kinds of wealth, sung by Kaalamega Pulavar. It is the 177th song in his collection called the *"Kaalamegam Thanippadalgal"*

*****

துதிவாணி வீரம் விசயம்சந் தானம் துணிவுதனம்
அதிதானி யம்சவு பாக்கியம் போகம் அறிவழகு
புதிதாம் பெருமை அறம்குலம் நோவகல் பூண்வயது
பதினாறு பேறும் தருவாய் மதுரைப் பராபரனே

*****

Thudhivani Veeram Visayam Sandhanam ThunibuDhanam
Adhidhaanyam Sowbhagyam Bhogam ArivuAzhagu
Puthithaam Perumai Aram Kulam Novakalpoon Vayadhu
Padhinaaru Paerum Tharuvai Madurai Paraparanae

*****

Thudhivani – Knowledge to Praise esp. GODs

Veeram – Courage

Visayam – Wisdom

Sandhanam – Children

Thunibu – Daring Attitude

Adhi Dhanam – Money

Madhi – Intellect

Dhaanyam – Food

Sowbhagyam – Prosperity

Bhogam – Harvest

Arivu – brainpower

Azhagu – Beauty

Perumai – Pride

Aram – Good things / Truth

Kulam – Class in Society

Novakalpoon Vayadhu – Long life without any ailment/disease

I have tried to give exact meaning to the the list above, however there are words that are used synonymously sometimes, for e.g. Veeru and Thunibu may mean the same thing in some contexts, but they have subtle differences though. Same goes for Madhi and Arivu.

The song above asks the Madurai Sundareswarar (Lord Shiva) to bestow all the 16 kinds of wealth.

There is one other song in Abirami Pathigam by Abirami Bhattar that also enlists the 16 kinds of wealth. The song is

*****

கலையாத கல்வியும் குறையாத வயதும் ஓர்
        கபடு வாராத நட்பும்
கன்றாத வளமையும் குன்றாத இளமையும்
        கழுபிணியிலாத உடலும்
சலியாத மனமும் அன்பகலாத மனைவியும்
        தவறாத சந்தானமும்
தாழாத கீர்த்தியும் மாறாத வார்த்தையும்
        தடைகள் வாராத கொடையும்
தொலையாத நிதியமும் கோணாத கோலுமொரு
        துன்பமில்லாத வாழ்வும்
துய்யநின் பாதத்தில் அன்பும் உதவிப் பெரிய

61

தொண்டரொடு கூட்டு கண்டாய்
அலையாழி அறிதுயிலும் மாயனது தங்கையே
ஆதிகடவூரின் வாழ்வே!
அமுதீசர் ஒருபாகம் அகலாத சுகபாணி
அருள்வாமி! அபிராமியே!

*****

Kalayaadha Kalviyum Kuraiyadha Vayadhum Ore
*   Kabadu Varadha Natpum*
Kandradha Valamaiyum Kundradha Ilamaiyum
*   Kazhupiniiladha Udalum*
Saliyadha Manamum Anbagalaadha Manaiviyum
*   Thavaradha Santhaanamum*
Thaazhaadha Keerthiyum Maaradha Vaarthaiyum
*   Thadaigal Vaaraadha Kodaiyum*
Tholaiyaadha Nidhiyamum Konaadha Kolumoru
*   Thunbamillaadha Vaazhvum*
Thuyyanin Paadhathil Anbum Udhavi Periya
*   Thondarodu Kootu Kandaai*
Alaiyaazhi Arithuyilum Maayanadhu Thangaiyae
*   Aadhikadavurin Vaazhvae*
Amutheesar Orubaagam Agalaadha Sugapaani
*   Arulvaami Abiramiyae*

*****

Meaning – Uninterrupted learning/education, long life, true friendship, undiminishing wealth, everlasting youth, healthy physique, brisk mind, loving wife, righteous kids, towering fame, unwavering word/promise, obstacle-free generosity, money that is not lost, a ruler who is righteous, life free of sorrows, unwavering faith in Your lotus feet. Apart from these sixteen wealths, being along with your devotees are the blessings you should bestow me Goddess Abirami!

The following song enlists the 10 characteristics

*****

மானம் குலம் கல்வி வண்மை அறிவுடைமை
தானம் தவம் உயர்ச்சி தாளாண்மை - தேனின்
கசிவந்த சொல்லியர் மேல் காமுறுதல் பத்தும்
பசி வந்திடப் பறந்து போம்

*****

Maanam Kulam Kalvi Vanmai Arivudaimai
Dhaanam Dhavam Uyarchi Thalanmai – Thaenin
Kasivandha Solliyarmael Kaamurudhal Paththum
Pasivandhida Parandhu Poam

*****

Maanam – Dignity

Kulam – Class in the Society

Kalvi – Education

Vanmai – Strength

Arivudaimai – Knowledge

Dhaanam – Donating Attitude

Dhavam – Penance

Uyarchi – Rank

Thalanmai – Generosity

Kamurudhal – Romance

Thaenin Kasivandha Solliyarmael Kaamurudhal – Romance with women uttering out words that are sweet as honey

The overall meaning of the song is that, if hunger strikes a human, then all the 10 characteristics mentioned above would go away from him/her until the hunger is over. None of the above in the list takes priority until the stomach is filled.

11. The Power of Yoga

Yoga, the catch-phrase of today. For anything metaphysical, the first resort is to yoga. If you are stressed, mentally pressurized, wanting some peace of mind, the first suggestion that everybody would give is to practise yoga. What is yoga actually? Well, it is an organised way to keep your mind and physique in good shape and condition. Apart from that, practising yoga is said to be a cure for some diseases and prevention from many. Well, as the old quote goes– Prevention is better than Cure. But in what ways! Thirumoolar describes in his masterpiece, Thirumandhiram, many facets of yoga. In the following one he describes about what are the ailments that yoga cures when practised during different times of the day

*****

அஞ்சனம் போன்றுடல் ஐயறும்அந்தியில்
வஞ்சக வாத மறுமத்தி யானத்திற்
செஞ்சிறு காலையிற் செய்திடிற் பித்தறும்
நஞ்சறச் சொன்னோம் நரைதிரை நாசமே

*****

Anjanam Pondrudal Iyy-arrum Andhiyil
Vanjaga Vaadham Arum Madhiyaanathil
Senchiru Kaalaiyil Seydhidil Pitharum
Nanjara Sonnom Narai Thirai Naasame

*****

Before explaining this song, let me digress a bit to tell something about the human body. Three main components drive the human body, called the Vaadham (Air), Piththam (Fire), Silaethumam or Saythumam (Water). The components in the appropriate proportions will have the body acting normally. Even if one of them decreases or increases in proportion it results in some ailment. Getting back to the song, our body is like the anjanam (kajal), soft, in which, the ailments due to disproportionate Silaethumam can be cured by practising yoga in the evening, and of Vaadham (Air) during the afternoon and of Piththam (Heat/Fire) during the early dawn. And as a closing note of this verse, Thirumoolar says that what he has told is the truth and practising yoga will ensure that your hair colour will remain black making you look young and you would not have any eye related diseases.

*****

புள்ளினும் மிக்க புரவியை மேற்கொண்டாற்
கள்ளுண்ண வேண்டா; தானே களிதரும்;
துள்ளி நடப்பிக்கும் சோம்பு தவிர்ப்பிக்கும்
உள்ளது சொன்னோம் உணர்வுடை யோர்க்கே

*****

Pullinum Mikka Puraviyai Merkondal
Kall Unna Vendadhavanai KaliTharum
Thulli Nadapikkum Sombu Thavirpikkum
Ulladhu Sonnom Unarvudayorkkay

*****

This song refers to breathing techniques practised in yoga, it means those who adopt the practise of taking in air that is faster compared to a bird, and then it gives the pleasure and briskness as you would drink the Kall (a drink prepared from the sap of toddy palm). The breathing practice will make you agile, will prevent fatigue. And Thirumoolar ends this with a quote that "I have told to those who can realise"

*****

புறப்பட்டுப் புக்குத் திரிகின்ற வாயுவை
நெறிப்பட உள்ளே நின்மல மாக்கில்
உறுப்புச் சிவக்கும் உரோமங் கறுக்கும்
புறப்பட்டுப் போகான் புரிசடை யோனே

*****

Purappattu Pukku Thirigindra Vaayuvai
Neripada Ullay Nin Malam Aakidil
Uruppu Sivakkum Romam Karukkum
Purappattu Pogaan Puri Sadaiyonae

*****

Meaning, "If channelised properly, within you, the air that goes around you, your skins and organs will get rejuvenated, the hair will get darker and the Lord Shiva (Puri Sadaiyone) will always reside in your body"

This chapter just scratches the tip of an iceberg. Yoga is not just for the body, but also for the mind. It is more of an exploratory aspect that each human has to explore himself/herself to really understand the power.

12. The Hidden Treasures in Tamil

In English, the phrase "To read between the lines" is famously used to infer something different from what is plainly indicated or to detect the real meaning as distinguished from the apparent meaning. Tamil has a wealth of such songs, information written by various poets, saints etc., which I refer to as hidden treasures. These treasures have to be unearthed meticulously to get the great meaning inside them. Now let's jump into the treasure hunt, with the first one,

*****

காணாமல் கோணாமல் கண்டு கொடு
ஆடு காண போகுது பார் போகுது பார்

*****

Kaanamal Konaamal Kandu Kodu
Aadu Kaana Pogudhu Paar Pogudhu Paar

*****

On the first look, the meaning looks as if it means something with charity. We could derive plainly like this

Kaanamal – Without seeing

Konaamal – Without deviating, without showing any grimace

Kandu – Seeing, Address

Kodu – Give

Aadu – Goat, Dance, Bathe

Kaana – On seeing

Pogudhu – Goes away

Paar – See

So clubbing it together, it might seem to be Without seeing the differences, Without deviating or showing grimace, address the needs of the poor and give them what you have and dance in merry then you will see your worries go away, go away

Nice try! However, the actual meaning is not that. It is a song that relates to the way to worshipping the Sun at different times during the day. History tells that Sun has been worshipped as a God in many civilisations and being worshipped even to this day. Many slogams in Sanskrit especially the Aaditya Hridhayam is in praise of the Sun God. Well let's get back to the song, it means

"At dawn, the sun should be worshipped without seeing (Kaanamal), that is, before He rises.

In the noon, without deviating (Konaamal), that is, when He is right above your head.

And in the evening, seeing (Kandu), that is, during sunset.

Then give (Kodu) your offerings.

Then Bathe (Aadu).

Then Realise and see the God in yourself (Kaana).

Then you can see your sins going way (Pogudhu Paar Pogudhu Paar)"

The next one might sound rather unacceptable in then normal case, but it is not actually, it conveys a greater meaning inside. Let's look at it now; it states three things that considered as purity or rather purest of the pure (Parisutham).

*****

எச்சில் பண்ணியது பரிசுத்தம்
இறந்தவனின் போர்வை பரிசுத்தம்
வாந்தி பண்ணியது பரிசுத்தம்

*****

Yechil Panniyadhu Parisutham
Erandhavanin Poravai Parisutham
Vaandhi Panniyadhu Parisutham

*****

Paraphrasing the above song, would mean the following,

Yechil (Saliva) Panniyadhu (being done) – The substance that has been mouthed by someone is purest of the pure

Erandhanvan (Dead person) Porvai (Blanket) – The blanket covering a dead person is purest of the pure

Vaandhi (Vomit) – The substance that has been vomitted is purest of the pure.

Totally unacceptable ain't it? However, digging the treasure in the song would reveal that it refers to three things that are considered sacred even though they have the above mentioned characteristics. The things are Milk, Silk and Honey.

Milk is normally milked from the cow after the calf has drunk some milk, not sure if this is the practice nowadays after the advent of modernized dairies, but still, in most places in India, this is the practice. So, the calf has mouthed the milk. But the milk that is obtained after the calf has mouthed it is considered sacred and even used in Poojas and when worshipping the Gods.

Silk is the blanket of the dead silk worm in its pupae stage. Silk is obtained by boiling the cocoon in hotwater and the silk threads being separated later by some process. So the blanket, of the silk worm that dies within the cocoon, is considered sacred and used to adorn the God statues and used by people in auspicious occasions.

Honey, is what the bee regurgitates after processing the nectar from flowers with some enzyme in its mouth. Honey has medicinal value and used for sacred, auspicious event and as an offering to the Gods.

Tamil literature holds such very interesting and valuable treasures that can be explored for a lifetime.

13. The Glorious Garuda

Garuda – The Brahmini Kite – is one of the most revered birds in India. It is the mount/vehicle of Lord Vishnu. It is also called the Krishnar Parundu/Kazhugu meaning the Kite/Eagle of Lord Krishna. The Garuda is so sacred that it is worshipped as a deity named Garudaazhwar in many Vishnu temples. It is even a strange phenomenon that it circles the temple in which auspicious events like the Kumbabishekam and other yearly festivals are being conducted. Garuda is believed to have strange powers that even its shadow would act as an antidote to the poison of a snake and alleviate the effects of the venom. The belief still exists in many places. There is even a sacred text, in Sanskrit, called *"The Garuda Puranam"* in its name. Tamil too has its part about Garuda. And seeing a Garudan is a good Sagunam (omen), a Tamil song goes like this

*****

செந்தலை கருடன்
வந்திடம் பாய்ந்தால்
கங்கையின் பொருளும்
தன்கையில் கிடைக்கும்

*****

71

Senthalai Garudan
Vandhidam Paainthaal
Gangayin Porulum
Thann Kayil Kidaikkum

＊＊＊＊＊

It means that if the vivid headed garudan crosses to your left when you start any important event, it indicates a good sagunam that you will get the rare and sacred items of the river Ganga in your hands. The river Ganges is said to be originating from the head of Lord Shiva and so it is so sacred that it cleanses all the sins of the humans. So, things gotten from the Ganga is considered rare and sacred. And obtaining things from the Ganges is not so easy in those days. So if a Garudan flies past to your left, then it indicates a good sagunam.

Senthalai – Red headed, vivid headed (in this context)

Vandhidam – Vandhu (Come) + Idam (Left) – Comes to your left

Paainthal – dive, pounce

Gangayin – Of Ganga (River Ganges)

Porul – Items, Substances

Thann – One's Own

Kayil – In hand (Kai)

Kidaikkum – Will be gotten

*****

ஆடிக்கெருடனை தேடிக்காண் ஆனந்தம் பொங்கும்
ஓடும்கெருடனை நாடிக்காண் வல்வினை போக்கும்
காலைகெருடனை பார்த்துக்காண் காவல் காக்கும்
மாலைகெருடனை கூட்டில்காண் மறுபிறப்பில்லையே

*****

Aadi Garudanai Thedi Kaan Anandham Pongum
Odum Garudanai Naadi Kaan Valvinai Pokkum
Kaalai Garudanai Paarthu Kaan Kaaval Kaakkum
Maalai Garudanai Kootil Kaan Marupirappillaiyae

Meaning, search and find the Garudan in the month of Aadi and you will find joy filling your life. Wait in expectation of the arrival of the Garuda in the morning and see it, it will be a sentinel in your life. Seek the elusive Garudan and envision it, it will destroy all your sins. See the Garudan accompanied by Lord Vishnu in the evening, you will cross the ocean of birth, attain salvation and will never be reborn to meet with all the suffering of birth.

Aadi – Dance; Tamil Month of Aadi (It falls between July and August), auspicious month for the Gods.

(Temples would be crowded during this month and it is not easy to worship the deities in the temple. So you would have to search amongst the crowd to find the deities. Garuda being one of the deities, should be searched and worshipped)

Thedi – Search

Kaan – See

Anandham – Joy, Merry

Pongum – Overflow, Abundance

Kaalai – Morning

Paarthu – verb. See; adjective – carefully; In this context Edhirpaarthu meaning in expectation

Kaaval – Watch, Sentinel

Kaakum – Protect

Odum – Running

Naadi – Seek

Valvinai – Sins, actions causing sins

Pokkum – Remove, eliminate

Maalai – Evening

Kootil – In the nest (Koodu); accompanied by someone or something

Marupirappillayae – Maru (Again) + Pirappu (Birth) + Illaiyae (No, Negation) – No rebirth

Not only the Garudan, but other birds and animals are venerated and associated with the gods in India. For example, the Snake (Lord Shiva), the mouse and the elephant (Lord Ganesha), the rooster (Lord Muruga), the monkey (Lord Hanuman), the cow (The Kamadhenu), the bull (Rishaba Devar – mount of Lord Shiva), the buffalo (mount of Yama), the tiger and the lion and so on and so forth. Even the dog is worshipped as the mount of Lord Bairava and even a scorpion has its place. The list goes on. The idea of venerating animals is not to start off any superstition among the people, but it has spiritual, biological and jurisprudential reasons. The spiritual being to the envision the Supreme being as the manifestation of all life forms, the biological being to conserve the ecology and those beings should be in existence, the jurisprudential being, that every animal has its right to existence. Elucidating the essence of such beliefs is that humans have to coexist with other species on the planet.

Apart from the Garuda, there are other birds known to indicate sagunam. One is the Sembothu or the Senbaga (Southern Crow–Pheasant). It would be in the size of a cuckoo and has a vibrant orangish brown colour in its body. The song that indicates is

*****

போத்திடம் பாய்ந்தால் மேத்தடம் வையாதே

*****

Pothidam Paainthal Maelthadam Vaiyaadhae

*****

Meaning, if the Sembothu flies past to your left, don't dare to step one more foot. Rather, it indicates a bad or an unsuccessful sagunam. To be more precise of the meaning, the belief is that if the Sembothu passes to your left while you are about to venture out something, it will not materialise whatever the effort you put.

Pothidam – Pothu (Sembothu) + Idam (Left) – Sembothu going to your left

Paainthaal – dive, pounce

Maelthadam – Mael (Top, Above, More) + Thadam (Path, Tread, footprint) – Treading foot on the path

Vaiyaadhae – Vai means Keep, Vaiyaadhae – negation of Vai

The other bird is the Karikkuruvi (The Black Drongo) is used to predict good omen. The song goes like this

*****

வால்நீண்ட கரிக்குருவி வலமிருந்து இடமானால்
கால்நடையாய் போனவரும் கனகதண்டி ஏறுவாரே

*****

Vaal neenda karikkuruvi valamirundhu idam aanal
Kaal nadaiyaai ponavarum kanaga thandi yaeruvaarae

*****

Meaning, if the Karikkuruvi flies from one's right to the left, even the person who goes by walk will return back being carried on a golden palanquin.

People associate birds and animals to predict the happenings, these beliefs can neither totally be believed nor can be disregarded as superstition. But we have to accept that every life has to be respected and they all have the right to coexist and we cannot hunt them or their habitat leading to their extinction. Maybe, our forefathers thought that at least these spiritual associations with the birds and animals could bring about some ecological balance.

14. Sagely Sivavaakiyar

Sivavaakiyar is a great poet who lived around the 10th century CE and is considered one of the siddhars. Some legends say that he was the first of siddhars who lived in the ancient times. He got the name Sivavaakiyar because he uttered the word "Shiva" when he was born. His works are extraordinary masterpieces that could be done only by a person who has transcended the materialistic aspects of the world and attained the connection with the ethereal bliss.

Sivavaakiyar lived a simple life and he did not have any desire except to get enlightened. He went to a siddhar whom he requested to show him the path to enlightenment. The siddhar agreed but wanted to test him before accepting him a disciple. He gave Sivavaakiyar a gold coin and asked him to leave the gold coin in the Ganga River when Sivavaakiyar immersed himself. Sivavaakiyar immersed himself in the Ganga and prayed to the Ganga River telling that his Guru wanted him to leave the gold coin in the river while immersing and he is doing so as per the words of his Guru. It is said that a hand with golden bangles appeared and got the gold coin from Sivavaakiyar.

Feeling blessed he went back to his Guru and narrated what happened. The Guru asked him if Sivavaakiyar was not worried in throwing away a gold coin. Sivavaakiyar replied that there is nothing more worthy than the words of a Guru. The Guru felt happy and taught Sivavaakiyar with his knowledge. Englightened by his Guru, it was time to leave his Guru and move on. He requested his Guru's permission and blessings on his way through life. The Guru blessed Sivavaakiyar, gave him the Pei Surakkaai, a bitter vegetable, and a some sand from the banks of the Ganges and told that he will have attain eternal bliss only after going through the phase of a family man. His Guru also told that whoever cooks the Pei Surakkaai and the sand as a meal for you without questioning will be Sivavaakiyar's wife.

Sivavaakiyar went on his way and there were offers coming from people to marry him. As soon as he showed the Pei Surakkaai and the sand and told what his Guru said, they would run away either at the sight of the Pei Surakkaai or thinking that he went mad. One lady agreed to cook them and indeed cooked him a sumptuous meal out to both the items. Pleased, Sivavaakiyar married her and lived a life of simplicity, helping out people in the places and also serving the siddhars and devotees. There was a siddhar who visited them often – some say that it was Konganar – and he tested Sivavaakiyar and his wife by giving them pieces of gold. But both of them did not budge an iota and did not get attracted to the gold. Sivavaakiyar even told the siddhar that Gold is a "human-killer". There is even an interesting story about this "human-killer".

Once, Sivavaakiyar was cutting bamboo in the forest, and when he cut one of the shoots, it started to ooze out gold powder. Seeing this, Sivavaakiyar was shocked and ran like hell, as if saving himself from a wild animal or a demon. One the way he met four men and shouted at them to run away as he has seen the "human-killer". Puzzled, those men asked the details, Sivavaakiyar showed them the gold powder and explained that a bamboo shoot was oozing out this thing and termed it as a human-killer and asked the man to save their lives. The men thought that he was stupid and went into the forest in the direction that Sivavaakiyar showed them. They found the gold powder oozing bamboo. They started packing in the sacks they brought with them and even after filling all the sacks, the bamboo was still oozing out golden powder.

Tired of filling the sacks, the men got hungry. So, they decided that two of them stay near the bags and the other two will go get some food from the nearby village. Two men who went to buy food, planned to kill the other two men who stood guard at the bags by poisoning the food they got for them, so that they can have all the gold powder. And once they reached, the men guarding the sack had a plan too. They asked the men who bought the food to fetch some water from the nearby well. When they went, these two pushed them into the well and killed them. Later they ate the poisoned food and died as well. The next day, when Sivavaakiyar passed along that way, saw all of them dead. He thought that even warning these idiots did not help save their lives.

His views might sound atheistic but what he professes is beyond what normal minds can be inculcated. For this reason of atheistic tinge in his songs, his works does not have prominence in the Shaiva Literature, however many people have realised the correctness of what he says. He greatly opposed idol worship and the practices that were followed with to idol worship; basically seeking the Almighty in a stone or a statue, confining the omnipresent in a small stone and considering the stone as GOD, etc. Let's see some of his songs.

*****

நட்டகல்லைத் தெய்வம் என்று நாலுபுட்பம் சாத்தியே
சுற்றிவந்து முணமுணேன்று சொல்லுமந்திரம் ஏதடா
நட்டகல்லும் பேசுமோ நாதன்உள் இருக்கையில்!
சுட்டசட்டி சட்டுவம் கறிச்சுவை அறியுமோ

*****

Nattakallai Dheivamendru Naalupushpam Saathiyae
Sutrivandhu MonaMonavendru Sollumandhiram Yaedhada
Nattakallum Pesumo Naadhan Ullirukayil
SuttaSatti Sattuvam Karichuvai Ariyumo

*****

Meaning, "You consider an erected stone as GOD and you adorn that stone with flowers, go around it chanting and muttering some mantras! How is that possible? Will that erected stone talk you when the the Almighty (Lord Shiva) is within you. Will the utensils used to cook the food realise that taste of its contents?".

Nattakallai – Natta (Erected, planted) + Kallai – possesive case of Kall (stone)

Dheivamendru – Dheivam (GOD) + Yendru – like, consider

Naalu – Four

Pushpam – flower

Saathiyae – Adorn

Sutrivandhu – Sutri (Going around, revolve, rotate) + Vandhu – Come

MonaMona – An interjection to denote murmuring and muttering

SolluMandhiram – Sollum (Utter, tell) + Mandhiram – Mantra

Pesumo – Interrogative of Pesum (Talk)

Naadhan – Lord Shiva (the Almighty)

Ullirukayil – Ull (Within, inside) + Irukayil (Staying, residing)

SuttaSatti – Sutta (Heated) + Satti (Pot, vessel)

Sattuvam – Spoon

Karichuvai – Kari (Vegetable cooked) + Chuvai (Taste)

Ariyumo – Interrogative of Ariyum (Knowing, being aware)

What he says is that, the act of being in oblivion without realising the supreme within oneself and searching elsewhere is like the utensils that do not realise the taste of food that is within them, being cooked. Understand the Almighty within yourself. Now let's see the next song.

*****

நினைப்பதொன்று கண்டிலேன் நீயலாது வேறிலை,
நினைப்புமாய் மறப்புமாய் நின்றமாயை மாயையோ
அனைத்துமாய் அகண்டமாய் அனாதிமுன் அனாதியாய்
எனக்குள்நீ உனக்குள்நான் நினைக்குமாற தெங்ஙனே

*****

Ninaipathondru Kandilaen Neeyaladhu Verilai
Ninapumaai Marappumai Nindra Maayai Maayaiyo
Anaithumai Agandamai Anaadhimun Anaadhiyaai
YenakkulNee UnakkulNaan Ninaikumaaradhu Yenganae

*****

This song is sung to the GOD Almighty himself, his humility, simplicity and divine faith is at its zenith. Let's see the meaning, "I have never known anything other than YOU (GOD) to think. Is the illusion of my consciousness and oblivion actually an illusion or is it YOU? YOU (GOD) have been both everything and nothingness, a being without beginning, who transcends all the beings without beginning. When will be the day when I could think that you are within me and I am within you?".

Ninaipathondru – Ninaipathu (Thinking, Imagining) + Ondru (Thing, One)

Kandilaen – Kandu (See, Imagine, Being Aware) + Ilaen – Negation

Neeyaladhu – Nee (You [GOD in this context]) + Aladhu – a variation if Illadhu indicating negation

Verilai – Veru (Other) + Illai – Negation

Ninapumaai – Ninaipu (Thought, Consciousness)

Marappumai – Marappu (Forgetting, Oblivion)

Nindra – Stand, Stay

Maayai – Illusion

Anaithumai – Everything

Agandamai – Nothing

Anaadhi – Thing without a beginning or origin

YenakkulNee – Yenakkul (Within me) + Nee (You)

UnakkulNaan – Unakkul (Within you) + Naan (Me)

Ninaikumaaru – Thinking so

Yenganae – When, how

The next one for the common man rather atheists,

*****

இல்லைஇல்லை என்றுநீர் இயம்புகின்ற ஏழைகாள்,
இல்லைஎன்று நின்றதொன்றை இல்லை
என்னலாகுமோ
இல்லைஅல்ல ஒன்றுமல்ல இரண்டும்ஒன்றி
நின்றதை
எல்லைகண்டு கொண்ட பேர் இனிப்பிறப்பது
இல்லையே

*****

82

Illailllai Illaiyendruneer Eyambukindra Yezhaikaal
Illaiyendru Nindrathondrai Illaiyennal Aagumo
Illaialla OndrumAlla ErandumOndri Nindradhai
YellaiKandu Kondapaer Inipirapadhu Illayae

*****

Meaning, "You poor people claiming that GOD does not exist; GOD does not exist! Will it be true that, a Being, existing as non-existent (not able to see physically) to actually not exist? Those who realise the bounds of that Being, that is existing as non-existent and existent will never be reborn to undergo the trials and tribulations of birth".

Illai – Negation, not existing

Eyambu – Claim, express

Yezhai – Poor

Nindra – Exist, Stand

Undu – Affirmative, Existing

ErandumOndri – Erandum (Both) + Ondri (Merge, Dependent)

Yellai – Bound, confines

Kandukonda – Found, obtain usually after searching

IniPirappadhu – Ini (Hereafter) + Pirappadhu (Being born)

Sivavaakiyar has transcended the boundaries of materialistic world as the above and other songs illustrate. He professes what the Brahmasutra (The origin of the Universe, the Composition of what is called Brahmam – not Brahma (The GOD of Creation)) says, "All of you and everything around you is Brahmam". In simple physics terms, all objects are manifestations of matter and so is all things in the entire Universe and the Universe itself is the manifestation of Brahmam. You have to realise the Brahmam with you first, don't try to give it a shape or visualise it as something or confine it to some object is what Sivavaakiyar says, a great sagely thought indeed. Let's try to think from his perspective and realise the Brahmam.

15. The Power of Aram (Truth)

Avaiyar and Kaalamega Pulavar were one of the great poets of Tamil. Avaiyar is a female icon and her works – Aathichudi, Nall Vazhi, Moothurai, Kondravendhan Vinayagar Agaval etc – are still recited and read in schools and many households. Kaalamega Pulavar is well known for his pun and is also called Silaydai Pulavar – Silaydai in Tamil denotes pun. Apart from their works, their songs have exhibited their special power – the power to sing Aram (Truth). Aram is a form of poem that describes a truth along with the wish or a curse that happens immediately as soon as the poet sings. We have already seen one such event that happened in the life of Pattinathaar where the Kazhumaram burnt. In this chapter, we will see the events in the life of Avaiyar and Kaalamega Pulavar that illustrate the power of Aram.

Thiruvalluvar wrote his exemplary work – The Thirukkural wanted to publish it to the world. During the Sangam period, it was necessary for anyone who wants to publish any work in Tamil, be approved by the Tamil Sangam at Madurai. So, Valluvar took his masterpiece for approval, but the lead poets (Pulavars) at Madurai rejected his work saying that it does not follow any of the grammatical category of Tamil Literature (Venba, Aasiriyappa..). But Valluvar said he categorises it as KURAL VENBA but the intelligent poets we not ready to accept his categorisation and rejected his work. Valluvar grew sad and walked out of Madurai Tamil Sangam. On the way, he met Avaiyar and then when they had a chat; Avaiyar came to know that Valluvar's work getting rejected at the Tamil Sangam. Avaiyar read the work and found it to be a masterpiece of all times and it should be made known to the world. So, she took Valluvar with her saying that she will help him get the approval and went to meet the King of

Madurai to talk about this. But the Poets and Ministers planned against Avaiyar and locked the gates with four chains and asked her to meet the King, if possible, by breaking the chains off. This made Avaiyar very angry and intolerable by the action of the Ministers and Poets and she sang the songs of truth that exhibited her power to sing Aram. Here are the songs; I will rather give the meaning of the stanzas rather than paraphrasing them.

*****

ஆர்த்தசபை நூற்றொருவர் ஆயிரத்தொன் றாம்புலவர்
வார்த்தை பதினாயி ரத்தொருவர் - பூத்தமலர்த்
தண்டா மரைத்திருவே தாதாகோ டிக்கொருவர்
உண்டாயின் உண்டென் றறு

*****

Aartha Sabai Nootru Oruvar Aayirathu Ondraam Pulavar
Vaarthai Pathinaayirathu Oruvar Pootha Malar
Thanda Marai Thiruvay Thatha Kodikku Oruvar
Undayin Undendru Aru

*****

Meaning – One in hundred could speak in a gathering/stage; One in thousand is a Poet; One in 10,000 will keep their word; And One in a crore (1,00,00,000) would have characteristics that they can be considered equal to GOD himself. If the above is true, let the chain break apart.

The first chain blew off!

*****

தண்டாமல் ஈவது தாளாண்மை தண்டி
அடுத்தக்கால் ஈவது வண்மை - அடுத்தடுத்துப்
பின்சென்றான் ஈவது காற்கூலி பின்சென்றும்
ஈயானெச் சம்போல் அறு

*****

Thandamal Eevathu Thaalanmai Aduthupin Sendrakkaal
Eevathu Vanmai Aduthupin Sendrakkaal Eevathu
Kaarkooli Aduthupin Sendrum Iyyathan
Echcham Pol Aru

*****

Now, we'll see the song about different names for different attitudes in providing help. Providing help or money just by understanding the situation of the persons is called (Thaalanmai) benefaction. And providing help or money after being asked is Vanmai (Donation). Providing help or money after going again and again is Kaarkooli (roughly Alm). And like the one who would be cursed for not helping even after persistent attempts for help asked, let the chains blow off. And there blew off the second chain.

*****

உள்ள வழக்கிருக்க ஊரார் பொதுவிருக்கத்
தள்ளி வழக்கதனைப் பேசி - எள்ளளவும்
கைக்கூலி தான்வாங்கும் காலறுவான் தன்கிளையும்
எச்சமறும் என்றா வது

*****

87

Ulla Vazhakku Irukka Ooraar Podhuvirukka
Thalli Vazhakadhanai Pesi Ell Alavum
Kaikooli Thaan Vaangum Kaal Aruvaan Thann Kilayum
Echcham Arum Endravathu

*****

This one is quite heavy in meaning and rather quite true, and it is for the people who are in the position to give a judgement and are entrusted to give a fair judgement. The song means – with the case before him and the people of the country watching the case, the judge who gives a biased judgement and gets the money for it, will perish and so will his descendants and family. If this is true, let the chains blow up. The third chain blew off.

*****

வழக்குடையான் நிற்ப வலியானைக் கூடி
வழக்கை அழிவழக்குச் செய்தோன் - வழக்கிழந்தோன்
சுற்றமும் தானும் தொடர்ந்தழுத கண்ணீரால்
எச்சமறும் என்றால் அறு

*****

Vazhakudaiyaan iruppa valiyarai koodi
Vazhakkai Azhivazhakku seithon Vazhakizhandhon
Sutramum Thaanum Thodarndhu Azhudha Kanneraal
Echcham Arum Endral Aru

*****

This one is heavier than the previous one. With the plaintiff before the court, the person who uses undue influence by joining hands with the stronger guy (in terms of power or money) and turns the case to his favour will perish by the effect of the tears in the eyes of the plaintiff and his people. If it is true, let the chains blow up.

This blew off the last of the four chains and Avaiyar met the king and then the Thirukural was put in the Por thamarai kulam (Pond with the Golden Lotus – which inside the Madurai Meenakshi Amman Temple even today) and the por thamarai accepted it, making Thirukural universally accepted.

This incident has been made as a scene in the good old movie named Avaiyar. Regardless of the fact that one can believe it or not, the power the Aram the song portrays is immense. There might not be any other record other than these songs about Avaiyar's Aram, but there is one that still exists even today, the place that was affected by the song of Kaalamega Pulavar–Koothanampatti near Madurai.

Kaalamega Pulavar, a great poet during that time had also the power of Aram. Normally, great poets of that era would not intend to save any wealth. The poets would sing songs in praise of the kings or Gods and the kings treat them well and gift them with money, gold, red carpet welcome and other valuables to make the poets happy. However, they never saved it for their own purpose rather they would help the kith and kin with that wealth earned, and they would become impecunious after that. This is one of the reasons that so many songs have been sung in Tamil Literature. Apart from that, some would never even mind to have a neat appearance. Kaalamega Pulavar is one such person.

He would travel to places and sing songs in praise of the king and take part in the contest of skill in Tamil literature, win prizes and donate to the poor and needy. Eat and sleep at places called Sathiram (A cottage), where food and shelter was provided for free. And, he had another habit of eating betel leaves and having a bunch of them in pouch tied to his hip. The characteristic of betel leaves is that it would stop the hunger for brief periods of time. This would be useful for him until he reaches the next sathiram.

Once, when he went to the place called Koothanampatti, near Madurai, he went to field where betel leaves where cultivated. Hoping that it would help if he gets some of the leaves for his reserves, he asked the farmer who was also the owner of the field for some leaves. That farmer thought Kaalamegam to be a beggar and chased him away and shouted that the beggars have started to beg right at the cultivation fields. Kaalamega Pulavar did not mind then thinking that the farmer is shouting for some reason and cleared off the place.

Later, while he was on his way near Nagapattinam, he was terribly hungry and when he looked into the pouch in his hip for betel leaves, the reserves were over and his hunger made him more frustrated. That's when he remembered someone shouting for asking betel leaves and right from where he was, that is, Nagapattinam – a distant place from Madurai – he sang his Aram which went like this, which was rather a powerful one!

*****

கூத்தானம்பட்டியிலே வடகிழக்கு மூலையிலே
பூத்தானமாய் புதுக்கொடிக்கால் உண்டுபண்ண
இலைகருக செடிகருக கொடிகருக

*****

Koothanampattiyilae Vada-Kizhakku Moolayilae
Poothaanamaai Pudhu Kodikaal Undu Panna
Ilai Karuga Sedi Karuga Kodi Karuga

*****

Meaning – in the north east part of Koothanampatti where betel leaves cultivation happens with the mercy and grace of the earth. Let the leaves, plants and climbers incinerate.

That was it; all the crops were just charred like anything. Even today no cultivation is possible in that area. Only a plant called Vellai Erukan (Calotropis Gigantea – White), that would survive extreme conditions and is not edible even to animals, would grow even today. Whether what Kaalamegam did was right or wrong might not be the point, but Koothanampattiis a proof for the power of Aram.

The interesting part happened next, when he was in search of a Sathiram for getting food to fill his tummy. He went in search of a sathiram, and he asked the kids who were playing Gilli (the older Indian version of cricket, played with a small stick and a small round stone or betel nut etc), in a rather poetic sense, "Siruvargaal, Ingae Saapaadu Engae Virrkkum" (Where the food would be available/sold). The kids in the playful mood said "Thondai-la thaan ayya vikkum" (it would hiccup in your throat). Here the words "Virrkkum" and "Vikkum" sound similar but have different meanings the former meaning availability for Sale and the later meaning hiccup.

This really fuelled fire to the already enraged Kaalamega Pulavar and he started off with the song and began writing on the wall.

*****

பாக்குத் தறித்து விளையாடும் பாலகர்க்கு நாக்குத் திரித்துப் போகக்கடவது

*****

Paaku Tharithu Vilaydum Palagarrkku Naakuth Thirithu Poga Kadavathu

*****

Meaning – "let the tongues (speech) of the kids who play with the betel nut, be destroyed". By the time he wrote "naakuth" (normally in Tamil songs, the last word of a line would end with a syllable that the word in the next line starts with), the bell in the sathiram rang indicating that food is ready to be served. Kaalamega Pulavar in great hunger left immediately hoping to complete after taking his food. And when he returned after his food to complete what he left incomplete, he found surprised for having it to be complete. It went like this.

*****

பாக்குத் தறித்து விளையாடும் பாலகர்க்கு நாக்குத் தமிழ்மணக்கும் நன்நாகை

*****

Paaku Tharithu Vilaydum Palagarrkku Naakuth Thamizh Manakkum Nann Naagai

*****

Meaning – "Let tongues of the kids spell the fragrance of good Tamil in the town of Naagai (Nagapattinam)". Kaalamega Pulavar on seeing the shrewdness of the kids; blessed them and went on his way.

The power of Aram is not something that the poets can throw at their whims and fancies; it works for those who are very austere and righteous in their conduct. The power of Aram was also the reason that poets were held in high reverence and regard by the Kings so that they would not meddle with them. Avaiyar had very high influence with the Kings of all the three kingdoms – The Cheras, The Cholas and The Pandyas.

16. Solving Sorrows – Part 1

Tamil Literature does not only have in abundance, great songs with indepth meaning but also songs about way of life. There are songs that guide people through the various trials and tribulations of life. Most people get vexed, depressed, disoriented due to the problems and the sorrows they face. Of course, those are parts and parcels of human life, but succumbing to these is not the point of living the life. Tamil literature has umpteen songs that guide people on how to deal with the sorrows and troubles they face. How to come out of it and how to attain a peaceful and sucessful life? Many of us have faced and are facing difficulties in our life each tuned for our own dimension. But how we have handled them makes what we are. So, what is the solution to all our sorrows and how to handle and live our life? Lets look at a song goes from the past.

*****

ஆஈன மழைபொழிய இல்லம் வீழ
அகத்தடியாள் மெய்நோவ அடிமை சாவ
மாஈரம் போகுதென்று விதை கொண்டோட
வழியிலே கடன்காரர் மறித்துக் கொள்ளக்
கோ வேந்தர் உழுதுண்ட கடமை கேட்கக்
குருக்கள் வந்து தட்சணைக்குக் குறுக்கே நிற்கப்
பாவாணர் கவிபாடிப் பரிசுகேட்க
பாவிமகன் படுந்துயரம் பார்க்கொணாதே

*****

Aaa eena Mazhai Pozhiya Illam Veezha
Agathadiyaal Mei Nova Adimai Saaga
Maaveeram Pogudhu Endru Vidhai Kondoda

Vazhiyilae Kadankaaran Mariththukkolla
Kovendhar Uzhudhunda Kadamai Ketka
Gurukkal Vandhu Datchinakku Kurukkae Nirkka
Paavanar Kavipaadi Parisu Kaetka
Paavimagan Padum Thuyaram Paarkonadhae

*****

The song illustrates a sequence of events that happen to a man in those days. Let's see the meaning.

"The man had a cow which gave birth to a calf;
At the same time, there was a heavy downpour
Even worse his house got destroyed by the rain.
Then, his wife got sick; His servant died.
And later the wetness in the land had was drying up, so ran with the
seeds to sow for cultivation;
On the way, a creditor – person who gave him a loan caught hold of him.
Then the officials from the king came asking for the tax money.
The Gurukkal – temple priest – came asking for donations.
Then a poet came wrote poems in praise and was waiting for the gift.
All these plight of the man is intolerable to see"

Aaa – Cow, King, God (in this context, Cow)

Eena – produce offspring

Mazhai – Rain; Pozhiya – Pouring

Illam – home, house; Veezha – Fall, destroy

Agathadiyaal – Wife (Agam: Home, Adiyaal: female companion)
Mei – Body;

Nova – Pain, suffer

Adimai – Servant; Saaga – dies

Maa – Land; Eeram – Wetness

Pogudhu – Going; Endru – like

Vidhai – seeds; Kondoda – Kondu (take, have) + Oda (run)

Vazhi – Way, Path;

Kadankaaran – Person who gave the loan; Mariththu Kolla – block, stop

Kovendhar – King;

Uzhudhunda – Uzhudhu (Cultivate) + Unda (derive benefit, Eat);

Kadamai – Duty, Tax; Ketka – Ask;

Gurukkal – Priest of the temple; Vandhu – come;

Datchinai – donations;

Paavanar – Poet

Kavi – Poem

Parisu – Gift, Prize

Now when you read the meaning of the poem, most of you would have had a gentle smile. It does not mean a sadist expression of laughing at the man in trouble. But all that you can do if you were in that situation would be to smile. That, is the solution to handle and tackle the troubles and sorrows in life. Take things in life with a smile, no matter how difficult it is and don't get dejected or depressed. This is what Thiruvalluvar says in his Kural.

*****

இடுக்கண் வருங்கால் நகுக அதனை
அடுத்தூர்வது அஃதொப்ப தில்

*****

95

Idukkan Varungaal Naguga Adhanai
Aduthoorvadhu Agudhu Oppadhill

$$\star\star\star\star\star$$

Meaning – "Laugh your trouble/sorrow away. There is no other way to conquer woes."

Idukkan – Sorrow, trouble

Varungaal – Varum (Come) + Kaal (Suppose)

Naguga – Smile, Laugh

Adhanai – a pronoun referring a thing, here, trouble

Aduthoorvadhu – Aduthu (Next, Other) + Thoorvadhu (conquer)

Agudhu – Like, similar

Oppadhil + Oppadhu (Comparing, Matching) + Ill – (Not existing)

So why worry, when you can laugh your sorrows away. Great people have realised this truth and gave it to us, which we should pass it on to the generations to come. Take life as it happens, what is destined to happen will happen. Prepare for the worst; expect the best; take what comes.

17. Solving Sorrows – Part 2

Laughing away the sorrows is not an easy task and everyone cannot take it that way because most are quite bound by their emotions that a verbal statement will not bring an effect immediately. It requires some practice and the mind needs to get trained to treat sorrows and joys equally. It requires a more composed state of mind to see those two as delusions in life rather than life itself. So what does Tamil literature has to offer for these people. Yes indeed it does have another way, though not a way for the atheists. Well, to summarise what it is – think every event, joyous or sad, to be an act of God, submit yourself to God continue with your work and that will save yourself from worries. A song by Avaiyar illustrates this point.

*****

இட்டமுடன் என்தலையில் இன்னபடி என்றேழுதி
விடசிவ நும்செத்து விட்டனோ-முட்டமுட்டப்
பஞ்சமே யானாலும் பாரம் அவ னுக்கன்னாய்
நெஞ்சமே யஞ்சாதே நீ

*****

Ittamudan (Ishtamudan) Enn Thalayil Innapadi Ezhuthi
Vida Sivanum Seththi Vittaano MuttaMutta
Panjamae Aanaalum Baaram Avanukku Annaai
Nenjamae Anjadhae Nee

*****

Meaning – Did Lord Shiva willingly determine to write the fate on my head that I should suffer, and He wrote so? Even if I suffer and fail in all my attempts in life, it is the burden of the God (Lord Shiva) I believe to relieve me out of the troubles. So don't worry my heart.

Ittamudan (Ishtamudan) – Willingly

Enn – My

Thalaiyil – in the head (Thalai: head)

Innapadi – Being so according to the context

Ezhuthivida – Determined to write (Ezhudhu – Write)

Sivanum – Lord Shiva

Seththi – Consider, thinking

Vittaano – Wrote

Mutta Mutta – expression used to indicate repetitive attempts

Panajam – Failure, Misery

Aanaalum – Happen to be so

Baaram – Burden

Avanukku – For Him (Lord Shiva in this context)

Annaai – A state of activity

Nenjamae – Heart, Mind

Anjadhae – Don't Worry

Nee – You

So, as the song explains, leave all your troubles to God and carry on with your work. Troubles would not hurt you much. There is yet another belief that still solves troubles better. That is, the thought that troubles are an act of God to test us. If you endure that toughness in life, you will shine as gold. Troubles and sorrows are rather things that shape us and brings out of us rare talents within that makes who we are. There is short story that speakers in some Upanyasam used to tell the gathering. Though the story might sound fictional, it has great meaning in it.

One day a man went to the temple and talked to the God statue. He told that he is facing a lot of troubles and worries in his life. There does not even seem to be any benefit to him in worshipping the God either. So, he wanted an answer for it and needs a solution to his problems and lives a peaceful life.

The God statue replied, "Long before I was carved into a statue and people started worshipping me, I was a solid rock lying in the mountains. There was no one to help me or heed to my troubles. I was under the hot sun, pouring rains and the cold winters. Later, a sculptor found me and carved me into a statue. Had I not tolerated the baking Sun, the lashing rains, and the chilly winters and apart from those, the hammer and the chisel of the sculptor; I would not have been worshipped now by many who come to this temple. So troubles in life are to shape what you are. Facing and tolerating them takes you to a new dimension you never expected."

Now satisfied with answer that the God Statue gave, the man got encouraged and started to live his life bravely.

To even illustrate this concept, there is a song written by the greatest poet of recent times. Rather the king of poets in the 20th century, Kavi Arasu Kannadhasan (Kavi Arasu means King of Poets). The song goes like this

*****

பிறப்பின் வருவது யாதெனக் கேட்டேன்
பிறந்து பாரென இறைவன் பணித்தான்!
படிப்பெனச் சொல்வது யாதெனக் கேட்டேன்
படித்துப் பாரென இறைவன் பணித்தான்!

அறிவெனச் சொல்வது யாதெனக் கேட்டேன்
அறிந்து பாரென இறைவன் பணித்தான்!
அன்பெனப் படுவது என்னெனக் கேட்டேன்
அளித்துப் பாரென இறைவன் பணித்தான்!
பாசம் என்பது யாதெனக் கேட்டேன்
பகிர்ந்து பாரென இறைவன் பணித்தான்!
மனையாள் சுகமெனில் யாதெனக் கேட்டேன்
மணந்து பாரென இறைவன் பணித்தான்!
பிள்ளை என்பது யாதெனக் கேட்டேன்
பெற்றுப் பாரென இறைவன் பணித்தான்!
முதுமை என்பது யாதெனக் கேட்டேன்
முதிர்ந்து பாரென இறைவன் பணித்தான்!
வறுமை என்பது என்னெனக் கேட்டேன்
வாடிப் பாரென இறைவன் பணித்தான்!
இறப்பின் பின்னது ஏதெனக் கேட்டேன்
இறந்து பாரென இறைவன் பணித்தான்!
அனுபவித்தேதான் அறிவது வாழ்க்கையெனில்
ஆண்டவனே நீ ஏன்' எனக் கேட்டேன்!
ஆண்டவன் சற்றே அருகு நெருங்கி
அனுபவம் என்பதே நான்தான்' என்றான்!

*****

Pirappil Varuvadhu Yaadhena Kaetaen
Pirandhu Paarena Iraivan Panithaan
Padippena Solvadhu Yaadhena Kaetaen
Padiththu Paarena Iraivan Panithaan
Arivena Solvadhu Yaadhena Kaetaen
Arindhu Paarena Iraivan Panithaan
Anbenap Paduvadhu Yaadhena Kaetaen
Aliththu Paarena Iraivan Panithaan
Paasam Enbadhu Yaadhena Kaetaen
Pagirndhu Paarena Iraivan Panithaan
Manaiyaal Sugamenil Yaadhena Kaetaen
Manandhu Paarena Iraivan Panithaan

100

Pillai Enbadhu Yaadhena Kaetaen
Pettru Paarena Iraivan Panithaan
Mudhumai Enbadhu Yaadhena Kaetaen
Mudhirndhu Paarena Iraivan Panithaan
Varumai Enbadhu Yaadhena Kaetaen
Vaadip Paarena Iraivan Panithaan
Irappin Pinnadhu Yaedhena Kaetaen
Irandhu Paarena Iraivan Panithaan
Anubavithaethaan Arivadhu Vaazhkkai Enil
Aandavanae Nee Yaen Yena Kaetaen
Aandavan Sattrae Arugu Nerungi
Anubavam Enbathae Naanthaan Endraan!

*****

Meaning,

I asked God, what do we realise by being born; God instructed me to be born
I asked God, what do we realise by learning, God instructed me to learn
I asked God, what does knowledge mean; God instructed me to seek the knowledge
I asked God, what does love mean; God instructed me to give it to the others
I asked God, what does affection mean; God instructed me to shower affection
I asked God, what is the pleasure of a wife; God instructed me to marry
I asked God, what is it to beget children; God instructed me to beget children
I asked God, what is with old age; God instructed to get old
I asked God, what is poverty; God instructed me to wither in poverty.
I asked God, what is after death; God instructed me to die
I asked God, if experiencing everything is what life is all about; Then why are you here.
God came a little bit closer and said; Experience is none other than me!

A great concept, in simple words! You just consider that all the experiences in life are not only act of God but God himself. The shifting of burden from ourselves to God, gives us the real strength to fight all the tussles and tribulations in life. Although atheists may question the existence of God, they might not feel the benefit they derive out of the invisible means of support. So, Tamil literature offers numerous ways to solve troubles and sorrows. It is up for the peoples' mind to choose what they can and what they need. But enduring the troubles makes us what we are and takes us to a new unimaginable dimension.

18. Exquisite Chithira Thaer

One of the most fascinating and exquisite works in Tamil Literature, that I searched for a long time and found in Kumbakonam, is the Chithira Thaer, meaning Artistic Car/Chariot. The literary eloquence really is awe-inspiring and is in a different dimension, that I have not seen/heard such a work in any other language. I found the Chithira Thaer at two places in Kumbakonam, one at the Saarangapani Temple (in praise of Lord Rama) and the other at the Kumbeshwarar Temple (in praise of Lord Shiva). The Chithira Thaer at Saarangapani Temple is a work by Thirumangai Azhwar, and this form of poetry is called the Thiru Ezhu Kootru Arikkai. The Chithira Thaer at Kumbeshwarar Temple is by Thiru Gnana Sambandhar.

The Chithira Thaer consists of many boxes in the form of a Chariot and each box containing a short verse. The speciality is that you can read the contents from the boxes from any line, but in order, and it will give you a meaningful verse. For e.g. take the content from box 1 in line 1 and then box 2 in line 3 and then box 3 in line 2 and so on – will give you a complete meaning. So the order of reading should be of the form.

1, 2, ... n , ... , 2, 1

Only the numbers need to be in that order, the content can be from any row. It is such a literary beauty that has to be treasured and to be felt proud of.

Take a look at the wonderful masterpiece.

Chithira Thaer at The Saarangapani Temple

The image that follows is nothing but the top section of the chariot, zoomed and rotated to the right to illustrate the masterpiece. The lower section is a mirror image of the upper section.

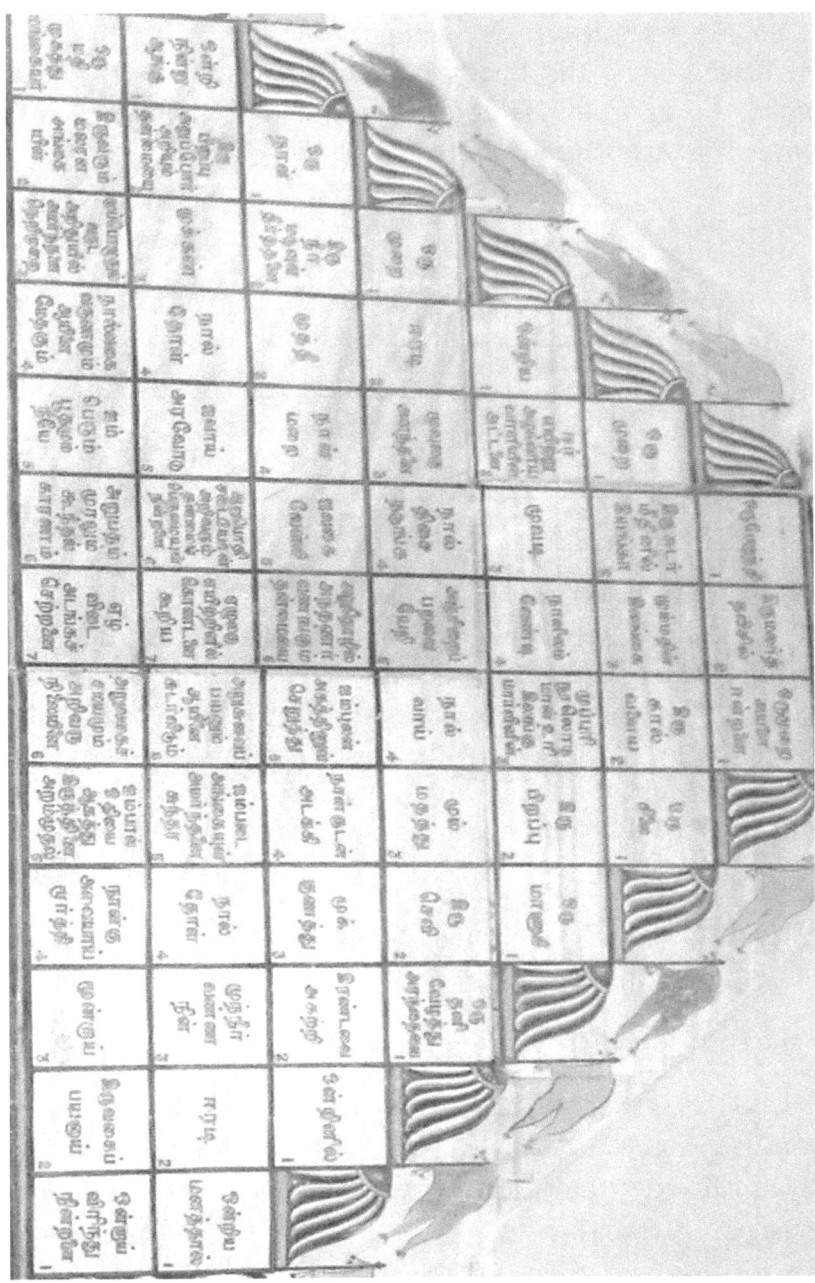

Top Section of the Chithira Thaer

The top section can be symmetrically divided vertically into two halves along the middle. There are seven rows, and the number boxes from the top increase in odd numbers starting from 3. The boxes are numbered as follows

					1	2	1					
				1	2	3	2	1				
			1	2	3	4	3	2	1			
		1	2	3	4	5	4	3	2	1		
	1	2	3	4	5	6	5	4	3	2	1	
1	2	3	4	5	6	7	6	5	4	3	2	1
1	2	3	4	5	6	7	6	5	4	3	2	1

As it can be seen, the right and left halves are numbered mirroring each other. We will have to collect the words in the boxes number from 1 to 7 and then from 7 to 1. Only the numbers have to be in that order but the boxes can be chosen from any row. Consider the following sequence [box-number, row-number(L/R)] – L/R indicates if the words were taken from the left portion or the right portion

[1, 3L], [2, 1], [3, 4L], [4, 4L], [5, 7L], [6, 7R], [7, 6], [6, 5], [5, 6L], [4, 3], [3, 5R], [2, 6R], [1, 7R]

The corresponding words in the boxes are

[1, 3L] – ஒன்றிய, [2, 1] – இருமலர் தவிசில், [3, 4L] – மூவுலகு அளந்தனை, [4, 4L] – நான்மறை, [5, 7L] – ஐம்பெரும் பூதமும்நீயே, [6, 7R] – அறுவகை சமயமும் அறிவரு நிலையினை, [7, 6] – ஏழுலக எயிற்றினில் கொண்டனை கூறிய, [6, 5] – அறுதொழில் அந்தணர் வணங்கும் தன்மையை, [5, 6L] – ஐவாய் அரவொடு, [4, 3] –

நானிலம் வேண்டி, [3, 5R] – முக்குணத்து, [2, 6R] – ஈரடி, [1, 7R] – ஒன்றாய் விரிந்து நின்றனை

Gathering all together, we get the following verse

*****

ஒன்றிய இருமலர் தவிசில் மூவுலகு அளந்தனை
நான்மறை ஐம்பெரும் பூதமும்நீயே அறுவகை
சமயமும் அறிவரு நிலையினை ஏழுலகு
எயிற்றினில் கொண்டனை கூறிய அறுதொழில்
அந்தணர் வணங்கும் தன்மையை ஐவாய் அரவொடு
நானிலம் வேண்டி முக்குணத்து ஈரடி ஒன்றாய்
விரிந்து நின்றனை

*****

Ondriya Irumalar Thavisil Moovulagu Alandhanai
Naanmarai Aimperum Boodhamum Neeyae Aruvagai
Samayamum Arivaru Nilaiyinai Ezhulagu Yeyitrinil Kondanai
Kooriya Aruthozhil Andhanar Vanangum Thanmaiyai Aivaai
Aravodu Naanilam Vendi Mukkunaththu Eeradi Ondraai
Virindhu Nindranai

*****

Meaning – Standing on a single small pedestal filled with flowers, you expanded and measured all the three worlds (Space, Land and the Underworld). You are the manifestation of the Four Vedas (Rig, Yajur, Sama, and Atharvana), the Five Elements (Air, Water, Fire, Soil, and Space), You are beyond the comprehension of the Shanmatham – Six Branches – (Vaishnavam, Saivam, Saaktham, Kaumaram, Gaanapathyam and Sauram); You carried the mother Earth in your tusks in the Varaha avatar; Your divine quality makes the priests, who perform the divine duties, worship You; You rest on the five-headed snake – Kaalingan; You went asking for three feet of land in the Vamana Avatar. You covered all the three parts of the expanse – Space, Land and Underworld – with your two feet covering everything as a Universal Being.

This is one random sequence; we will be able to create verses that are meaningful whatever the permutations we use in picking the words from the boxes provided the order is maintained. The literary eloquence, brilliance of Thirumangai Azhwar and the flexibility of the Tamil Language definitely blows our mind!

19. Sensible Senses

How many senses does a human have? Many would readily come with an answer, SIX. This was really an interesting question and I went in search if some more could be found. Then I hit with something quite interesting and intriguing too! As usual, Thirumoolar had the answer to this interesting question and I was really amazed at his classification and the visualisation of the senses, which he did thousands of years back. Well, let us not prolong the suspense anymore. Thirumoolar in his masterpiece Thirumandhiram states that humans have 10 senses, yes T...E...N, ten senses. His classification is quite awesome and we would agree that it is indeed true. Well, the song goes like this

*****

உற்றறி வைந்தும் உணர்ந்தறி வாறேழும்
கற்றறி வெட்டும் கலந்தறி வொன்பதும்
பற்றிய பத்தும் பலவகை நாழிகை
அற்ற தறியா தழிகின்ற வாறே

*****

Uttrarivu Aindhum Unarndha Arivu Aaru Yaezhum
Katrarivu Yettum Kalandha Arivu Onbadhum
Patriya Paththum Palavagai Naazhigai
Attradhu Ariyaadhu Azhigindra Vaarae

*****

Meaning – The five senses, Sight, Hearing, Touch, Taste and Smell are the inherent ones. The sixth and the seventh senses are those that are realised – Common sense and the sense that we get out of Realisation and Experimenting. The eighth sense is the one that we get out of our Learning and Experience. The ninth sense is the one that blending with the Supreme Being with the faith. And the tenth one being, the grasp the faith of the Supreme Being. Getting all these ten senses will take a long time, but most people perish without realising and acquiring these senses

Uttra – Inherent

Arivu – Sense

Unarndha – Realised

Aaru – Six

Yaezhu – Seven

Katra – Learnt, Experienced

Kalandha – Mixed, Relating

Onbadhu – Nine

Patriya – Grasping the hold (of the Supreme Being)

Paththu – Ten

Palavagai – Lots of types (in this context, lots of amount of time)

Naazhigai – In a general sense – time. Otherwise it refers to a unit of time that is equal to 24 mins. 60 Naazhigai's make one day

Attradhu – Word that refers to the above senses

Ariyaadhu – Without knowing or realising

Azhigindra – Perish, get destroyed

Vaarae – Hence

To think beyond the usual classification of six senses, requires some great thought. Though we might contain the others senses as being a part of common sense. However, the way Thirumoolar perceives is that they are distinct on their own, that those senses deserve to be separate on their own. Let's take the case one by one. We will consider the senses that have been listed after common sense that is 7 to 10.

The Seventh Sense – got by realisation of the Supreme Being. It is similar to the experience obtained by the feel of something. Like putting the fingers in a candle flame to sense of how fire is. Or like tasting honey, or an electric shock which could not be explained verbally.

The Eighth Sense – got by acquiring knowledge something over time, esp. the Supreme Being; that takes time and faith to understand and experience. Like the experienced people in any field can do things more or less instinctively than the new ones, experiencing the Supreme through faith is more of an instinctive thing.

The Ninth Sense – is blending with the Supreme with the help of the focused thought.

The Tenth sense – is the culmination in the attainment of senses. It is realisation of the Supreme Being within. In simple terms, all objects that exist in the world are manifestations of the basic form – matter. Their shape and composition varies, but the matter inside it is the same; so is the Supreme Being. Realisation of the Supreme Being within is the ultimate level; it is not just the knowledge of it but also the experience. At that level all things around are recognized as some form of the Supreme Being.

And as Thirumoolar rightly says, most people perish even before they realise that these senses exist and it is possible for humans to achieve those senses through effort. In each of that step, the perception of the Supreme Being takes a different dimension. Each level transforms the person into different human being. They would start seeing the world in a different perspective, including the dimension of time, even the past, present and future would appear the same to them. A man would be able to transcend this materialistic dimension of the world he lives, only if he achieves all these 10 senses. We need to think, how many of these senses we have acquired so far and what we need to do to acquire the others too.

20. Classy Kaalamegam – Part 1

Kaalamega Pulavar is known for his great poetic knowledge. We already seen a bit about him in the Power of Aram, where, he appears to be notorious for singing Arams against persons. But actually he is revered as a great poet of all times. His original name was Varadhan and he was serving the Vishnu temples and was a Vaishnavite. He had fallen in love with a lady called Mohana, who was a Shaivite, a dancer among the group of dancers called Deva Daasis. In those days, there was a strong opposition between the Shaivite and Vaishnavite followers.

Initially Mohana fell in love with Varadhan but her Shaivite friends started insulting her for having relationship with a Vaishnavite whom the Shaivites hate. So, Mohana avoided Varadhan for this reason and this made Varadhan to become a Shaivite and he became one.

Later one day, Varadhan was waiting in a temple mandapam for Mohana to return. At that time, Goddess Parvathi took the form of a young girl in order to bless a disciple who prayed rigorously. She appeared before that disciple and asked him to open his mouth so that she can spit the divine mixture of betel leaves etc called Thamboolam. The disciple did not realise that the young girl was Goddess Parvati incarnate and shooed her away for disturbing his prayer.

Goddess Parvathi thought that the disciple's mind is not mature yet to attain the knowledge he wishes. So she went back and on the way she saw Varadhan sleeping in the temple. She went near him and asked to open his mouth. Varadhan just getting out of his sleep opened his mouth without any question and the Goddess spit the Divine mixture, indicating Her grace for him. From then on, Varadhan got the ability to sing songs in a blink of an eye and later on became a poet who would shower poems as the heavy clouds would shower rain and hence the name Kaalamegam.

Kaalamegam's use of pun in his songs is so remarkable and so seamlessly merged with the real meaning in the songs, earning him the name "Silaydai Pulavar" (see Interesting use of Pun in Tamil Literature). But he is much more famous for another form of songs that is using only the letters in the sequence of alphabets. For e.g., some of his songs, would use only the letters in the Ka sequence (Ka, Kaa, Ki, Kee and so on). This is the most difficult of all songs that, to my knowledge, he is the only one who has sung such songs.

A word is nothing but a permutation and combination of letters, and a language a permutation and combination of words. But how deep should be one's knowledge to come up with a poem with only the letters of the same series of alphabets, and how vast should be a language's vocabulary to accommodate his thoughts! Now let's get into his songs. The following song uses only the letters in the Ka sequence

*****

காக்கைக்கா காகூகை கூகைக்கா காகாக்கை
கோக்குகூ காக்கைக்குக் கொக்கொக்க கைக்குக்குக்
காக்கைக்குக் கைக்கைக்கா கா

*****

KaakaiKaa KaaKoogai Koogaikkaa KaaKaakkai
Koakkukkoo Kaakkaikku KokkuKokka Kaikaikkuk
Kaakaikkuk KaiKaikkuKaa Kaa

*****

Indeed, a very tough song to understand. Let's rephrase the song as follows

*****

Kaakaiku Aagaa Koogai Koogaikku Aagaa Kaakkai
Koakku Koo Kaakkaiku Kokku Okka Kaikaiku Kaakkaiku
Kaikku Aiykku Aaga Kaa

*****

Still tough ain't it. Well let's see the meaning of the song. It means in the night, the crow's enemy is the owl that can see in the night, whereas the crow cannot. In the day, the crow is the enemy for the owl as the crow can see in daylight whereas the owl is nocturnal. However, the owl is stronger than the crow. Likewise the king who wishes to protect his country from enemies by waiting like the stork, that waits patiently to make its meal before making an attack, will sometimes be defenceless like the owl though he is more powerful than the enemies are.

Kaakai – Crow

Aagaa – Will not go together, disagreement, enmity, inability to do,

Koogai – Owl

Ko – King, Cow, God. In this context, King

Koo – Land, Territory, Country

Kaakkai – The act of protecting (Kaaval)

Kokku – Stork

Okka – Resembling in action or appearance

Kaikkai – Opposing the enemies

Kai – Talent, Hand

Aiy – King

Kaa – Protecting

Very great usage of the language and the eloquence exhibited is really marvellous. Kaalamegam has other similar songs to his credit. The next song, that uses the 'Tha' sequence, goes like this

*****

தத்தித்தா தூதுதி தாதூதித் தத்துதி
துதித் துதைததி துதைத்ததா தூதுதி
தித்தித்த தித்தித்த தாதெது தித்தித்த
தெத்தாதோ தித்தித்த தாது

*****

Thathithaa Thoodhi ThaaThoodhi Thaththudhi
Thuthi Thudhaithi Thudhaidha Thaadhoothi
Thithitha Thithitha Thaadhedhu Thithitha
Theththaadho Thithitha Thodhu

*****

The song is sung as a question to the bee. The meaning of which is as follows: You go jumping from flower to flower tasting the nectar from the flower. When jumping from a flower to a flower, you squeeze the flowers oozing the nectar out of them and then drinking that nectar. You have drunk nectar from various flowers. Which of those flowers had nectar that tasted sweet? Tell me those flowers that had the nectar that tasted sweet.

Let's rephrase the song to have a better understanding

116

*****

Thathi Thaadhu Oodhi Thaadhu Oodhi, Thaththudhi
Thuthi Thudhaithi Thudhaidha Thaadhu Oodhi
Thithitha Thithitha Thaadhu Yedhu Thithithadhu
Yeth Thaadho Thithithadhu Odhu

*****

Thathi – Jump, Hop

Thaadhu – Nectar from flowers

Oodhi – blowing, drinking. In this context, drinking

Thaththudhi – form of root word Thathudhal, meaning hopping

Thuthi – Drink, Eat

Thudhaithi – Crushing, Forcing together

Thudhaidha – Pouring of liquid when squeezed, esp oozing of nectar from flowers

Thithitha – Sweet Taste

Yedhu – which

Odhu – tell, utter, and chant

The song above really elevates Kaalamegam as one the greatest poets in the history of Tamil Literature. And being gifted with such a prowess is really marvellous. And composing poems with an in-depth meaning using a single letter sequence is really a great feat to be admired. The next song of Kaalamega is left as an exercise for the reader. Just kidding, we will see the meaning of this song in the next chapter.

*****

தாதிதூ தோதீது தத்தைதா தோதாது
தூதிதூ தொத்தித்த தூததே தாதொத்த
துத்தித் தாதே துதித்துத்தே தொத்தீது
தித்தித்த தோதித் திதி

*****

ThaadheeThoo ThoTheedhu Thaththaithoo Thodhaadhu
ThaadheeThoo Thothitha Thoodhadhae Thaadhotha
Thuthithath Thaadhae Thudhithuthae ThothTheedhu
Thithitha Thothith Thithi

*****

21. Classy Kaalamegam – Part 2

Kaalamegam really is a great poet, as we saw in the previous chapter, his eloquence is unmatched. Now, let us see the meaning of the last song in the previous chapter.

*****

தாதிதா தோதீது தத்தைதா தோதாது
தூதிதா தொத்தித்த தூததே தாதொத்த
துத்திதத் தாதே துதித்துத்தே தொத்தீது
தித்தித்த தோதித் திதி

*****

ThaadheeThoo ThoTheedhu Thaththaithoo Thodhaadhu
ThaadheeThoo Thothitha Thoodhadhae Thaadhotha
Thuthithath Thaadhae Thudhithuthae ThothTheedhu
Thithitha Thothith Thithi

*****

As usual, let's rephrase this song to have a better understanding

*****

Thaadhee Thoodho Theedhu Thaththai Thoodhu Odhadhu
Thaadhee Thoodhu Othiththa Thoodhu Adhae Thaadhu
Oththa
Thuthi Thathaadhae Thudhithu Thae Thothu Theedhu
Thithitha Thodhi Thithi

*****

Meaning – the servant girls will not act as messengers correctly and they will not convey the message correctly to her lover. The parrot that she has as a pet will go as a messenger for her, though it talks beautifully. Even if the servant girls take the message, it will get days for the message to be conveyed back and forth, so it will not be useful. The skin is becoming pale as a lesions start to appear and spread all over her body as the nectar from flowers would spread if poured. Worshipping the Gods to have a peace of mind is not going to help either. So, just utter my man's name to make me feel better.

Thaadhee – Servant girl

Thoodhu – message conveyed

Theedhu – Bad, Not useful

Thaththai – Parrot, Young woman (in this context, parrot)

Odhadhu – Negation of Odhu meaning utter, chant, convey

Othiththa – Procrastinate, postpone

Adhae – Reflexive Pronoun, indicating the subject mentioned previously, in this case, the message to be sent to her lover

Thaadhu – Nectar, Ore

Oththa – Resembling

Thuthi – Lesion appearing in the skin, lichens

Thaththaadhae – Negative of Thaththu meaning spreading

Thudhithu – Praise, Worship

Thae – God, King, Head of a family etc

Thothu – Climb, Grasp or, Clasp. In this context, grasping the feet of God

Thithitha – Tasting good, Sweetness

Odhi – Utter, Chant

Thidhi – Exist, Stay

The song reflects the sadness in the mind of the young woman who is separated from her man. Her mother comes to her consolation telling her to just divert her thoughts into divine aspects, but the girl refuses all the options and settles down saying that her lover's name soothes her more than anything else in the world.

This reflects a marvellous piece of work by Kaalamega Pulavar. This is not all; Kaalamega Pulavar has gone to various extremes, in the following song, he using a single word (Aaruthalai) in different meanings so beautifully and elegantly associating Lord Shiva, Lord Vishnu, Lord Vinayagar and Lord Murugan and the worshippers of Lord Shiva in a single song. The song goes like this

*****

சங்கரர்க்கு மாறுதலை சண்முகர்க்கு மாறுதலை
ஐங்கரர்க்கு மாறுதலை யானதே - சங்கைப்
பிடித்தோர்க்கு மாறுதலை பித்தாநின் பாதம்
பிடித்தோர்க்கு மாறுதலை பார்

*****

Sankararukku Maaruthalai Shanmugarkku Maaruthalai
Aingararkku Maaruthalai Yaanadho Sangai
Pidithorkku Maaruthalai Pithaa Nin Paadham
Padithorkku Maaruthalai Paar

*****

Meaning, Lord Shiva has a river in his head, Lord Murugan (Shanmugan meaning Six faces) has six faces. Lord Vinayagar has a different head. Lord Vishnu on the other hand has a Water source as His home. And the worshippers and disciples of Lord Shiva get consolation or in other words have a great good change in their lives as result of their worship

Sankarar – Lord Shiva

Aaruthalai – Aaru (River) + Thalai (Head) – Lord Shiva having a the Ganga River in his head

Shanmugar – Lord Murugan

Aaruthalai – Six heads

Aingarar – Having five hands – Lord Vinayagar

Maaruthalai – Maaru (Changed) + Thalai (Head) – Lord Ganesh has an elephant's head that is different from the other Gods

Sangai Pidithor – Sangu (Conch) + Pidithor (Holder) which is Lord Vishnu

Aaruthalai – Aaru (River) + Thalai (Head) – Lord Vishnu having a Water body as his home. His other name Narayana means person residing in water.

Pithaa – Another name for Lord Shiva

Nin Paadham – Your (Lord Shiva) feet

Padithor – People who have realised, learned etc

Maaruthalai – Can be interpreted in two ways. Aaruthalai means Consolation, Solace. Maaruthal – Change or betterment in life

Truly Kaalamegam stands out of the crowd and his proven his mastery of poetry. He is a man to be honoured for ages come. There were other interesting incidents that happened in the life of Kaalamegam, one such event is the tussle with Kambar, the Kavi Chakravathi. Usually when poets fight, it will be a war of words that will be very interesting and of course they maintain the diplomacy, political correctness and the decency, yet insult each other with words very tactfully that makes things more interesting. Let's see more about this in the next chapters.

22. Classy Kaalamegam – Part 3

Kaalamegam was a true poet, in the sense, he amassed wealth by singing songs in praise of Kings and Gods at all the places he went. But, he was so generous and had a helpful tendency that he would give away that money to the needy and poor and move on to other places. This behaviour of the poets of the Sangam age is also one of the reasons, for so many songs in Tamil Literature. When poets sing songs in praise of the kings, those kings used to be lavishly generous that they gave lots of money, gold and other prizes to those poets. In some cases, the kings would even make them part of the group of honoured poet in their kingdom. The poets were not too focused on saving that wealth for themselves, they would distribute it to their kith and kin and the needy without minding that giving all that they have would lead them to poverty again. They had the confidence in their knowledge and poetic abilities and, of course, the kings' generosity, so they could sing more songs in praise and earn the money. Kaalamegam was one such poet, who led a simple life and would stay at any place, be it a small hut or a temple mandapam or even Sathiram.

So, what has this to do with Kaalamegam's tussle with Kambar? Kaalamegam was a wanderer and was not associated with any king or kingdom. However, Kambar though he too was generous and had a helping heart, he held high positions in the kingdom, from being the head of the poets to being advisor to the kings. He was held in high respect.

Though some literary and historical people say that Kaalamegam and Kambar belong to different periods and Kambar lived a century before Kaalamegam. Some say that they were contemporaries. In those days, casteism was prevalent and there was a class difference between higher and lower castes. Not only in those days, even today it is much like a cold war, where people organise communal societies for their welfare. Let us not aberrate from what we were to see. There is even an argument about the caste of Kambar, some say that he belonged to a higher class and some say that he belong to a lower caste called Valaiyar. Well, let's not bring any caste disputes or arguments here. And let us not probe into the truths about this. We shall just see the interesting legend that has stayed for years since Kambar's and Kaalamegam's time. And this will not cause any harm to the respects that both the poets have earned in history.

Well, the legend goes like this. Once upon a time, Kaalamegam was taking rest in the temple mandapam. By then, Kambar with all his servants bearing him in a palanquin went around the city. Kambar was accompanied by his wife. When he reached the temple, he saw Kaalamegam sitting in the temple mandapam. Judging by the appearance of the Kaalamegam, Kambar's pride knew no bounds. He holding a higher position in the kingdom and Kaalamegam being so simple and not as popular as him increased his pride. So he just looked slyly at Kaalamegam as if he was denigrating him. Kaalamegam provoked by this act, stayed cool and just started to sing and he sang the first line of the song

*****

கம்பா! கலைஞா!

*****

Kambaa! Kalaignaa!

*****

Meaning — Oh Kambaa! a great poet and artist! But Kambar knew that Kaalamegam was provoked and he is intending to insult him. He asked his palanquin bearers to stop immediately. Came rushing to Kaalamegam, gave a bag of gold that he had with him, praised him and went silently. The others just considered this act of Kambar's as being generous and Kambar having a great respect for a fellow poet. But only Kaalamegam and Kambar knew its inner meaning.

Now Kaalamegam on seeing Kambar coming to him stopped singing after the first line and he too paid the same respect that Kambar gave him in front of the other people. The people around thought that, though Kaalamegam being a great poet was humble enough to praise a contemporary poet in front of the people. So both the poets, maintained their political correctness and decency, but the insults were known only to them.

Kambar got back onto the palanquin, and his wife asked in curiosity, why Kambar gave the bag of gold for Kaalamegam who just sang a simple one liner about Kambar. Now Kambar explained that had he not rushed to give the bag of gold. Kaalamegam would have sung the next line which would have been a great insult to him, because he is from a lower caste. The song would have been like this

*****

கம்பா! கலைஞா!
வம்பா! வளைப்பயலே!

*****

Kambaa! Kalaignaa!
Vambaa! Valaippayalae!

*****

Meaning –Oh Kambaa! a great poet and artist! Poking fun at me? You Valaiyar (low caste) kid! Had Kambar left Kaalamegam to sing the next line, it would have insulted him for the position he was holding in the kingdom. The point of the legend is not about the casteism, but the shrewdness and meticulousness of the both the poets that they maintained the decency of each other in a public place.

There is also another instance where Kaalamegam criticised Kambar on the use of the language his songs. The song goes like this

*****

நாரா யணனை நரணனென் றேகம்பன்
ஓராமற் சொன்ன வுறுதியால் - நேராக
வாரென்றால் வர்ரென்பேன் வாளென்றால்
வள்ளென்பேன்
நாரென்றால் நர்ரென்பேன் நான்

*****

Naaraayananai Narraayanan Endrae Kamban
Oraamal Sonna Urudhiyaal Naer Aaga
Vaar Endral Varr Enbaen Vaal Endral Vall Enbaen
Naar Endral Narr Enbaen Naan

*****

Meaning, for the reason that the Kamban wrote Naaraayanan as Narraayanan, I will make the mistake as he did by uttering the word Vaar as Varr, Vaal as Vall and Naar as Narr.

Why Kaalamegam said this, is because he felt offended when Kambar mentioned Lord Vishnu as Narraayanan meaning residing in a human (Kambar referred Lord Rama in this context, however) but Naaraayanan means the one who resides in a water body. Kaalamegam felt that Kambar should not have used the word Narraayanan to mean it differently altogether. So, Kaalamegam instead of criticising Kambar directly, he said that Kambar being a great poet, pertaining to the usage of the words, he used Kaalamegam too would follow, Kambar's track. This not only criticised Kambar but also point out the mistake in a decent manner.

Poets in those days were shrewd enough to understand these indirect and hidden criticisms, so were Kambar and Kaalamegam. Though they had tussles between them, they are poetic stalwarts history has ever seen. They had respect for each other and stand out as great poets of all times.

23. Classy Kaalamegam – Part 4

Kaalamegam being well known for his pun in his song, did not spare even the Gods from his pun. His pun also includes a form of poetry in Tamil Literature called the Vanja Pugazhchi Ani, in which the poet would seem to have sung a song in praise of someone but actually the inner meaning of it would have cursed or denigrated the image of the person; and vice versa. Kaalamegam has sung many such songs and two of such songs fascinated me, just because of the use of language in it.

The first song is about Lord Murugan. Though the song might sound very insulting in the first look, the more indepth study has a good meaning in it. The song goes like this

*****

அப்பன் இரந்துஉண்ணி; ஆத்தாள் மலைநீலி
ஒப்பரிய மாமன் உறி திருடி ; சப்பைக்கால்
அண்ணன் பெருவயிறன்; ஆறுமுகத்தானுக்கு
எண்ணும் பெருமை இவை

*****

Appan Iranthunni Aathaal Malai Neeli
Oppariya Maaman Uri Thirudi Sappaikaal
Annan Peruvayiran Arumuga Thaanukku
Ennum Perumai Ivai

*****

The superficial meaning is His father is a beggar who lives by begging food. His mother is a mountain devil. His incomparable uncle is a great thief. His flat footed brother has a large tummy. These are things that Lord Murugan has to be proud of.

But the actual meaning is His father took the form of Bichaadanar, meaning person begging food. This means that He did away with the feeling of acquiring wealth and lives a simple live getting food what others provide. His mother Parvathi, means mountain Goddess, is a queen of the mountains. His incomparable uncle, Lord Vishnu, stole butter from the pots called Uri, which is the major play of Lord Vishnu in his Krishna Avatar. His brother, Lord Ganesh, is an elephant that has flat feet and a big stomach. These are the things Lord Murugan has to be proud of because His family has people who are all popular. However, the immediate meaning of the poem looks like an insult but the inherent meaning is actually a praise.

Appan – Father

Irandhu – Beg

Unni – Person who eats

Aathaal – Mother

Malai – Mountain

Neeli – Mountain devil, another name for Goddess Parvathi, a plant called Karu Nochi

Oppariya – Incomparable

Maaman – Uncle, either Brother of mother or Husband of Father's Sister.

Uri – Stacked up pots that are used to store butter

Thirudi – Thief

Sappaikaal – Flat feet

Annan – Brother

Peru Vayiran – Peru (Big) + Vayiru (Stomach); Vayiran – person with a big stomach

Arumugan – another name for Lord Muruga, which means Six faces

Ennum – Thinking

Perumai – Pride

Ivai – Pronoun to describe a group of things

There is another song that has a similar impact, but that was sung to denigrate, but when the person concerned came and apologised for his mistake, the meaning was totally the opposite and was in praise of him. The song goes like this

*****

கத்துக் கடல்சூழ்நாகைக் காத்தான்தன் சத்திரத்தில் அத்தமிக்கும்போதில் அரிசி வரும் - குத்தி உலையில் இட ஊரடங்கும் ஓகைப்பை அன்னம் இலையிலிட வெள்ளி எழும்

*****

Kaththukadal Soozh Naagai Kaathaan Thann Sathirathil Aththamikkum Podhil Arisi Varum Kuthi Ulaiyil Ida Oor Adangum Ore Agappai Annam Elayil Ida Velli Mulaikkum

*****

The first meaning is, In the Sathiram of Kaathan in Naagapattinam which is surrounded by noisy sea waters. Rice will arrive only in the evening. The people in the town would have gone to sleep when the rice is being put in the boiler after

131

husking. The pole star called the Vidi velli, that indicates dawn, will rise when a scoop of cooked rice is being served.

The people working in that Sathiram told this song to Kaathan Varunakulaadhithan, the owner of that Sathiram, who realised his mistake of not providing food on time to the people who come to his Sathiram, went to meet Kaalamega Pulavar and apologised for his mistake and asked Kaalamega Pulavur to rewrite that song. Kaalamegam told that there is no need to change the song as the song has the following meaning.

In the Sathiram of Kaathan in Naagapattinam which is surrounded by noisy sea waters. Rice will arrive throughout the day till dusk, normally in other places; it arrives only in the morning. This explains how busy that Sathiram would have been and how many people would have been fed by the Sathiram. When the rice is put into the boiler for cooking after husking, the noisy crowd of the town will become quiet expecting the food any moment. And when the scoop of food is being served, the smile that is comparable to a bright star will be found in the faces of the people who are waiting for the food

Kaththu – Noisy, Making noise

Soozh – Surround

Naagai – Nagapattinam

Kaathan – Kaathan Varunakulaadhithan

Thann – one's own

Sathiram – Place where free food and accommodation was available

Aththamikkum – Dusk

Podhil – Word indicating time

Arisi – Rice Varum – Arrive, come

Kuthi – Stab, Strike, Punch, in this context husking

Ulai – Boiler

Ida – Put

Oor – Town, city

Adangum – Settle down, Sleep, Become silent

Ore – One

Agappai – Utensil used to serve food, a scoop

Annam – food

Elayil – Plantain leaf

Velli – Silver, Pole star, in a funny context, Shiny teeth

Mulaikkum – Grow, Raise above

Awesome work by Kaalamegam, how eloquent he should have been to sing a song that has two diametrically opposite meanings. He is really a bestowed person with the gifts that most of us yearn to acquire. He is true a remarkable person whose name will stay in the hearts of millions for the ages to come.

24. Classy Kaalamegam – Part 5

Kaalamegam's uniqueness is in his pun filled songs is the ability to compare and represent different things in the same song. He uses the words so gracefully that he describes two things in the same song, like Castor and Elephant, Hay and Elephant, Snake and Banana, Snake and Gingelly seeds, Snake and Lemon etc. This feat is really remarkable and this is what has earned Kaalamegam his reputation. Let's see two of those songs.

The first song goes like this

*****

வாரிக் களத்தடிக்கும் வந்துபின்பு கோட்டைபுகும்
போரிற் சிறந்து பொலிவாகும் - சீருற்ற
செக்கோல மேனித் திருமலைராா யன்வரையில்
வைக்கோலும் மால்யானை யாம்

*****

Vaari Kalathu Adikkum Vandhu Pinbu Koattai Pugum
Poril Sirandhu Polivaagum Seerutra
Sekkola Maynee Thirumalai Raayan Varaiyil
Vaikolum Aal Yaanaiyaam

*****

The first meaning refers to hay, Hay is being beaten in the fields after harvesting (Vaari Kalathu Adikkum) and then the hay stack is brought into the fort (Vandhu Pinbu Koattai Pugum). The bigger the haystack the brighter and better it looks and it also indicates a good harvest (Poril Sirandhu Polivaagum). The haystack is big indicating the fertile nature of the bright coloured mountain regions of Thirumalai Raayan's territory (Seerutra Sekkola Maynee Thirumalai Raayan Varaiyil).

The second meaning is about the elephant. The elephant in the war field, thrashes soldiers on the ground (Vaari Kalathu Adikkum). After the war it goes into the fort victoriously (Vandhu Pinbu Koattai Pugum). Being a war machine, it has a very good reputation in times of war (Poril Sirandhu Polivaagum). The elephant being in the army indicates the power of the Thirumalai Raayan (Seerutra Sekkola Maynee Thirumalai Raayan Varaiyil).

So, the delicate use of the words that convey different meaning that is applicable to both haystack and elephant respectively makes the poet to compare them as equal (Vaikolum Aal Yaanaiyaam), because the usage of the same words to describe them

Vaari – Pull and lift by holding the legs or the bottom most part of the thing

Kalathu – Rice field (context of haystack), War field (context of elephant)

Adikkum – Beat, Thrash

Vandhu – Come

Pinbu – Later

Koattai – Fort

Pugum – Enter

Poril – haystack, War (context of elephant)

Sirandhu – Best

Polivaagum – Glitter, look better, have a reputation

Seerutra – Orderly

Sekkola – Bright looking

Maynee – Body, landscape

Varaiyil – Territory

Vaikol – Hay

Aal Yaanai – Aggressive Elephant

The comparison has nuances that are seamlessly intricate, and are really out of this world.

The next song is about Snake and Gingelly.

*****

ஆடிக் குடத்தடையும் ஆடும்போ தேயிரையும்
மூடித் திறக்கின் முகங்காட்டும் - ஓடிமண்டை
பற்றின் பரபரெனும் பாரிற்பிண் ணாக்குமுண்டாம்
உற்றிடுபாம் பெள்ளெனவே யோது

*****

Aadi Kudathadaiyum Aadumbodhay Eraiyum
Moodi Thirakkin Mugamkaatum Odi Mandai
Pattril Parapara Vennum Paaril Pinnakkum Undam
Uttridum Paambu Ell Enavae Odhu

*****

The first meaning is about the snake. The snake dances and then goes into the pot that the snake charmer has (Aadi Kudathu Adaiyum). While dancing it makes a hissing noise (Aadumbodhay Eraiyum). When you open the lid it shows its face (Moodi Thirakkin Mugamkaatum). If you run behind it and catch its head it just curls around the person catching it (Odi Mandai Pattril Parapara Vennum). In this world, snakes have a split tongue (Paaril Pinnakkum Undam).

136

Now, let's see the meaning for gingelly. Gingelly will get crushed in the oil mill and will reach the pot as oil (Aadi Kudathu Adaiyum). When it is being crushed, it makes a noise (Aadumbodhay Eraiyum). When the lid of the pot is being opened, it shows face of the person opening of the lid as a reflection (Moodi Thirakkin Mugamkaatum). When you pour it in the head and rub it cools the body immediately (Odi Mandai Pattril Parapara Vennum). In this world, the oil cake remains after crushing (Paaril Pinnakkum Undam).

Thus the comparison between the Snake and Gingelly (Uttridum Paambu Ell Enavae Odhu)

Aadi – Dance (context of snake), Crushing (Context of Gingelly)

Kudathadaiyum – Kudathu (Pot) + Adaiyum (Reach and settle)

Aadumbodhey – while dancing

Eraiyum – Make noise

Moodi – Lid

Thirakkin – Open

Mugam – Face

Kaatum – Show

Odi – Running (while chasing for snake, and pouring in the head)

Mandai – Head

Pattril – Catch

Parapara Vennum – Curls around for snake,

Paaril – In this world

Pinnakkum – Split tongue for snake, Oil cake after crushing

Undam – Having

Uttridum – Existing

Paambu – Snake

Ell – Gingelly

Enavae Odhu – Tell as so

Kaalamegam, truly a great poet of all times and his poems truly represent his literary knowledge and eloquence. He stands out of the crowd and his name will live for ages in the minds of all the people who read Tamil Literature.

25. Rain – The elixir of life

Rain is a natural phenomenon of water precipitating, but the interesting fact is that people associate it with good deeds, well-being etc. More precisely, people tend to associate the amount of rainfall with the good deeds performed. If there are many good deeds performed then, there would be a good amount of rain and if bad deeds increase, rainfall decreases. Let us see what Tamil Literature has to offer. There is even a phrase in Tamil – *"Maadham Mummaari"* meaning *"three rains a month"*. Let's begin with Avaiyar with her song that goes,

*****

நெல்லுக் கிறைத்தநீர் வாய்க்கால் வழியோடிப்
புல்லுக்கும் ஆங்கே பொசியுமாம் தொல்லுலகில்
நல்லார் ஒருவர் உளரேல் அவர்பொருட்டு
எல்லார்க்குமாம் பெய்யும் மழை

*****

Nellukku Iraitha Neer Vaaikaal Vazhi Odi
Pullukkum Aangae Posiyumaam – Tholl Ulagil
Nallaar Oruvar Ularel Avar Poruttu
Ellaarkkum Peyyum Mazhai

*****

Meaning –The water that flows in a stream to irrigate the paddy also irrigates the grass and weeds around. Likewise, for the reason that one good person who exists on this old earth, it rains for the benefit of all.

Nellukku – *(possesive case of) Nell – Paddy*

Iraitha – Poured, Irrigated

Neer – Water

Vaaikaal – Stream, a shallow passage for water to flow

Vazhi – Path

Odi – Run

Pullukkum – For the grass (Pull), in this context, weed

Aangae – There

Posiyumaam – Flow, Drip

Tholl Ulagil – Old (Tholl) Earth – (Ulagu)

Nallaar – Good persons

Oruvar – (denoting count of persons) One

Ularael – Ula – Exist; in conjunction with Oruvar – if one such person exists

Avar Poruttu – Avar: Them, respected tone of a single person; Poruttu – For a particular purpose

Ellarkkum – For all (Ellar)

Peyyum Mazhai – pour down, used in conjunction with rain (Mazhai)

Now, let's see what Vivega Chinthamani has for the rains. The first song goes like this

*****

வேதம் ஓதிய வேதியர்க்கு ஓர் மழை
நீதி மன்னர் நெறியனுக்கு ஓர் மழை
மாதர் கற்புடை மங்கையர்க்கு ஓர் மழை
மாதம் மூன்று மழையெனப் பெய்யுமே.

*****

Vedham Odhiya Vedhiyarkku Ore Mazhai
Needhi Mannar Neriyanukku Ore Mazhai
Maadhar Karppudaya Mangayarkku Ore Mazhai
Maadham Moondru Mazhaiyena Peyyumae

*****

The meaning,

"A rain for the priests enchanting the Vedhas.

A rain for the king who follows good virtues and upholds justice.

A rain for the women who maintain their chastity.

So in all three rains a month".

Vedham – Vedhas

Odhiya – Enchanted, Recited

Vedhiyar – Priests or persons following the Vedhas

Ore – One

Mazhai – Rain

Needhi – Justice

Mannar – (plural of Mannan) Kings

Neriyan – Follower of good virtues

Maadhar – (plural of Maadhu) Women, normally used in a collective sense

Karppu – Chastity

Mangayar – (plural of Mangai) Women

Maadham – Month

Moondru – Three

Peyyum – downpour, fall (esp rain)

This song above is a representation of the fact that if the good deeds grow and good virtues are upheld, the nature will bestow good rains that will help the planet flourish with all good things. Now, here the opposite where if good deeds dwindle, then nature punishes those act. The following song can be interpreted in two ways, one as nature grieving the situations that would have caused the persons involved to perform such acts; the other as a punishing measure for those who are expected to follow good virtues but they stray away blatantly.

*****

அரிசி விற்றிடும் அந்தணர்க்கு ஓர் மழை
வரிசை தப்பிய மன்னருக்கு ஓர் மழை
புருடனைக் கொன்ற பூவையர்க்கு ஓர் மழை
வருடம் மூன்று மழையெனப் பெய்யுமே

*****

Arisi VittridUm Andhanarrkku Ore Mazhai
Varisai Thappiya Mannarkku Ore Mazhai
Purushanai Kondra Poovaiyarkku Ore Mazhai
Varudam Moondru Mazhaiyena Peyyumae

*****

The meaning,

"A rain for the priests who sell rice.

A rain for the kings stray away from their virtues.

A rain for the women who kill their husbands (Rather in the non-literal sense, women who betray their husbands).

So in all, three rains a year".

Arisi – Rice

Vittridum – Selling

Andhanarr – Priests

Varisai – Duties, Order, Queue

Thappiya – Escape, Default, Missing to perform duties

Purushan – Husband

Kondra – Kill, Destroy

Poovaiyar – (plural of Poovai) Women

Varudam – Year

Some people say, that the only one of the three rains mentioned in the first song actually happens and that too not every month – (A rain for the women who maintain their chastity). And all the three rains mentioned in the second song occur without fail. The points in the two songs of Vivega Chinthamani and in Avaiyar's song bear some correlation – "For the purpose and the benefit of the few good people, nature will bestow goodness for all."

26. Who am I?

Who am I?, a question that has baffled and intrigued many philosophers and metaphysicists. The question, that most don't find an answer. If they find an answer to this question, most would not be able to express that verbally. It is not the social identity a person is given. It is about the inner-self, the soul, your ethereal identity – rather shortly – *"The Real You"*. Bit confusing? Well, let's a take a look at what Thirumoolar says and see our thoughts get provoked and intrigued. Here goes the song

*****

இட்டான் அறிந்திலன் ஏற்றவள் கண்டிலள்
தட்டான் அறிந்தும் ஒருவர்க் குரைத்திலன்
பட்டாங்கு சொல்லும் பரமனும் அங்குளன்
கெட்டேன் இம்மாயையின் கீழ்மைஎவ் வாறே

*****

Ettaan Arindhilan Yaetraval Kandilal
Thattaan Arindhum Oruvarkkum Uraithilan
Pattaangu Sollum Paramanum Angulan
Kettaen Immaayaiyin Keezhmai Yevvaray

*****

Meaning – "The sower of the genetic seed (Father) does not know who I am. The acceptor of the genetic seed (Mother) does not know who I am. The creator (Lord Brahma), though he knows who I am, does not tell anyone about that. Even Lord Shiva – the God of Destruction, the foreteller of the end of life – is present there at that time. See! I have been spoilt and just imagine the meanness I have been put into by illusion/oblivion that caused this"

Ettaan – The person who gives; in this context, sower of genetic seed

Arindhilan – Arindhu (know) + Elan (negation a form of Ellai, masculine gender) = the referred person does not have the knowledge

Yaetraval – Yaetra (accept) + Aval (addressing the second person feminine gender) = the person who accepts

Kandilal – Kandu (See, be aware) + Elal (negation a form of Ellai, feminine gender) = The referred person is not aware

Thattaan – Blacksmith; the one who shapes object by striking; in this context, the creator – Lord Brahma

Arindhum – Having knowledge

Oruvarkkum – Even for a single person

Uraithilan – Uraithu (tell) + Elan – He will not tell

Pattaangu – End of world, life etc

Sollum – Telling

Paramanum – (Paraman – Lord Shiva) Even Lord Shiva

Angulan – Angu (there) + Ulan (exists)

Kettaen – Kettu – Become Spoilt

Immaayai – This (Im) illusion (Maayai)

Keezhmai – Lowest point, meanest

Yevvaray – imagine how

Intriguing! Thirumoolar mentions that most people interpret that their perceived identity – the physical body, name and the attributes that are immediately visible – to be who they are. But discovering the inner self, their real identity is not attempted by many. Their purpose of existence is not realized. Even the parents, who are the ones who gave the physical form, do not know about our purpose and who we are. That discovery and realisation is a journey to be embarked by the individual. This is what great philosophers, saints and siddhars have professed all their life that is – "Know thyself!"

Of course, it is a great and a difficult thing to achieve. In order to do that, what siddhars have shown as a way is to meditate. Get detached from the materialistic distractions and start focusing with an empty mind, the real self will start to reveal itself. Let's start on a journey to find who we are for ourselves!

27. Esoteric Edaikaadar – Part 1

Edaikaadar or Edaikaatu Siddhar is one of the 18 Siddhars. He is known to have mastered the art of astrology besides the 8 maha-siddhis called the Ashtama Siddhis which are as follows

- **Aṇimaa:** reducing one's body to the size of an atom
- **Mahimaa:** expanding one's body to an infinitely large size
- **Garimaa:** becoming infinitely heavy
- **Laghimaa:** becoming almost weightless
- **Praapti:** ability to be anywhere at will
- **Parakamyam:** realizing whatever one desires
- **Isithuvam:** supremacy over nature
- **Vasithuvam:** control of natural forces

He is known to have won what fate had for him and the country with his Siddhis. Of all his work, the awesome and the great work is the one describing what happens each year in the world. It is quite esoteric that you have to believe it to understand it. It cannot be considered as a prediction or specific statement of what happens during particular year, but rather it seems to me as more or less a mathematical calculation.

Describing what would happen each year in the world is not an easy task and that too in a generic way. What Edaikaadar has done, is that he has divided the time frame into 60 years, named from Prabava to Akshaya, and has given the generic happenings for each of those years. Those 60 years repeat as a cycle and each year starts from April 14 to the April 13 of the next year, i.e., the Chitirai month to the Panguni Month, in the Tamil Calendar. The following list enlists the names of the years (1-60). The current 60-years cycle started on 1987 and runs till 2047.

Year Name	From 14th Apr	To 13th Apr
Prabava	1987	1988
Vibava	1988	1989
Sukila	1989	1990
Pramogadha	1990	1991
Prajorpaththi	1991	1992
Aangirasa	1992	1993
Srimuga	1993	1994
Bhava	1994	1995
Yuva	1995	1996
Thadhu	1996	1997
Easwara	1997	1998
Vegudhanya	1998	1999
Pramadhi	1999	2000
Vikrama	2000	2001
Vishu	2001	2002
Chithirabanu	2002	2003
Subanu	2003	2004
Dharana	2004	2005
Parthiba	2005	2006
Viya	2006	2007
Sarvasiththu	2007	2008
Sarvadhari	2008	2009
Virodhi	2009	2010
Vikrudhi	2010	2011
Kara	2011	2012
Nandhana	2012	2013
Vijaya	2013	2014
Jaya	2014	2015
Manmadha	2015	2016
Thunmughi	2016	2017
Hayvilambi	2017	2018
Vilambi	2018	2019
Vigari	2019	2020

Sarvari	2020	2021
Pilava	2021	2022
Subhakridhu	2022	2023
Sobakridhu	2023	2024
Kurodhi	2024	2025
Visuvavasu	2025	2026
Parabhava	2026	2027
Pilavanga	2027	2028
Keelaga	2028	2029
Sowmiya	2029	2030
Saadharana	2030	2031
Virodhikridhu	2031	2032
Paridhabi	2032	2033
Pramadheesa	2033	2034
Aanandha	2034	2035
Rakshasa	2035	2036
Nala	2036	2037
Pingala	2037	2038
Kaalayukthi	2038	2039
Siddharthi	2039	2040
Rowdhri	2040	2041
Thunmadhi	2041	2042
Thundhubi	2042	2043
Rudhrodhgaari	2043	2044
Rakthakshi	2044	2045
Kurodhana	2045	2046
Akshaya	2046	2047

The generic predictions of the happenings in each of these years have been sung by Edaikaadar as Verses called Venba in Tamil Literature. Following are some those verses with their meanings

*****

PARTHIBA - (பார்த்திப)

தேச மிசைபார்த் திபவருடஞ் சிங்களத்தார்
தேசங் கேடுமனந்த தேசத்து ராசர்
அநியாயஞ் செய்வா ரதமேறு மாரி
இனிதாம் விளைவுமுள தாம்

*****

Desamisai Parthiba Varudam Singalathar
Desathar Nesam Kedum Ananda Desathu – Rajar
Aniyayam Seivar Radham Yerum Maari
Inidhaam Vilaivum Ulavaam

*****

Meaning – during the year Parthiba, the Srilankans would have a bad time, having their internal and external relations spoiled. Kings and Rulers of other countries would do blatant injustice. Rains will batter the world. The yield on crops would be very good.

*****

DHAARANA - (தாரண)

தாரணத்தின் மாரியறுந் தாரணியிற் கேடுமல்கும்
ஒரிலுயிர் வரக்கமவை யுய்யாவாற் பார்ப்பிணியால்
ஐய மடியுமே ய:கங் குறையுமே
வெய்யர் பயமே மிகும்

*****

Dhaaranathil Maari Arum Dharaniyil Kaedum Undaam
Oraai Seevangalukku Uyyadhu – Paarpiniyaal
Ayyamadiyumae Yakkam Kuraivaamae
Veiyar Bayame Migum

*****

Meaning – in the year Dhaarana, rains will fail, catastrophe and bad events would occur. The beings on earth would not attain comfort or salvation. The world would die of difficulties etc, divine activities like yaagams etc will reduce. Terrorist / Enemical threats would increase.

*****

SUBANU - (சுபானு)

சொன்னேன் சுபானுதனிற் றோன்றுமழை
கொஞ்சமாம்
மின்னே விளைவு பெருகாது மன்னேதுன்
மத்திமக்கோ ளுண்டா மடியுநாற் காற்சீவன்
சற்றுஞ் சுகமில்லைத் தான்

*****

Sonnaen Subanuthanil Thodrum Mazhaikonjamam
Pinnae Vilaivu Perugathu Manne Munn
Mathima Kolundaam Madium NaarkaalJeevan
Sattrum Sugam Illai Than

*****

Meaning – in the year Subanu rainfall will dwindle as a result crops would not yield in the later part of the year. Moderate benefits during the middle of the year. Cattle would die in large proportions. In total, not a good year even to a small extent

151

*****

CHITHIRABANU - (சித்திரபானு)

சித்திர பானு சிறக்க மழைமிகுத்து
வித்துள்ள வெல்லாம் விளையுமே எத்திசையும்
பார்ப்பாருக் காகாது பார்வேந்தர்க் கேநலமாந்
தீர்ப்பாகப் பூமியயஞ் செப்பு

*****

Chitirabanil Sirakka Mazhai Migundhu
Vithulla vellaam Vilayumae – Ethisaiyum
Parparukku Aagadhu Paarvendharkkolamam
Theerpaga Bhoomi Bayam Seppu

*****

Meaning – in the year Chithirabanu, rains will be good and adequate resulting in good agricultural yield. Though the year is quite good with people living a king-like life, those involved in divine activies may have a bad time. Territorial disputes/natural land disasters/threats/fears will exist.

*****

VISHU - (விஷு)

பாரில் விஷுவருடம் பாலர்க்குப் பீடையுண்டாம்
கார்பொழிவ தில்லைமுற் காலத்தில் ஏரி
பெருகாது பிற்காலம் பெய்யுமே மாரி
இருகால முஞ்சமன்னெ றென்

*****

Paaril Vishu Varudam Paalagarkku Peedaiundaam
Kaarpozhivadhillai Murkaalathil – Yeri
Perugadhu Pirrkaalam Peyyumae Maari
Irukaalamum Samannedru Enn

*****

Meaning, during the year Vishu, children will have a bad time, rains will fail during the early part of the year and water sources like lakes, reservoirs would not have their water levels increased. In the later part of the year rains will be good and consider the two parts of the year to be equal in giving benefits

*****

VIKRAMA - (விக்கிரம)

விக்கிரம வாண்டதனின் மேவியநன் மாரிகொஞ்சம்
அக்க ணுயிர்க எழியுமே தொக்க
பயிர்தீயும் நோயும் பழியுமாம் பின்பு
செயிர்தீர்ந்த வோர்மழையாஞ் செப்பு

*****

Vikrama Aandathanil Meviya Nannmaari Konjam
Akkanuyar Kalazhiyumae – Thokka
Payirtheethaam Noyum Pazhiyumamam Pinbu
Seyirtheerndha Mazhaiyaam Seppu

*****

Meaning – during the year Vikrama, the expected rains will be lesser, crops will perish, diseases and curses will spread and during the later part of the year the rains would be remedial to the past effects

*****

PRAMADHI - (பிரமாதி)

வெய்யபிர மாதியினில் வேந்தர் கொடுமையுறும்
ஐயகேள் பஞ்ச மடுக்குமே செய்ய
பசுக்கள் மெலியுமே பாரிற் குடிகள்
சிசுக்க ஞடனலைவார் தேர்

*****

Veyya Pramadhiyil Vendhar Kodumaiyilum
Ayyakael Panjamadukkumae – Seyya
Pasukkal Meliyum Paarir kudigal
Sisukaludan Alaivaar Thaer

*****

Meaning – in the year Pramadhi, even the kings will be in a torment, and heed with fear that famine will strike. As a result, all the cattle would starve, and the people of the world would make an exodus with their children.

*****

VEGUDHANYAM - (வெகுதான்யம்)

வெகுதா னியவருட மேதினியி லெல்லாந்
தகுமாரி பின்பெய்யுந் தான்முன் முகில்சோர்ந்து
கொஞ்சமழை பெய்யுங் குலவு தழைதழைக்கும்
பஞ்சும் பருத்தியுப்புப் பாழ்

*****

Vegudhanya Varuda Maydhaniyil Vellaam
Tharumari Perryumthaan munn – Mugil Soarndhu
Konja Mazhai Peyyum Kulavu Thazhai Thazhaikkum
Panjum Paruthi Uppu Paazh

*****

Meaning – during the year Vegudhanyam, rains will set a record though during the early part of the year rains will be less. But agricultural yields will be good, but wool, cotton and salt would be destroyed.

*****

PRABAVA - (பிரபவ)

ஆதி பிலவத்தி லம்புவியின் மானுடர்க்குச்
சோதனையாய்ச் சாவுதுன்பந் தோன்றுமே
தருப்பொலியுந் ம:கமிகுந் தண்மாரி யோங்கும்
பருத்தியுப்பு மாமணக்கும் பாழ்

*****

Aadhi Pilavathil Ambuviyil Maanidarkku
Sodhanaiyai Saavu Thunbam Thonumae – Needhi
Tharu Pasukkal Maeya Thalaimazhai Undaam
Paruthiuppu Aamanukku Paazh

*****

Meaning – during the first year Prabava, humans will see deaths, problems and difficulties. Rains will be sufficient enough to grow the grass grazed by cattle. Cotton, castor and Salt will get destroyed.

*****

AKSHAYA - (அக்ஷய)

மானேகே எஷயத்தின் மாரியற்ப மானாலுந்
தானே நலமுண்டு தாரணியில் வானூருங்
கார்பொழியும் வேளாண்மை கானமெங்குந்
தோன்றுமே
சீர்பொழிய வோங்கும் திரு

*****

Maanae Kael Achayathin Maari Arrpam Aanaalum
Thanae Nalamundu Thaaraniyil Vaanoorum
Kaarpozhiyum Velaanmai Kaanmengum Thondrumae
Seerpozhiya Ongum Thiru

*****

Meaning – during the Akshaya, though crops would give a meagre yield, good deeds would be on the rise and rains will be adequate to cultivate paddy and all things will get into order.

Though I don't have a historical track of the things to prove the above songs but with the happenings we could clearly estimate that these are indeed true. We would have to wait to see if these are correct. My belief, it works!

28. Esoteric Edaikaadar – Part 2

We have already seen about Edaikaadar and his predictions in the previous chapter. Edaikaadar is also believed to be a disciple of another Siddhar called Bogar. Bogar is the one who installed the Navapaashana Statue at Palani Hills. He travelled to China to spread the knowledge of Siddha sciences. Edaikaadar being the disciple of Bogar is illustrated in his songs as he mentions about China in his predictions. So, it seems that he would also have visited China with Bogar.

Let us see the predictions for the years Viya, Sarvasithu, Saravadhaari, Virodhi, Vikrudhi, Kara, and Nandhana. The songs go like this

*****

VIYA - (விய)

வியவருட மாரி விளைவுண்டாஞ் சீனம்
சுயவாழ் வுடனே சுகமாம் உயர்வாம்
பதினெட்டு வித்தும் பதிவாய்ப் பலிக்குஞ்
சதிர்பெறுநல் லஃகமிகுந் தான்

*****

Viyavarudam Maari Vilaivundaam Cheenam
Suya Vaazvudanae Sugamaam Uyarvaam
Pathinettu Viththum Pathivaai Palikkum
Sathir Peru Nallakkam Migumthaan

*****

Meaning – In the Viya year there will very good rainfall and all the 18 major crops will grow well. China will grow to be self-sufficient. And good deeds and yaagams will rise on this planet.

Viya Varudam – Viya Year

Maari – Rains

Vilaivu – Growth of Crops

Cheenam – China

Suya Vaazhvu – Self Sufficiency

Sugam – Comfort, Happiness

Uyarvu – Promotion and good fortune

Pathinettu – Eighteen

Viththum – Crops

Pathivaai – Register (usually an event), Surely

Palikkum – Happen for sure

Sathir – Boundaries

Perum – Receive

Nall – Good

Yakkam – Yaagams

Migum – Rise

I guess China was establishing itself at a global level and there was indeed a good rainfall during that year.

*****

SARVASITHU - (சரவசித்து)

சருவசித்து தன்னிற் றலத்திற் பலவும்
ஒருபதி னெட்டுவித்து மோங்கும் பெருமையுடன்
மிக்கவிளை வுண்டாகு மேன்மேலு மரியுண்டாந்
தக்க சுகம்பெருகுந் தான்

*****

158

Sarvasithu Thannil Avathil Palavum
Ore Pathinettu Vithuthum Ongum Perumaiyudan
Mikka Vilaivindaam Menmaelum Maariyundaam
Thakka Sugam Perugum Thaan

*****

Meaning – during Sarvasithu all the 18 crops will have good yield. Rains will pour continuously in quantities more than required. All happiness and comfort will last throughout the year.

Sarvasithu Thannil – During Sarvasithu

Avathil – Planet, world

Ore Pathinettu – one 18

Viththu – Crops

Ongum – Gain, have good growth

Perumai – Pride

Mikka – Excess

Vilaivu – Growth of crops

Menmael – Over and Over again

Maari – Rains

Undaam – Affirmative

Thakka – Appropriate

Sugam – Comfort

Perugum – Rising

*****

SARVADHAARI - (சர்வதாரி)

நற்சருவ தாரிதனி நல்லமழை யுண்டாகும்
அற்பவித் தனவெல்லா மாகாது சொற்பெரிய
ஐந்து வகைவிளைவு மாகுஞ் சுகமுடனே
மைந்தரெல்லாம் வாழ்ந்திருப்பர் மற்று

*****

Narr Sarvadhaarin Nalla Mazhai Undaam
Arppa Vithaanadhellam Aagadhu Sorrperiya
Aindhu Vagai Vilaivum Aagum Sugamudanae
Maindhar Ellam Vaazhndhiruppar Matru

*****

Meaning – during Sarvadhaari rains will be good, but only the 5 major crops will have a good yield, the rest would not. And people will live a comfortable life.

Narr – Good

Sarvadhaarin – year Sarvathaari

Nalla – Good

Mazhai – Rains

Undaam – Affirmative

Arppa – Mean

Vithu – Crops

Aagadhu – Negation, Will not happen

Sorrperiya – Things worth mentioning

Aindhu – Five

Vagai – Variety

Vilaivum – Harvest

Aagum – Happen

Sugam – Comfort

Maindhar – People, Children

Ellam – All

Vaazhndhu – Live

Iruppar – Exist

Matru – the rest of it

*****

VIRODHI - (விரோதி)

நீடு விரோதி நிலத்தின் மழைமிகுதி
மேடுகா டெல்லாம் விளைவுண்டாம் நீடும்
அரசர்போ ராலே யழியு முலகந்
திரமிகுநோய் சேருமெனச் செப்பு

*****

Needu Virodhi Nilathin Mazhai Migudhi
Medu Kaadellam Vilaivundaam Needum
Arasar Peraalae Azhiyum Ulagam
Thiramigu Noi Saerumena Seppu

*****

Meaning – during Virodhi rains will pour everywhere, and hence there will be good growth of crops everywhere, be it plains or hills. Rulers and Kings (can be interpreted as countries) will fight with each other and cause devestation and destruction. Contagious diseases will be on the rise.

Needu – Long

Virodhi – year Virodhi

Nilathin – On this land

Mazhai – Rain

Migudhi – Excess

Medu – Mounds

Kaadu – Forest, Plains

Ellam – All

Vilaivu – Harvest

Undaam – Affirmative

Arasar Peraalae – Because of Kings

Azhiyum – get destroyed

Ulagam – World

Thiramigu – More potent and powerful

Noi – Disease

Saerum – Will reach

Seppu – Tell

*****

VIKRUDHI - (விக்ருதி)

வையந் தனில்விகிர்தி மாரி விளைவதிகளு்
செய்ய வளங்கள் சிறக்குமே ஐயகேள்
மாடு கழுதை வயப்பரி நோய்மிக்குச்
சட மெலியுமே தான்

*****

162

Vaiyam Thanil Vikrudhi Maari Vilaivadhigam
Seiyya Valangal Sirakkumae Aiyya Kael
Maadu Kazhudhai Vayapari Noi Mikku
Saada Meliyumae Thaan

*****

Meaning – during Vikrudhi, rains and crop harvest will be good. All the resources will be abundant, but cows and donkeys (to be interpreted as cattle) will catch disease and die in large numbers

Vaiyam Thanil – In the earth (Vaiyam – Earth)

Vikrudhi – The year Vikrudhi

Maari – Rain

Vilaivadhigam – Vilaivu (harvest) + Adhigam (Excess)

Seiyya – Beauty, usually used as an adjective

Valangal – Resources

Sirakkumae – Get better

AiyyaKael – Hear with caution

Maadu – Cow

Kazhudhai – Donkey

Vayapari – Contagion

Noi – Disease

Mikku – Too much

Meliyumae – Get weak, die

*****

KARA - (கர)

கரவருட மாரிபெய்யுங் காசினியு முய்யும்
உரமிகுத்து வெல்லமெங்கு மோடும் நிரைமிகுத்து
நாலுகாற் சீவ னலியுநோ யான்மடியும்
பாலுநெய்யு மேசுருங்கும் பார்

*****

Kara Varudam Maari Peiyum Kaasiniyum Uyiyum
Uramigundha Vella Engum Odum Nirai Migundhu
Naalukaal Seevan Azhiyum Noiyaal Madiyum
Paal Neiyumae Surungum Paar

*****

Meaning – during Kara year, rains will be good and the people in the world will attain bliss and salvation, but floods will inundate everywhere and four legged cattle will die in large numbers because of diseases. And hence, milk and ghee will go scarce.

Kara – The year Kara

Varudam – Year

Maari – Rain

Peiyum – downpour of rain

Kaasiniyum – Earth

Uyiyum – Salvation

Uramigundha – Forceful

Vella – Flood

Engum – Everywhere

Odum – Flow

164

Nirai – word used refer cattle

Migundhu – in excess

Naalukaal – Four legged

Seevan – Beings

Azhiyum – Destroy

Noiyaal – Disease

Madiyum – Die, Perish

Paal – Milk

Neiyumae – Ghee

Surungum – Shrink

*****

NANDHANA - (நந்தன)

நந்தனத்தின் மாரியறு நாடெங்கும் பஞ்சமிகும்
நந்துமுயிர் நோயா நலியுமே அந்தரத்தின்
மீனுதிருந் தூமமேழும் மிக்க கெடுதியுண்டாம்
கோன்மடிவ னென்றேநீ கூறு

*****

Nandhanathin Maariyarum Naadengum Panjam Migum
Nandhumuyir Noyaal Naliyumae Andharathin
Meenu Thirundhu Thooman Ezhum Mikka Keduthi Undaam
Kone Madivan Endrae Nee Kooru

*****

Meaning – during Nandhana year, rains will fail and famine will strike throughout the world. Beings will die as a result of diseases. Comet will appear indicating a bad omen. Kings and Rulers will die in this year.

165

Nandhanathin – In the year Nandhana

Maariyarum – Maari (Rain) + Arum (Fail)

Naadengum – All over the country

Panjam – Famine

Migum – Excess

Nandhumuyir – refers to cattle being grown

Noyaal – Disease

Naliyumae – Become weak, or perish

Andharathin – Space

Meen Irundhu – Stars

Thooman – Comet, indicating bad omen

Ezhum – Rise

Mikka – In Excess

Keduthi – Bad Things, Mishaps

Undaam – Affirmative

Kone – Kings, Rulers

Madivan – Die

Kooru – Tell

It is not about the belief that it works or not, but the thing that makes us wonder is Edaikaadar's ability was able to predict the happenings in a generic fashion even with no technological advancements. By probing more into those ancient texts, we would be able to realise and reveal it to the world, what our ancestors have left for us.

29. Esoteric Edaikaadar – Part 3

In this chapter we will see the predictions for the years Vijaya, Jeya, Manmadha, Dhunmugi, Heyvilambi and Vilambi along with a few legends associated with this Siddhar. First, let us see the predictions and the interesting legend about how Edaikaadar evaded the famine for 12 years and manipulated the planetary positions to reverse the effects of the famine.

*****

VIJAYA - (விஜய)

மண்ணில் விஜய வருடம் மழை மிகுதி
எண்ணு சிறு தானியங்களெங்கும் நண்ணும்
பயம் பெருகி நொந்து பரிவாரமெல்லாம்
நயங்களின்றி வாடுமென நாட்டு

*****

Mannil Vijaya Varudam Mazhai Migudhi
Ennum Siru Dhaniyangal Engum Nannnum
Bayam Perugi Nondhu Parivaaram Ellam
Nayangalindri Vaadum Ena Naatu

*****

Meaning – In this land, during the Vijaya year, rainfall will be abundant. Pulses (Crops) will grow well. Fear will mount, and as a result, the army and people will become unhappy and weak.

*****

JEYA - (ஜெய)

ஜெய வருடந்தன்னிலே செய்புலங்களெல்லாம்
வியனுறவே பைங்கூழ் விளையும் நயமுடனே
அஃகம் பெரிதாமளவில் சுகம் பெருகும்
வெஃகுவார் மண்ணிறை மேல்

*****

Jeya Varudam Thannilae Sei Pulangal Ellam
Viyanuravae Painkoozh Vilayum Nayamudanae
Akkam Peridhaam Alavil Sugam Perugum
Vekkuvaar Mannirai Mael

*****

Meaning – during the Jeya year, crops will yield a good harvest in both the Nanjai and Punjai lands. Divine activities like Yaagams and Poojas will be on the rise. Everyone will be happy and comfortable. The rulers will become greedy and proud.

*****

MANMADHA - (மன்மத)

மன்மததின் மாரியுண்டு வாழும் உயிரெல்லாமே
நன்மை மிகும் பல்பொருளு நண்ணுமே
மன்னவரால்
சீனத்தில் சண்டை உண்டு தென் திசையிற்
காற்று மிகுதி
காணப்பொருள் குறையும் காண்

*****

Manmadhathin Maariyundu Vaazhum Uyirellamae
Nanmai Migu Palporulum Nannumae Mannavaraal
Seenathil Sandai Undu Then Disayil Kaatru Migudhi
Kaanapporul Kuraiyum Kaan

*****

Meaning – In the year Manmadha, rains will be good. People will live well and be bestowed with good things. Because of the decisions made by the rulers, China will have to face war. The southern regions of India will have more winds. As a result, items obtained from the forests in those regions will get reduced.

*****

DHUNMUGI - (துன்முகி)

மிக்கான துன்முகியில் வேளாண்மை யேறுமே
தொக்க மழை பின்னே சொரியுமே மிக்கான
குச்சர தேசத்தில் குறை தீரவே விளையும்
அச்சமில்லை வெள்ளை அரிதாம்

*****

Mikkaana Dhunmugiyil Velanmai Yaerumae
Thokka Mazhai Pinnae Soriyumae Mikkaana
Kuchara Desathil Kurai Theeravae Vilayum
Achamillai Vellai Aridhaam

*****

Meaning – In the year Dhunmugi, agriculture will flourish, good amount rains will fall during the later part of the year. Gujarat will see good harvest. There is nothing to fear in this year, but products that are white – milk, salt, cotton etc will become scarce.

*****

HEYVILAMBI - (ஹேவிளம்பி)

ஹேவிளம்பி மாறியற்பமெங்கும் விளை
குறையுமே
பூவில் விளைவரிதாம் போர்மிகுதி சாவதிகம்
ஆகுமே வேந்தர் அநியாயமே புரிவர்
வேறுமே மேதணி தீ மேல்

*****

Heyvilambi Maari Arpam Engum Vilai Kuraiyumae
Poovil Vilaivaridhaam Pormigudhi Saavadhigam
Aagumae Vendhar Aniyayamae Purivar
Yerum Maedhani Thee Mael

*****

Meaning – during Heyvilambi, rains will fail and harvests will fall. Countries will wage war against each other. Rulers will begin to do injustice as a result; the world will burn in fire.

*****

VILAMBI - (விளம்பி)

விளம்பி வருடம் விளைவு கொஞ்சம் மாறி
அளந்து பொழியும் அரசர் கலங்க்முடன்
நோவான் மெலிவரே நோக்கரிதாகும் கொடுமை
ஆவா புகலரிதாம்

*****

Vilambi Varudam Vilaivu Konjam Maari
Alandhu Pozhiyum Arasar Kalangmudan
Novaan Melivarae Nokkaridhaagum Kodumai
Aava Pugalaridhaam

*****

Meaning – Vilambi year will see less harvests, rainfall will be just sufficient. Rulers will commit blatant injustice, torture and tyranny. Successful happenings will become scarce.

Now, let's see the interesting legend where Edaikaadar manipulated the planets to bring prosperity. Edaikaadar was a shepherd and was herding his goats in the Podhigai hills. One day, one Siddhar was passing by those hills and Edaikaadar provided him with the goat's milk and other food items. As a token of gratitude, that Siddhar bestowed Edaikaadar with the knowledge of self-realisation. With that knowledge and realisation he was able to predict things beforehand and thus he calculated that the next 12 years is going to suffer from drought and famine. He started to train his goats to eat the Erukkilai (Madar plant), it is one of the plants that will survive even the toughest drought. Though it has medicinal properties, raw intake could cause a lot of problems that includes skin irritation. He also mixed the Kuruvaragu (a kind of millet) along with mud and started to construct a small hut in that region.

On the onset of the drought, grazing grounds started to dwindle and the goats were left with no other choice than to eat the Erukkilai. As a result, it will start to itch which in turn will make them to rub their skin against the walls of the hut. After the goats scratch themselves against the walls, the kuruvaragu will fall off along with the dried mud. Edaikaadar collected these, prepared food and made his living.

Soon, all the people in that place, fled to other areas because of the severe drought. But Edaikaadar stayed there, as he had the way to endure the drought. The Navagrahams (Nine planets) who influenced everything on this planet were confused when they saw Edaikaadar being able to survive the drought, wanted to find out how he did.

The Navagrahams went to Edaikaadar's place to find out how he managed the drought. Edaikaadar realising that they are the

171

Gods that represent the Navagrahams, received them well and his hospitality was great that he provided them with the Varagu food and goat's milk. Having had a good meal, the Navagrahams dozed off. At that time, Edaikaadar changed their positions and thereby ending the drought. When the Navagrahams woke up they realised that their positions have been altered, grew furious, but the hospitality of Edaikaadar prevented them from cursing him, instead they blessed him and left the place.

Though the legend might not sound logical or even humanly possible to manipulate the planets, but Edaikaadar's predictions and his presence of mind enabled him to endure the drought and also maintain a herd which is appreciable.

30. Esoteric Edaikaadar – Part 4

Edaikaadar's messages have been quite cryptic and with a deep meaning. In this chapter let's explore the predictions of a few more years and delve into the details of his cryptic messages. Now, let's see the predictions

*****

VIKARI - (விகாரி)

பார் விகாரிதனிற் பாரணநீ ருங்குறையும்
மாரியில்லை வேளாண்மை மத்திமமாம் சோரர்
பயமதிக முண்டாம் பழையோர்கள் சம்பாத்
தியவுடைமை விற்றுண்பார் தேர்

*****

Paar Vigarithanil Paarana Neerum Kuraiyum
Maariyillai Velaanmai Maththimamaam Sorar
Bayam Adhigam Undam Pazhaiyorgal Sambaathiya
Udaimai Vitrunbaar Thaer

*****

During Vigari rains will fail, there will be shortage of potable water. Agricultural yield will be average. Thievery and robbery will rise. People will sell their belongings to make a living.

*****

SAARVARI – (சார்வரி)

சாருவரி யாண்டதனிற் சாதிபதி னெட்டுமே
தீரமறு நோயாற் றிரிவார்கள் மாரியில்லை
பூமிவிளை வில்லாமற் புத்திரரு மற்றவரும்
ஏமமின்றிச் சாவா ரியம்பு

173

*****

Saruvari Andathanil Saadhi Pathinettumae
Theeramaru Noyaal Thirivaargal Maari Illai
Boomi Vilaivillaamal Puththirarum Matravarum
Yaemam Indri Saavaar Iyambu

*****

In the year Saarvari, people across the country will be hit by epidemics. Rain and crops will fail. People and their progeny will die out of food scarcity.

*****

PILAVA - (பிலவ)

பிலவத்தின் மாரிகொஞ்சம் பீடைமிகும் ராசர்
சலமிகுதி துன்பந் தருக்கும் நலமில்லை
நாலுகாற் சீவனெல்லா நாசமாம் வேளாண்மை
பாலுமின்றிச் செயபுவனம் பாழ்

*****

Pilavathin Maarikonjam Peedai Migum Raasar
Salam Migudhi Thunbam Tharukkum Nalamillai
Naalukaal Seevan Ellaam Naasamaam Velaanmai
Paalum Indri Sei Puvanam Paazh

*****

In the Pilava year, rains will be scanty, sorrows will mount. Rulers will be angry and will cause harm to the subjects of the country. Cattle will die in large numbers as a result, crops will fail and milk production will go down. People will suffer because of the scarcity.

*****

SUBAKRIDHU – (சுபகிருது)

சுபகிருது தன்னிலே சோழதே சம்பாழ்
அவமாம் விலைகுறையு மான்சாம் சுபமாகும்
நாடெங்கு மாரிமிகு நல்லவிளை வுண்டாகுங்
கேடெங்கு மில்லையதிற் கேள்

*****

Subakridhu Thannilae Chola Desam Paazh
Avamaam Vilai Kuraiyum Maansaam Subamaagum
Naadengum Maarimigum Nalla Vilaivu Undaagum
Kaedengum Illayadhil Kael

*****

In the year Subakridhu, Chola kingdom will be devastated and things there will go of waste. Aromatic consumables will go down in price. Rains will be very good and will bestow good harvest but the rainfall will not do any damage to the country.

*****

SOBAKRIDHU - (சோபகிருது)

சோப கிருதுதன்னிற் றொல்லுலகெல்
லாஞ்செழிக்குங்
கோப மகன்று குணம்பெருகுஞ் சோபனங்கள்
உண்டாகு மாரி யொழியாமற் பெய்யும்மெல்லாம்
உண்டாகு மென்றே யுரை

*****

Sobakridhu Thannil Tholulagellaam Sezhikkum
Kobam Agandru Kunam Perugum Sobanangal
Undaagum Maari Ozhiyaamal Peyyum Ellam
Udaagum Endru Urai

*****

In the year Sobakridhu, the whole world will flourish. People's thoughts and actions will be good. Good deeds will increase. Rains will be abundant and agricultural harvests will be good. All the goodness will happen.

Now let's look at the events where he gave us cryptic messages that are interesting and deep in meaning. One such incident is when a person coming to know about Edaikaadar's realisation powers asked him which God to worship. He said

*****

"ஏழை இடையன் இளிச்சவாயனை வணங்கு"

*****

"Ezhai Edaiyan Elichavaayanai Vanangu"

*****

The man gave a confused look and Edaikaadar smiled gave the following explanation

விளக்கம்:

ஏழையாய் பிறந்தவன் (சிறையில் வாசுதேவருக்கும் தேவகிக்கும் ஏழையாய் பிறந்தான்), இடையானாய் வாழ்ந்தவன் (ஆயர் குலத்திலே நந்தகோபன், யசோதை மகனாய் வளர்ந்தான்) , சிரித்த முகத்துடன் இருப்பவனான கண்ணபிரானை வணங்கு"

Meaning – The One who was born poor (Lord Krishna was born to Vasudevar and Devaki in a prison as a poor child), The One who lived as herding cows and goats (Lord Krishna grew up as the son of Nandhagopan and Yasodha, among the people who herd cattle called Edaiyars), The One who always has a smiling face should be worshipped.

Then the person asked when should He be worshipped for which the Edaikaadar said

*****

காணாமல் கோணாமல்
கண்டு கொடு
ஆடு காண
போகுது பார்
போகுது பார்

*****

Kaanaamal Konaamal
Kandu Kodu
Aadu Kaana
Pogudhu Paar
Pogudhu Paar

*****

The person was confused more than he was earlier and gave another puzzled look. Edaikaadar explained.

விளக்கம்:

கதிரவனை காணும் முன்பு, கதிரவன் நேர் உச்சியில் (கோணாமல்) இருக்கும்போதும், கதிரவன் அத்தமிக்கும் போதும் வணங்கி. நீராடி கண்ணனை கண்டு வணங்கினால் உன் பாவங்கள் எல்லாம் போகுது பார்.

Meaning - Before the sunrise, and when the sun is at the top, and during the sunset, you offer your prayers. Take a bath, go see Lord Krishna and pray, you can see your sins going away.

The person again asked what he should provide as offering to Lord Krishna when worshipping, for which Edaikaadar said to worship with the purest of things *(பரிசுத்தமானதை படைத்து வணங்கு)*. For which the person asked what are the purest of things, Edaikaadar said.

*****

எச்சில் பண்ணியது பரிசுத்தம்
இறந்தவனின் போர்வை பரிசுத்தம்
வாந்தி பண்ணியது பரிசுத்தம்

*****

Echchil Panniyadhu Parisuththam
Irandhavanin Porvai Parisuththam
Vandhi Panninadhu Parisuththam

*****

Which, literally means the following

பரிசுத்தமான பொருட்களாவன எச்சில் பண்ணியது,
இறந்தவன் போர்த்திய போர்வை, வாந்தி பண்ணின
பொருள்

The food already tasted by someone, the cloth covering the dead and the food that is spewed out, are the purest of things

Now the person was extremely puzzled and also gave a disgusted look. Edaikaadar understood his expression and gave the explanation because though at the outset the aforesaid might look disgusting and gross but it has deep meaning in it.

பால், பட்டுத்துணி, தேன் இவை மூன்றும்
பரிசுத்தமான பொருட்கள். எவ்வாறெனின், பசுவிடம்
இருந்து பால் கறக்கும் முன்னர் கன்றுக்குட்டியை
முதலில் குடிக்கவிட்டு பின்னர் பால் கறப்பர்,
அதனால் பால் கன்றின் எச்சில். பட்டு நூல்
எடுக்கும்போது உள்ளை பட்டுப்புழு இறந்து இருக்கும்
ஆகவே அது இறந்தவனின் போர்வை. தேன் என்பது
தேனீ மலர்களில் சேகரித்து உமிழ்வது (வாந்தி).

178

Milk, Silk and Honey are the purest forms of things. Milk before it is drawn from the cow; the calf is made to drink, so the milk is echil. Silk when it is woven, has the silkworm dead inside. So Silk is the cover of the dead. Honey is collected by the bees and then spewed. All three are the purest of things.

Now enlightened, the person bowed before Edaikaadar imagined the depth of knowledge Edaikaadar had. His major works include Gnanasuthiram 70 (ஞானசூத்திரம் 70) and some songs in Aganaanooru (அகநானூறு), Puranaanooru (புறநானூறு) etc., however the Gnanasuthiram 70 and the 60 year predictions are more popular.

People say history repeats itself in some form or the other. Likewise, Edaikaadar's 60 year cycle repeats itself and the verses match close enough to the events of the years. (The appendix at the end of the book provides the predictions for all the 60 years). We should praise and wonder the amount of knowledge he had amassed and enlightened people with that knowledge though he was just a simple person herding cattle.

31. Austere Aasaarakkovai

These days, we hear a lot of people talking about environment safety, etiquettes etc, but it is quite amazing to know that our ancestors had this consciousness thousands of years ago. Such a fabulous thought process has been rendered as a treatise that defines the rules of life and etiquette that has to be followed to lead a disciplined and a happy life.

The treatise is "**Aasaarakkovai**" by Peruvaayin Mulliyanar which is one of the Pathinen Keezhkanaakku Group of literary works in Tamil literature. Written about 1500 to 2000 years ago, by around (100CE–500CE) consists of 100 stanzas, in which the author defines that rules governing food, dress code, decorum with kings and elders, conserving and non-pollution of natural resources, eschewing evil habits and bad company.

It is quite intriguing and amazing to see that Peruvayin Mulliyanar had envisioned about a lot of aspects that are applied even today. The name aasaaram itself means discipline, etiquette, decorum etc. Kovai means collection, aggregation. Let's see a few stanzas. The first one enlists the characteristics of discipline

*****

நன்றி அறிதல் பொறை உடைமை இன்சொல்லோடு
இன்னாத எவ்வுயிர்க்கும் செய்யாமை கல்வியோடு
ஒப்புரவு ஆற்ற அறிதல் அறிவுடைமை
நல்லினதாரோடு நட்டல் இவை எட்டும்
சொல்லிய ஆசார வித்து

*****

Nandri Aridhal Porai Udaimai Innsollodu
Innadha Evvuyirkkum Seyyaamai Kalviyodu
Oppuravu Aatra Aridhal Arivudaimai
Nallinathaarodu Nattal Ivai Ettum
Solliya Aasaara Viththu

*****

Meaning – The eight traits of good decorum are Gratitude, Patience, Pleasantness in speech, Refraining Unharming attitude towards other beings, Being Educated and Learned, Concordance with people, Understanding things thoroughly, Being Knowledgeable, Association with good people define aacharam (disciplined way of life).

To maintaining these traits one has to be much disciplined otherwise the traits cannot be achieved, this defines the basis for the remaining 99 stanzas. However, the poet goes into defining more on, who an educated person is, who a respectable person is etc. Let us see a few songs and their meaning to unravel what the poet has actually got for us.

*****

அரசன் உவாதியாயன் தாய் தந்தை தம்முன்
நிகரில் குறவர் இவரை
தேவரை போல தொழுது எழுக என்பதே
யாவரும் கண்ட நெறி

*****

Arasan Uvvathiyaayan Thaai Thandhai thammun
Nigaril Kuravar Ivarai
Devarai Pola Thozhudhu Ezhugha Enbadhae
Yaavarum Kanda Neri

*****

Meaning – The King, the Teacher, the Father, the Mother and Elder Siblings are respectable people in one's life, so they should

181

be treated and respected like the Gods and that is the etiquette which our ancestors found out

The next stanza is the basic etiquette about serving food or table manners

*****

விருந்தினர் மூத்தோர் பசு சிறை பிள்ளை
இவர்க்கு ஊன் கொடுத்தல்லால் உண்ணாரே என்றும்
ஒழுக்கம் பிழையார்

*****

Virundhinar Moothor Pasu Sirai Pillai
Ivarkku Oon Koduthallal Unnare Endrum
Ozhukkam Pizhaiyar

*****

Meaning – The disciplined, before they eat, will serve the food for the guests, elderly people, the cow, the birds and the children first. This is what is considered as table manners

Even today, many people serve food for the birds before they eat their meal during the day. It is even considered, that the ancestors eat the food in the form of birds. Such an act of providing food to the cattle and the birds is to some extent a conservation of the ecological system.

The next is about keeping the environment clean and pollution-free, which is the buzzword that every person or organisation is talking about these days, but the same thought have been introduced thousands of years back.

*****

புல் பைங்கூழ் ஆப்பி சுடலை வழிதீர்த்தம்
தேவகுலம் நிழல் ஆனிலை வெண்பலி என்று
ஈரைந்தின் கண்ணும் உமிழ்வோடு இருபுலனும்
சேரார் உணர்வுடையோர்

*****

Pul Painkoozh Aapi Sudalai Vazhitheertham
Deva Kulam Nizhal Aanilai Vennpali Endru
Eeraindhin Kannum Umizhvodu Irupulanum
Saeraar Unarvudaiyor

*****

Meaning – Grasslands, Agricultural lands, Cow dung (the dried form of cow dung is used to burn alongwith wood while cooking and during pujas), Graveyard, Waterbodies like ponds, lakes etc, Temples and places of sanctity, Shades under trees etc where people rest, Stable where cows are tied and Ash that is obtain by burning wood etc – are the 10 places where disciplined people would not pollute by spitting, passing excrements or otherwise

This environmental consciousness is the paramount statement of today's environmentalists, but this consciousness was widespread with our ancestors even in those days.

The next song is about strict discipline and self control

*****

பிறர்மனை கள் களவு சூது கொலையோடு
அறனரிந்தார் இவ்வைந்தும் நோக்கார் திறனிலர்
என்று
எல்லபடுவதும் அன்றி நிரயத்து
செல்வழி உய்த்திடுதலால்

*****

Pirarmanai Kall Kalavu Soodhu Kolaiyodu
Aranarindhaar Ivvaindhum Nokkaar Thiranilar Endru
Ellapaduvadhum Andri Nirayaththu
Sellvazhi Uithiduthalaal

*****

Meaning – Being flirtatious on other's wives, Booze, Larceny, Gambling and Murder are the five things that learned and disciplined people would never dare to commit because it not only brings blame and bad name, but also paves the way to hell

The next stanza details about how one should conduct his life

*****

நந்தெறும்பு தூக்கணம் புள் காக்கை என்று இவைபோல்
தம் கருமம் நல்ல கடை பிடித்து தம் கருமம் அப்பெற்றியாக முயல்பவர்க்கு ஆசாரம் எப்பற்றியாயினும் படும்

*****

Nandherumbu Thookanam Pull Kaakai Endru Ivaipol
Tham Karumam Nalla Kadai Pidithu Tham Karumam
Appettriyaga Muyalbavarkku Aasaram
Eppatriyaayinum Padum

*****

Meaning – The one who is working hard like an ant, protective like the weaver bird, Active like a bird, Social like the crow and does his duties correctly, then discipline will automatically attribute to him.

It is quite amazing about how the poet can bring about all these nuances of discipline. The problem is that how it could be followed by everyone equally, so considering that, the poet has also given exceptions to people who might not be able to follow the rules of discipline or etiquettes or in other words, it describes the people who are exempted from these rules. The following stanza enlists those poeple

*****

அறியாத தேயத்தான் ஆதுலன் மூத்தான்
இளையான் உயிர் இழந்தான் அஞ்சினான் உண்பான்
அரசர் தொழில் தலைவைத்தான் மணாளன் என்று
ஒன்பதின்மர் கண்டீர் உரைக்குங்கால் மெய்யான
ஆசாரம் வீடு பெற்றார்

*****

Ariyadha Theyatthan Aadhulan Moothaan
Ilayaan Uyir Ilandhan Anjinaan Unbaan
Arasar Tholizh Thalaivaithaan Manaalan Endru
Onbadhinmar Kandeer Uraikkunkaal Meiyaana
Aasaram Veedu Pettrar

*****

Meaning – The people who are exempt from following the rules described are Foreigner, Beggar, Aged people, Kids, Dead person, Frightened/Panicked person, Persons on deputation of King's or Governmental order, Persons about to get married are the nine people enlised to be exempt from maintaining the aasaram.

Though some of the stanzas might not be relevant to this day or cannot be followed as mentioned, some stanzas might even appear to be discriminating. But, if we construe it in the right sense, the point of discrimination disappears. However, we have to appreciate the knowledge and the awareness we had, even before the most other parts of the world knew that there are such principles to govern discipline for a citizen and for a society as a whole.

32. What to tell and what not to tell

Privacy, Confidentiality and Sensitive Information are very important things that all of us tend to be careful about in this Internet-enabled world. The information that are considered private, confidential, and quite personal to each individual, where revealing them makes one feel insecure, ashamed etc. So, what are the factors that are considered as privacy? Nowadays, the list goes like credit card numbers, mobile phone numbers, bank account numbers etc. The fact about privacy is not an awareness that was created recently. It dates back to the eighteenth century, where a poet named Ambalavana Kavirayar in his work, Arappaleeswara Sadhagam, has described about what to tell and what not to tell to the world. His work is in praise of Arappaleeswarar (Lord Shiva) of Arappaleeswaram, in the place called Sadhuragiri in the town of Seergazhi.

His literary work, the Arappaleeswara Sadhagam, consists of 100 songs that praise Lord Arappaleeswarar. Sadhagam is one of the 96 Prabandhams. It consists of 100 songs that either praises the Gods or describes about Love etc. This Arappaleeswara Sadhagam not only praises Lord Shiva, but also tells about good deeds, morals and characteristics of various things. And this is where Ambalavana Kavirayarar has sung about what to tell and what not to tell. The song goes like this

*****

சென்மித்த வருடமு முண்டான வருத்தமுந்
தீதில கிரகச் சார முஞ்
தின்றுவரு மௌடதமு மேலான தேசிகன்
செப்பிய மகா மந்த்ரமும்
புன்மையவ மானமுந் தானமும் பைம்பொனணி

186

புளையுமட வார் கல்வியும்
புகழ்மேவு மானமு மிவையொன்ப துந்தமது
புந்திக்கு ளேவைப் பதே
தன்மமென் றுரைசெய்ய சொன்னார் கருத்தையுந்
தன்பிணி யையும் பசியையுந்
தான்செய்த பாவமு மிவையெலாம் வேறொருவர்
தஞ்செவியில் வைப்ப தியல்பாம்
அன்மருவு கண்டனே மூன்றுலகு மீன் றவுமை
அப்பனே யருமை மதவே
எனுதினமு மனதினினை தருசதுர கிரிவள
றறப்பளீ சுர தேவனே

*****

Senmitha Varudamum Undaana Aththamum
Theedhil Gragachaaramum
Thindru Varum Oudathamum Maelanaa Desikan
Seppiya Maha Mandhiramum
Punmai Avamanamum Dhaanamum Paimpon Ani
Punaiyum Madavaar Kalaviyum
Pugazh Mayvum Maanamum Ivai Onbadhum Thamadhu
Pundhikkullae Vaipadhae
Dharmam Endru Urai Seivar Onnaar Karuthaiyum
Thann Piniyaiyum Pasiyaiyum
Thaan Seidha Paavamum Ivai Ellam Veru Oruvar
Thann Seviyil Vaipadhu Eyalbaam
Annmaruvu Kandanae Moondru Ulagum Eendra Umai
Anbanae Arumai Madhavael
Anu Dhinamum Manadhil Ninai Tharu Sadhuragiri Vala
Arappaleeswara Devanae

*****

Meaning – The year of birth, The wealth acquired, Planetary positions when they are good in one's zodiac chart, The medicines being taken, The mantra uttered by the Guru, The mean insults, The donations and benefactions, Intimacy with women, The dignity that brings fame – all these nine things should be kept within oneself as they are considered as private and should not be publicised to the world. The intentions of the enemies; The troubles one has, Hunger, The sins committed will usually be shared with someone else. Concluding with this moral, this stanza is completed with the praise of Lord Arappaleeswarar stating that his throat is dark as He ate the great poison obtained along with the divine potion called Amirdham, after churning the ocean of milk. And He is the consort of the Goddess Parvathi, who created all the three types of worlds. And this Lord Arappaleeswarar is being worshipped daily by the patron of the poet called Madhavael.

Senmitha – Being born

Varudam – Year

Undaana – Created, Acquired, Resulted

Aththamum – Wealth

Theedhil – Theedhu (Bad) + Ill (Negation), which means without being bad

Thindru Varum – Thindru (Eat) + Varum (Come, Continuing something)

Oudatham – Medicines

Maelana Desikan – Guru, Teacher

Seppiyya – Uttered, Said

Maha Mandhiram – The great or important mantra or advice

Punmai – Mean, Cheap, Misery

Avamaanam – Insult

Dhaanam – Donations

Paimpon Ani – Pure gold ornaments

Madavaar – Women

Kalavi – Intimacy

Ivai – These

Onbadhu – Nine

Thamadhu – Oneself

Pundhikkullae – In the mind

Vaipadhu – Keeping, holding

Dharmam – Good deed, Moral etiquette

Onnaar – Enemies

Karuthu – Intentions, Thoughts

Thann – Oneself

Pini – Troubles, Diseases etc

Pasi – Hunger

Paavam – Sin

Veru Oruvar – Other persons

Seviyil – Ears

Vaipadhu – Put, Tell, Hold, Keep

Iyalbu – Natural, Usually

Anmaruvu – Dark part

Kandam – Throat

Moondru Ulagam – Three Worlds

Eendra – Give birth, Create

Umai – Goddess Parvathi

Anbanae – Lover, Person showing Kindness

Madhavael – Patron of Ambalavana Kavirayar

Anu Dhinam – Every Day

Manadhil – Mind

Ninai – Think

Tharu – Giver, Tree

Sadhuragiri – Place in Seergaazhi

Arappaleeswara Devanae – Lord Arappaleeswarar

Some of the details like year of birth could not be hidden these days, but the actual intention to not reveal the year of birth was that the general characteristics of the person could be found if the year of birth is known. But the other things are considered private even today. Let's honour the great mind Ambalavana Kavirayar for his excellent work – The Arappaleeswara Sadhagam – and let his work be propagated for generations to come.

33. Graceful Kumaresa Sadhagam!

Our Tamil poets had eloquence in Tamil Language that they were capable of writing hundreds of songs at a stretch. Those songs were so elegant that those songs/poems sought to inculcate morals and facts of life. They have stood for hundreds of years as a moral reference. We already came across one such work – The Arappaleeswara Sadhagam by Ambalavana Kavirayar. There is one more Sadhagam (100 songs in praise of some deity inculcating some moral throughout – forms part of the 96 Prabandhams), the Kumaresa Sadhagam by Gurupaadha Daasar. The song is in praise of Lord Kumaresan (Murugan), hence the name Kumaresa Sadhagam, in the place called Pullvayal. The 100 songs sung in praise of Lord Kumaresan (Murugan) is full of elegance and grace in explaining the ethics. These songs were sung some 250 years ago and being recited in many homes. The facts and morals explained in it are applicable even today. There are songs explaining on how to get the Thiruneeru (Viboothi – The sacred ash) and how the Thiruneeru should be applied on the forehead and other parts of the body. We will see two songs that are really exemplary of the grace of the songs.

The first song is about the things that are useful to many people.

*****

கொண்டல்பொழி மாரியும், உதாரசற்குணம்உடைய
கோவும் ஊருணியின் நீரும்
கூட்டம்இடும் அம்பலத்து உறுதருவின் நீழலும்,
குடியாளர் விவசாயமும்,
கண்டவர்கள் எல்லாம் வரும்பெரும் சந்தியில்
கனிபல பழுத்தமரமும்,

கருணையுடனே வைத்திடும் தண்ணீர்ப் பந்தலும்
காவேரி போல்ஊற்றமும்,
விண்தலத்துஉறைசந்திர ஆதித்த கிரணமும்,
வீசும்மாருத சீதமும்,
விவேகிளினும் நல்லோர் இடத்தில் உறுசெல்வமும்
வெகுசனர்க்கு உபகாரமாம்,
வண்டுஇமிர் கடப்பமலர் மாலைஅணி செங்களப
மார்பனே வடிவேலவா
மயில்ஏறி விளையாடு குகனே புல்வயல்நீடு
மலைமேவு குமரேசனே.

*****

Kondal Pozhimariyum Udhara Sarrgunam
Udaiya Kovum Ooruniyin Neerum
Kootamidum Ambalaththu Urutharuvin Nizhalum
Kudiyalar Vivasayamum

Kandavarkal Ellarum Varum Perum Sandhiyil
Kanipala Pazhutha Maramum
Karunayudanae Vaithidum Thanneer Pandhalum
Kaveripol Ootramum

Vindalathu Urai Chandraadhitha Kiranamum
Veesu Maarutha Seedhamum
Vivegi Enum Nalloridathil Ooru Selvamum
Vegu Sanarkku Ubagaaramaam

Vandimir Kadappamalar Maalai Ani Senkalaba
Maarbanae Vadivelava
Mayil Yeri Vilayadu Kuganae Pullvayal Needu
Malaimevu Kumaresanae

*****

Meaning –The rain giving clouds, the generous hearted king, the water from the lake in the country, the shade of the tree where people gather, the agriculture of the farmer.

The tree bearing lots of fruits that grows in a place beneficial for the people. The Thanneer Pandhal, place where water is served free for passers-by. The spring has water flowing like the river Kaveri.

The rays of the Sun and the Moon in the sky; the gentleness of the breeze; the wealth in the hands of a Wiseman; all of the things mentioned above will benefit many in the country

I worship the Lord Kumaresan who is adorned with the Kadamba Flower Garland in which the bee gathers nectar and who goes around everywhere on top of a peacock in the hilly region of Pullvayal.

The next song is about the activities that happen in this Yugam – The Kali yugam. The Hindu cosmology has cyclic period has Four successive periods called Yugams. The four yugams are

- The Sathya or Krita Yugam (17,28,000 years),

- The Treta Yugam (12,96,000 years),

- The Dvapar Yugam (8,64,000 years) and

- The Kali Yugam (4,32,000 years).

In 2019 just 5121 years have passed in the Kali Yugam. There is a lot to tell about these yugam calculations but we will see that in a later chapter. In Kumaresa Sadhagam, Gurupaadha Daasar explains what activities will happen in this Kali Yugam. The song goes like this

*****

தாய்ப்புத்தி சொன்னால் மறுத்திடும் காலம்,உயர்
தந்தையைச் சீறுகாலம்
சற்குருவை நிந்தை செய்காலம்,மெய்க் கடவுளைச்

சற்றும் எண்ணாதகாலம்
பேய்தெய்வம் என்று உபசரித்திடும்காலம்
புரட்டருக்கு ஏற்றகாலம்
பெண்டாட்டி வையினும் கேட்கின்ற காலம்,நல்
பெரியர்சொல் கேளாதகாலம்
தேய்வுடன் பெரியவன் சிறுமைஉறு காலம்,மிகு
சிறியவன் பெருகுகாலம்
செருவில்விட்டு ஓடினார் வரிசைபெறு காலம்வசை
செப்புவோர்க்கு உதவுகாலம்
வாய்மதம் பேசிடும் அநியாய காரர்க்கு
வாய்த்தகலி காலம்ஐயா!
மயில்ஏறி விளையாடு குகனேபுல் வயல்நீடு
மலைமேவு குமரேசனே!

*****

Thaai Buddhi Sonnal Maruthidum Kaalam Uyar
Thandhai Seeru Kaalam
Sarrguruvai Nindhai Seikaalam Meikadavulai
Sattrum Ennadha Kaalam

Peidheivam Endru Ubasariththidum Kaalam
Purattarukku Yetra Kaalam
Pendaati Vaiyinum Kaetkindra Kaalam Narr
Periyar Soll Koladha Kaalam

Thaeivudanae Periyavan Sirumayurum Kaalam Migu
Siriyavan Perugu Kaalam
Seruvil Vittu Odinor Varisai Perr Kaalam Vasai
Seppuvorkku Udhavum Kaalam

Vaaimadham Pesividum Aniyaya Kaararkku
Vaaitha Kalikaalam Ayya
Mayil Yeri Vilayadu Kuganae Pullvayal Needu
Malaimevu Kumaresanae

*****

Meaning – The time when people don't heed the words/advice of their mother. The time when the children fight with their respectable father. The time when their guru is being insulted. The time when people don't think about the real God.

The time when the ghost are hailed as Gods. The time for all the liars. The time when people hear to the wife shouting and scolding them. The time when the words of the wise people are neglected.

The time when great people are being denigrated and mean and useless people grow. The time when the person who ran from the war field is being awarded. The time when people help those who vituperate them.

It is the time for all the people who commit blatant injustice. And all these events happen in the time period called the Kali Kaalam.

I worship the Lord Kumaresan who goes around everywhere on top of a peacock in the hilly region of Pullvayal.

Though quite simple in the use of language, but Kumaresa Sadhagam has in-depth meanings in its song. The great man who bestowed these songs surely would have been blessed by the God of the Tamil Language – God Murugan.

34. Kali Yugam – The Yugam with an infamous spell

Kali Yugam, the last of the four Yugams in the Hindu Cosmology. It is a dreaded yugam where things will be a haywire, where virtues (dharmam) are ignored and neglected. The Kali Yugam lasts for 4,32,000 years according to the Hindu Cosmology and once Kali Yugam ends, the cycle of the other Yugams – Satya or Krita (17,28,000 years), Treta (12,96,000 years), Dwapar (8,64,000 years) – take over. Don't hasten yet about Kaliyugam's end because we are just in the beginning, only about 5120 years have passed we still have a lot to go. Kaliyugam is dreaded because, legend says people live a short life unlike the people in the other yugams; in Krita yugam, people have life until their bones exist; in Treta, until their flesh lasts; in Dwapar, until the last drop of blood – remember Bhishma; and in Kali Yugam, people live until they eat food, once the food reserves in the body are gone, they die. That is the reason the saints and the enlightened profess people to donate food which is a good deed in the Kali Yugam.

We have already seen about the happenings in the Kali Yugam in one of the earlier chapters on Kumaresa Sadhagam. However, there is an interesting legend, an upakadhai of the Mahabharatha that illustrates the effects on the onset of the Kaliyugam. Mahabharata and the Kurukshetra War happened at the end of the Dwapar Yugam. The story beautifully explains the infamous nature of the Kali Yugam.

Now the legend – The Kurukshetra War was over, the Pandavas won the battle. Dharmaraja (Yudhistra) also called Dharmar, is known for holding the values of Truth (Satya) and Righteousness

(Dharma) and hence the name Dharmar. He ascended the throne after the Kurukshetra War and his subjects lived peacefully and happily in his righteous reign and then came this strange but interesting case.

Dharmar was in his court, along with his brothers and Lord Krishna. Two farmers came to him for deciding on a certain case. Of the two farmers, one sold his land to the other, lets call them the buyer farmer and the seller farmer. The deal was done and the seller received his payment from the buyer. The buyer after a few days of buying that land from the seller, starting ploughing and digging that land, and he struck some priceless treasure of rare gems and gold. The buyer was honest enough, so he took that treasure and went to the seller saying that he had paid only for the land and not for the treasure in it and the rightful owner of the treasure is the seller. The seller being equally honest told that the sale of the land has been done and anything from the land does not belong to him anymore and he said that the rightful owner was the buyer.

Both did not come to an agreement and that's when the dispute started (Strange isn't it, but remember that was in the Dwapar Yugam☺) and finally they decided to have it settled at Dharmar's court. The next day they went to Dharmar's court and explained the situation. Dharmar was really happy to see his subjects so righteous and he said that he felt really proud of both of them because of their righteousness. And Dharmar told that he does not want to give a verdict that will cause other to feel bad and asked them to both make a decision in his court. The farmers decided unanimously that the treasure be in possession of Dharmar until they come up with a decision and once they have decided who is to have the treasure, they will get it from Dharmar. Dharmar felt that it sounded like a plan and gave a nod. The farmers went for the moment leaving the treasure in Dharmar's possession. Dharmar felt really proud of the farmers' act.

Time passed by and things went on fine, until the same farmers who came to Dharmar's court earlier, came again with a different view of the earlier case. The buyer farmer now claimed that the treasure is his as he has paid the seller for the land and whatever he gets, either crops or whatever, is his. The seller farmer's argument was that he sold only the land and not the treasure, if he had known about that treasure, he would have either took it himself before the sale or would have charged the amount in the sale price. The farmers were arguing with the points reversed from their stand in the case when came earlier to Dharmar. Lord Krishna who watched all this smiled at Dharmar, who was confused a lot about this case. It was a case where the plaintiff and defendant had self-contradictory views over a period of time. He thought for a moment and gave the verdict that the treasure belongs to the government giving his explanation as follows.

The land of the buyer, which was previously with the seller before that sale, falls into his Empire. So, all the things belong to his Empire unless it was a reward for some effort made towards a claim. In addition, the treasure was not the benefit of any effort made by either of them and hence the King (himself) vests all the right to property and possession of the treasure. The treasure shall be used for the benefit of the people of his Kingdom. The farmers were disappointed, but they could not fight the King and went back.

Now, Lord Krishna rose to the fore and told Yudhistra that the time has come for them to leave this planet as He has seen the indications that Kali Yugam has started. And once Kali Yugam starts, they had no business there. Dharmar asked how Lord Krishna told that there are indications of Kali Yugam. Lord Krishna replied, that Dharmar who had the held the values of Truth and Righteousness, has slipped in the above case. Lord Krishna proceeded saying that though Dharmar had mentioned that the treasure will be used for the benefit of the people of his Kingdom, he had no right on the treasure and yet he found out justifications in the name of righteousness. And that, is the indication of Kali Yugam's arrival, even the most righteous will fall victims to circumstances and try to plunder and covet other's property. Dharmar realised his mistake and did as Lord Krishna suggested and the left Earth in a vimanam for good.

The aforesaid story clearly explains the spell Kali Yugam has even on the people who are determined. Think about the common man like you and me, unless the person has a great grit and determination to stand for the good, circumstances will lead him to unrighteous and immoral paths very easily, thereby taking them spiritually away from the path of Salvation. Of course, we can realise that with the events happening around us today, Kali yugam has a bad spell on everything that is on the planet, but this is just the beginning and there is a long way to go. Imagine the plight and sorrow people will have at the end. Legend says that at the end of the Kali yugam, human race will get to be contained within one foot or so. The mention about human race getting contained within a feet or so is unclear whether humans will grow only a feet or so tall, or will be contained within something that is a feet or so high, however a movie that has brought this legend to visual interpretation is "The Matrix" and the avatar, Kalki, will incarnate to rescue the people from their sorrows and plight. Nobody knows how the Kalki Avatar will be, but it is mentioned as the most modern of Avatars. Time has the answer, we will have to wait for nearly 4,27,000 years to see that...

35. Stupendous Saarangapani Temple

The Saarangapani Temple adorns the heart of the divine city Kumbakonam. Built around the time of the Pallavas and renovated and reconstructed and repaired by the Nayak Kings around the 15th century, is a masterpiece that stands 12 storeys and a staggering 150 ft high. The main gopuram has exquisite sculptures that symbolise the creativity and the hard work of our ancestors. The temple is devoted to Lord Rama.

Saarangapaani Temple is the place where the human race was bestowed with the blessings of Lord Vishnu to get the Naalayira Dhivya Prabandham, the collection of 4000+ songs sung by the Azhwars and considered the Vedas themselves by the Vaishnavites.There is an interesting legend that is related to the obtaining of Naalayira Dhivya Prabandham

Naadhamuni, a devout Vaishnavite, who went on to worship the Divyadesams, came to Saarangapaani Temple. There a devotee was singing the Paasurams of Azhwars at that time. Immersed in the divinity of the Paasurams, Naadhamuni went to the devotee and asked if he knew or had all the Paasurams, but the devotee said he does not know or have anything more than what he sang then. Disappointed, Naadhamuni prayed to Lord Vishnu on when he would be blessed to get Prabandhams. That's when he heard the divine voice directing him to Azhwar Thirunagari, where he would get the answers from a person living in the hole of a tamarind tree – Nammazhwar.

Naadhamuni immediately travelled to Azhwar Thirunagiri, where he met Nammazhwar residing in the hole of the Tamarind tree, which still is there to this day. He and Madhurakavi Azhwar together with the instructions of Nammazhwar gathered the Prabandhams and Naadhamuni collated it in the form that we now read it. Both Naadhamuni and Madhurakavi Azhwar took great efforts to gather those divine Paasurams. All of it began at this very Saarangapani Temple, and Vaishnavites who know this detail are still grateful to the Lord Saarangapani for bestowing His blessings to the human race to get the Prabandhams.

The deities are named Saarangapani and Komalavalli Thaayar. Let's see the amazing and the wonderful pics of the great temple.

Sri Saarangapani Temple Raja Gopuram

Close-up view of the Raja Gopuram

Raja Gopuram from inside the Prakaram

Another view of the Gopurams

36. Truthful Thirumangai Azhwar!!!

Thirumangai Azhwar one of the twelve Azhwars. He proved that one's faith and determination can take anybody near the Supreme – Lord Vishnu. There are other Azhwars who are equally worshipped as the incarnation of Lord Vishnu except Aandal who is worshipped as the incarnation of Goddess Lakshmi, but Thirumangai Azhwar inspires me a lot. His endurance in his devotion to Lord Vishnu has exalted him to the position of an Azhwar. He has travelled extensively to all the 108 Dhivya Desams, of which 106 are in this Earth and the remaining two are in the Heavenly Abode. He is said to have lived for 105 years and then attained salvation at the Lotus feet of Lord Vishnu at a place called Thirukurungudi. He has sung a majority of the songs in "The Naalayira Dhivya Prabandham", a collection of 4000 hymns, sung in praise of Lord Vishnu. His works in the Naalayira Dhivya Prabandham are Periya Thirumozhi, Thiru Kurunthaandagam, Thiru Nedunthaandagam, Thiruvelukootrarikkai, Siriya Thirumadal and the Periya Thirumadal which count to over 1200 hymns in all. He was a crude person before he became an Azhwar, same as what Valmiki was before writing the Ramayana.

His original name is Kaliyan, born to the Army Chief Command Neelan (as Abithana Chintamani states), he was chieftain of the Chola Empire and later crowned as King by the Chola Emperor for a small kingdom called Thirumangai as a token of the friendship and the gratitude for winning the war on the enemy, and hence the name Thirumangai Mannan – subsequently Thirumangai Azhwar. He explains in his songs that he slayed innocent lives, has not even uttered kind words to the poor and needy, plundered the wealth of people and had an affinity towards women. But later when he was crowned as a King he was attracted to a great lady called Kumudhavalli, who was the main reason for Kaliyan to divert his attention to the devotion to Lord Vishnu. He wanted her in marriage, but Kumudhavalli accepted his proposal conditionally stating that she would marry only a person who feeds 1000 devotees of Lord Vishnu daily and the one who helps the construction of the Vishnu temple at Srirangam. Kaliyan agreed and Kumudhavalli married him. He ardently carried on with the tasks. Troubles started to crop up, his reserves started to dwindle and there was pressure from the Chola Emperor, on the dues of taxes to be paid to the Chola Empire, but Thirumangai King was very serious in completing the work of the temple he started and feed the devotees of Vishnu. He was imprisoned for not respecting the orders of the Chola Emperor. Later, while in the prison he heard the instructions from the voice of Lord Vishnu (Lord Kariaperumal) asking him to come to Kanchipuram to pay off the dues to the Emperor. He informed the Emperor about it and Lord Vishnu directed Kaliyan to the place where there was treasure and he paid the dues, but he was dethroned out of his kingdom and he wandered lonely in the forests, where he got into the company of thieves. But even at that time, his intention and endurance was to complete the temple for Lord Vishnu. Before he got into the company of thieves, he begged the wealthy people in his kingdom telling the reason that he needed money to complete the temple and their help is very much needed, but in vain. Then he started the pillage and started plundering from the wealthy men. His looting continued and he got a lot of wealth enough to complete the temple work.

One fine day, he planned looting a marriage party, he intimidated the people of the marriage party to put all the jewels and valuables in one place and it happened. But when he tried to lift the ransom, he could not. This surprised him as he has lifted more that what he had plundered now, but he was still struggling to move the bundle, but it didn't budge. Then, Lord Vishnu and Goddess Mahalakshmi revealed themselves from the incarnation they took as a groom and the bride respectively and then he realised and fell at Lord Vishnu feet and pleaded mercy and apologized. Lord Vishnu blessed him and told that the hardships he went under were to test his endurance in his commitment and thereafter Kaliyan be called "Thirumangai Azhwar" thereby exalting him to an Azhwar. Later he got back his kingdom and wealth, and started to continue with the good deeds and devotion to Lord Vishnu. After this he sung the Periya Thirumozhi in praise of the Lord Vishnu.

The enthralling effect and the greatness of his songs are simply out of this world. In most cases, we would try to justify our faults or mistakes that we committed, but Thirumangai Azhwar accepted all his crimes, mistakes and faults at their face value without any justification offering his complete surrender to Lord Vishnu. The songs not only consist of repentance, but also the eloquence in the praise that shows the devotion and the high regard and respect he had for Lord Vishnu. This along with his endurance has exalted him to an Azhwar. Let us see some of his songs

*****

குலம்தரும் செல்வம் தந்திடும் அடியார்
படுதுயராயினவெல்லாம்
நிலந்தரஞ் செய்யும் நீள்விசும்பருளும்
அருளொடு பெருநிலமளிக்கும்
வலந்தரும் மற்றும் தந்திடும் பெற்ற
தாயினும் ஆயின செய்யும்
நலம்தரும் சொல்லை நான் கண்டுகொண்டேன்
நாராயணா என்னும் நாமம்

*****

Kulam Tharum Selvam Thandhidum
Adiyaar Paduthuyar Aayinavellaam
Nilandharam Seyyum Neel Visumbarulum
Arulodu Perinilam Alikkum

206

Valam tharum mattrum thandhidum Petra
Thaayinum Aayina Seyyum
Nalam Tharum Sollai Naan
Kandukondaen Narayana Ennum Naamam

*****

Meaning – It gives you status, wealth, eliminates sorrow by demolishing them to the ground. It bestows you with lengthy heaven along with lots of land. It blesses you with strength and all sorts of good things. It does more than what a mother would do to a child. And I found the all-good-bestowing name, Narayana. Here land means not only the materialistic property land, but grounds on which the person is recognised.

Kulam – status

Tharum, Thandhidum – provides

Selvam – Wealth

Adiyaar – devotees

Paduthuyar – sorrow

Aayinavellaam – all of the sorrows

Nilandharam – ground level

Seyyum – Does

Neel – Lengthy

Visumbu – Heaven

Arulum – Blesses

Arulodu – Along with the blessings

Perunilam – A huge piece of land

Alikkum – Provide

Valam – Strength

Mattrum – Others

Petra Thaai – Mother who begets a child

Nalam – Goodness

Soll – Word,

Kandukondaen – Found and realised

Narayana – Lord Vishnu's name

Naamam – Name

The next songs illustrate his meekness and great devotion. His acceptance of his mistakes at their face value without any justification, but all he requests was salvation

*****

வாடினேன் வாடி வருந்தினேன் மனத்தால்
பெருந் துயர் இடும்பையில் பிறந்து
கூடினேன் கூடி இளையவர்-தம்மோடு
அவர் தரும் கலவியே கருதி
ஓடினேன் ஓடி உய்வது ஓர் பொருளால்
உணர்வு எனும் பெரும் பதம் திரிந்து
நாடினேன் நாடி நான் கண்டுகொண்டேன்
- நாராயணா என்னும் நாமம்

*****

Vaadinaen Vaadi Varundhinaen Manaththaal
Perunthuyar Idumbaiyil Pirandhu
Koodinaen Koodi Ilayavar Thammodu
Avartharum Kalaviyae Karudhi
Odinaen Odi Uyivadhor Porulaal
Unarvenum Perum Padham Thirindhu
Naadinaen Naadi Naan Kandukondaen
Narayana Ennum Naamam

*****

208

Meaning — I anguished, felt weak and sad in my heart just because I was born in this whole lot of sorrow and distress. I had friendship with the mean and cheap people, just for the mean pleasures they gave me. Then I ran and ran because the Supreme Being changed my instincts and senses to search for the Supreme Being. Then because of the search I found the Supreme Being in the name of Lord Narayana.

*****

மானேய் கண் மடவார் மயக்கில் பட்டு மாநிலத்து
நானே நானாவித நரகம் புகும் பாவம் செய்தேன்
தேனேய் பூம்பொழில்சூழ் திருவேங்கட மாமலை என்
ஆனாய் வந்தடைந்தேன் அடியேனை
ஆட் கொண்டருளே

*****

Maanei Kann Madavaar Mayakkir Pattu Maanilathu
Naane Naanavidha Naragam Pugum Paavam Seidhaen
Thaenei Poompozhilsuzh Thiruvenkatamaa Malai Enn
Aanai Vandhadainthaen Adiyaenai Aatkondarulae

*****

Meaning — I fell for the attractive deer like eyes of women and committed sins that will take me to all the four kinds of hell. The Lord, Lord Venkatachalapathy, of the Thiru Venkata Mountains, that have flowers bearing nectar; I have come to surrender at your feet, please accept me and bless your devotee.

*****

தெரியேன் பாலகனாய் பல தீமைகள் செய்துமிட்டேன்
பெரியேன் ஆயின பின் பிறர்க்கே உழைத்து ஏழை
ஆனேன்
கரி சேர் பூம்பொழில் சூழ் கனமாமலை வேங்கடவா
அரியே வந்தடைந்தேன் அடியேனை
ஆட்கொண்டருளே

*****

Theriyaen Paalaganai Palatheemaigal Seithumittaen
Periyaen Aayinapin Pirarkae Uzhaithu Yaezhaiyaanaen
Karisaer Poompozhilsuzh Kanamaamalai Venkatava
Ariyae Vandhadainthaen Adiyaenai Aatkondarulae

Meaning – As a young child that commits mistakes, I have committed a lot of sins. And when I grew up (mental maturity), I became a poor fellow just by working for others (Feeding 1000 people daily as per Kumudhavalli's request). The Lord Venkatachalapathy of the great mountains that have majestic elephants – Lord Hari, I have come to Tirupathi to fall at your feel, grant me an asylum in your heart and bless me.

*****

கொன்றேன் பல்லுயிரை குறிக்கோள்
ஒன்றிலாமையயால்
என்றேனும் இரந்தார்க்கு இனிதாக உறைத்தறியேன்
குன்றேய் மேகமதிர் குளிர் மாமலை வேங்கடவா
அன்றே வந்தடைந்தேன் அடியேனை
ஆட்கொண்டருளே

*****

Kondraen Palluyirai Kurikkole Ondrillamayinaal
Endranum Irandhaarkku Inidhaga Uraiththariyaen
Kundraei Megamadhir Kulirmaamalai Venkatavaa
Andrae Vandhadaidhaen Adiyaenai Aatkondarulae

*****

Meaning – I killed many lives aimlessly, I never spoke benignly to those who came for help. Lord Venkatachalapathy, the lord of the mountains covered with misty chill clouds, I have come then to surrender at your feet and take asylum in your heart, bless me.

As already told, the greatness of Thirumangai Azhwar was his simplicity and the attitude to accept his mistakes at their face value, and most of all his endurance and the devotion to Lord Vishnu and his incarnations. His poetic eloquence has bestowed us great songs that have to be remembered for days to come and indeed sung in all the Bramhotsavam's celebrated in Tirupathi and various other Dhivyadesams. One such masterpiece is the Thiruvelukootrarikkai covered in the the chapter about Chithira Thaer in the Saarangapani temple of Kumbakonam. Thirumangai Azhwar stands as an example of how a devotion to their God should be, whatever religion be it. Let us worship Thirumangai Azhwar and get the blessings of Lord Vishnu.

37. The Wealth called Health

These are the days where most people appear to be pompously conscious of the calories in the food they eat, but actually they are not. Also, there are people who just think very low that the body is just a thing made of waste. There is even a song that says that the human body is just air filled bag and is just an illusion. The song goes like this

*****

காயமே இது பொய்யடா
வெறும் காற்றடைத்த பையடா

*****

Kaayamae Idhu Poiyada
Verum Kaatradaitha Paiyada

*****

Meaning – the human body is just an illusion and it is just an air filled bag, when the air being breathed goes out it becomes an empty shell that is useless

Kaayam – The human body

Idhu – A reflexive pronoun referring the body in this context

Poi – Lie, Illusion, Imaginary

Verum – Simply

Kaatradaitha – Kaatru (Air) + Adaitha (Filled, blocked)

Though this might be correct from one perspective, but in this world most people do not have the super natural capabilities to exceed their limits of their human nature and physiology. And thus came another song, on the same line

*****

காயமே இது மெய்யடா
அதில் கண்ணும் கருத்தும் வையடா

*****

Kaayamae Idhu Meiyada
Adhil Kannum Karuthum Vaiyada

*****

Meaning – The body exists in reality, so take the utmost care to maintain it carefully.

Mei – Truth

Adhil – Word referring to the body

Kannum Karuthum – The eye and the mind, meaning focus your attention in nurturing the body

There are many advices in the form of songs that emphasize the point of having good health. Because all that a man could achieve would be when he is in good health, once his health is gone everything is gone, his wealth, his fame. Many writers emphasize the one of the greatest wealth that a man could have is his health. There is one song that might sound funny and almost everybody knows it, but the actual meaning it emphasizes is really great. This song was sung by a Siddhar and it emphasizes the need for maintaining one's health. The song is

*****

நந்தவனத்தில் ஓர் ஆண்டி - அவன்
நாலாறு மாதமாய்க் குயவனை வேண்டி
கொண்டு வந்தான் ஒரு தோண்டி - மெத்தக்
கூத்தாடிக் கூத்தாடிப் போட்டுடைத்தாண்டி

*****

Nandhavanathil Ore Aandi Avan
Naalaaru maathamai Kuyavanai Vendi
Kondu Vandhan Oru Thondi Meththa
Koothadi Koothadi Pottudaithaandi

*****

The meaning at the first look would seem funny. It means that a poor man in the garden begged for a pot for ten months from the potter. And he got it finally after ten months, but the poor man carelessly played and played with the pot and broke it. The above meaning might look as if the poor man's effort was a waste as he could not save the pot he begged, but the actual meaning is different and has an indepth meaning, but before that let us meaning of the words in the song.

Nandhavam – Garden, Earth

Ore – one

Aandi – Man without anything with him

Avan – Personal Pronoun

Naalaaru – Naalu + Aaru – Four + Six that is ten

Maatham – Month

Kuyavan – Potter, Creator

Vendi – Beg, Ask

Kondu – Bring

Vandhan – Refers to the Aandi

Oru – One

Thondi – Pot, Container

Adhai – Pronoun referring the pot

Koothadi – Play

Pottu – Drop

Udaithaan – Breaking

The actual meaning is as follows. Nandhavam means the Earth and Aandi refers to the human. A human born in the face of the Earth garden comes with nothing in his hand, so he is a poor man. He comes into existence on this earth after ten months. So those ten months is being interpreted as the human begging the creator (God) for his existence by bringing his physical body on this Earth garden. His body being referred to the pot that holds his life and hence the Potter is God. And all his ten months of penance goes of waste once he carelessly roams on the face of the earth unconcerned about his health and thereby breaking the Pot (body) – his life and existence – which he brought into this Garden (Earth) after ten months of effort.

The greatness of this song is that it emphasizes a great meaning with a funny context. Thirumoolar in his masterpiece Thirumandhiram has written about the need to have good health. Even the greatest poet of the recent times, Kaviarasu Kannadhasan, has mentioned his experiences of having good health in his work Arthamulla Hindu Madham (Hinduism and its meanings). Let's see what Thirumoolar has mentioned about this in his songs. The first song goes like this

*****

உடம்பார் அழியில் உயிரார் அழிவர்
திடம்பட மெய்ஞ்ஞானஞ் சேரவு மாட்டார்
உடம்பை வளர்க்கும் உபாயம் அறிந்தே
உடம்பை வளர்த்தேன் உயிர்வளர்த் தேனே

*****

Udambaar Azhiyil Uyiraar Azhivar
Dhidampada Meignanam Seravum Mataar
Udambai Valarkkum Ubaayam Arindhae
Udambai Valarthaen Uyir Valarthaenae

*****

Meaning – "Those who have their health destroyed, its as though they have destroyed their life. They would never attain salvation or realise the Supreme Being. Hence I learned the way to nurture my health. And thus I was able to nurture my life"

Udambu – Physical body

Azhiyil – If destroyed

Uyir – Life, Soul

Azhivar – Die, Destroyed

Dhidampada – Healthiness

Meignanam – Salvation, Knowledge about the Supreme Being

Valarkkum – Nurturing

Ubaayam – Way, Method

Arindhae – realising, learning

What Thirumoolar says is 100% true, if a man does not have good health, then he will not find time to realise the Supreme

216

Being as he has to mind his own health to keep him alive. And it is a pain to see people suffering from health disorders.

His next song states what our very first song of this chapter states and then later realises the importance of the human body.

*****

உடம்பினை முன்னம் இழுக்கென் றிருந்தேன்
உடம்பினுக் குள்ளே உறுபொருள் கண்டேன்
உடம்புளே உத்தமன் கோயில்கொண் டான்என்று
உடம்பினை யானிருந் தோம்புகின் றேனே

*****

Udambinai Munnam Izhukkendru Irundhaen
Udambinukku Ullae Uru Porul Kandaen
Udambullae Uththaman Koyil Kondan Endru
Udambinai Yaanirundhu Ombukindraenae

*****

Meaning —"Earlier, I had the thought that the body is a disgrace. Then within it, I realised the existence of the Supreme Being. In my body, the Supreme Being (Lord Shiva) has a temple within which he resides. Therefore, I worship and nurture my physical body".

Udambu – Physical body

Munnam – Earlier

Izhukku – blemish, blame

Irundhaen – have an opinion, in this context

Ullae – Inside

Uru Porul – refers to the Supreme Being

Uththaman – Flawless, Divine Human

Koyil – Temple

Kondan – Have, Reside

Yaanirundhu – Yaan (refers to self – Thirumoolar) + Irundhu (exist, remain)

Ombukindraen – Worshipping, Nurturing

The religious attitude that God resides in one's body, is a great thought that the religiously inclined will consider the body to be divine thing and will start to maintain it in good health. For the others who are not religiously inclined, they understand that their body health is of utmost importance for them to survive. Both ways, the emphasis is to have a good health throughout life. There are various ways humans can maintain their health. The following song explains one – Yoga. There are others ways like knowing about the food we eat and thereby eating the good food, more about this in a subsequent chapter – Priceless Padhartha Guna Chinthamani.

So, conclusively, all the siddhars, doctors and wise men talk about conserving one's health. There has been ancestral knowledge on home remedies in every culture like the Paati Vaidhiyam that was passed on from one generation to another for many generations. It was was followed and used to cure many common ailments and people also had good healthy food that helped keep the body fit. The knowledge is getting lost as many in this fast-paced world do not have the patience to learn those and they also are looking for a quicker relief than attempting to have a right and permanent cure. The people who forget the most treasured knowledge that is priceless will realise only when health is lost. Let us bring back those practices back into life to live long and prosper!

38. Elusive Illusions – Maayai

Maayai – Illusions in life – is an elusive term that reflects the unsteady state of human life. Philosophers and Saints who achieved realisation say that everything around us and we, ourselves, are the facets of illusion or illusion itself. But that definition does not seem to give a complete insight or understanding to a layman about what Maayai actually is. This is where our great epics – The Ramayanam and The Mahabharatham – come to deal with such situations. Though the mainline of these epics is well known to the world, there are many stories/legends that come along with the mainline of these epics. The ancillary legends are called the Upakadhai meaning stories that form as an ancillary part. The line and the situations mentioned in these Upakadhais are a bit different from the main epic, but the characters involved in the Upakadhais are the same as those in the main epic.

Well, lets get back to our Maayai concept. Though people have explained pages and pages of things about this, the Upakadhais explain it in a very simple manner that whole concept is understood to people of all categories. One such story comes from Mahabharatham. The story goes like this.

Once, Naradhar had the same question that we have raised here. What is Maayai? He asked various people and saints he knew, but nobody gave him an answer that was so satisfactory. So he wanted to know a concrete answer to that question. Finally he went to Lord Krishna and asked the question. Lord Krishna promised to give him an answer so concrete that Naradha would completely understand what Maayai was. Lord Krishna also told Naradha that He will take him somewhere the next day to show and explain what Maayai was. Naradha agreed.

The next morning, Lord Krishna and Naradha started very early that Naradha could not find time to take his bath. On the way, Naradha found a pond and said to Lord Krishna that he will be back in a few minutes after taking his bath immersing himself in the pond. Lord Krishna agreed to it and asked him to be back quickly as they would be late to where they are heading. Naradha consented and went ahead to the pond. This is when the Omnipotent Being, Lord Krishna, got prepared to unleash the Maayai. When Naradha immersed completely inside the water, Lord Krishna unleashed Maayai and that's where things started for Naradha.

Then later, both were walking for a long distance. Lord Krishna felt very thirsty and asked Naradha to go get some water in house that visible at short distance from where they were. Until then Lord Krishna said that he will take rest under a tree.

Naradha went to that house to get some water. When he went inside the house calling for people in there, a beautiful and charming young lady appeared from the house and asked what he wanted. He was taken aback by the beauty of that girl and he lost himself. He fell madly in love with that girl and wanted to marry her. Naradha completely forgot about Lord Krishna asking water. He was completely obsessed, that, only the girl's beauty was in his eyes.

He wanted to marry her and spoke to her father saying that he was Naradha, son of Lord Brahma – The Creator. The girl's father consented to Naradha marrying his daughter. The wedding was over and the couple lived happily for twelve years. They had 12 children; the family became big and so was its burden. The family was getting into poverty as Naradha could not manage such a big family. Every day was painfully bad because of the increasing poverty.

One day rain poured heavily that started to cause floods in that area. Naradha with all his family members was sitting together in the old dilapidated hut. He grasped as many children as the others cuddled together. Slowly the flood waters began to rise and washed away Naradha's home and children. He grasped to the hands of as many children as he could and took a few in his shoulders so that they could be in safety. When the floods washed them, Naradha caught hold off a branch of a tree and stayed in safety with a few children on his shoulder and in his grasp. Slowly the floods started to gain speed and washed away all the children. Naradha was exhausted, that he could not move or hold on anymore and the floods were continuously rising and he was immersed completely.

Finally, he mustered all his energy to pull himself out of water and with a big gasping sound for a breath of air; he came out of the water. Then suddenly, he realised that he was in the pond that he immersed himself to take bath while coming along with Lord Krishna. He was shocked to see that he did not move out of the pond and yet he had the pleasurable and worst experiences in life. By then he heard Lord Krishna saying, "Naradha, why is it taking you 45 minutes to immerse yourself and take a bath?" Naradha was more shocked when Lord Krishna said this.

He came out of the pond and asked Lord Krishna about all that happened. He said that he had spent 12 years of life that was peaceful and miserable, but how come just 45 mins have passed. Lord Krishna smiled at Naradha and told – "That is Maayai (that 12 years of his life)". Naradha fell at his feet.

Well, that is one fine story that explains a subtle concept in a simple manner. These stories are not only easy to understand, but they also contain a great message that does not need any special learning to understand it. Though these stories might sound like a fairy tale suitable for children, they explain concepts that have been explained in Physics (Concept of time dilation as in this story), Management etc. These stories have to be interpreted correctly that they will serve a greater purpose to every aspect of human life.

Let us find out and preserve these Upakadhais as we do with our epics so that they are not only interesting to hear, but hold great philosophical knowledge.

39. Divinely Unique – Aandaal

Andaal – Kodhai Naachiyaar – a name that is held is very high respect in the Vaishnavite world and is exalted to the status of a Goddess. She is unique in various respects. Of the twelve Azhwars, she is the only female Azhwar. She had an unwavering devotion to Lord Vishnu and married him at Srirangam

She started the ritual called the Paavai Nonbu that is followed to this day. This ritual is followed by unmarried girls so that they get a husband of a good character. She is considered to be the incarnate of Goddess Lakshmi, the consort of Lord Vishnu

Her birth place is Srivilliputur and the temple for her at Srivilliputur stands as an official symbol in the seal of Government of the Tamil Nadu, as a symbol of the Art and Architecture of the Tamil Civilisation

Let us see the life history of Aandaal. Legend says that Goddess Lakshmi wanted to praise Lord Vishnu, by being the daughter of the famous Azhwar, Vishnu Sitthar, famously known as Periazhwar. Periazhwar found her as a baby under the Thulasi plant in the temple garden. From then on, Periazhwar considered her to be a gift that Lord Vishnu gave him and brought her up as his own daughter. He taught her all the philosophies and stories he knew about Lord Krishna and also taught her to attain poetic eloquence in the Tamil language. He named her Kodhai meaning Garland.

Kodhai grew up as a kid just thinking about Lord Krishna and she would consider herself as playing with Lord Krishna when her father was away to perform the temple rituals. Everyday Periazhwar gathers flowers from the garden and makes a garland out of it to be presented to Lord Ranganathar. Everyday after making the garland, he would go away to his garden to maintain it and then return back to take the garland to the temple. So, when he was away, Kodhai would wear the garland to see if it suited her, only if it did, she thought that it should be offered to the Lord.

One day, Periazhwar saw Kodhai doing this and got very angry as it is considered a sacrilege in Hinduism that anything that has been used by the humans should not be offered to the Lord. He shouted at her telling her to get out of his sight, but Kodhai told that she was unaware and she thought she was playing with Lord Krishna. But later Periazhwar composed himself and told her not to repeat it and that he will get a fresh garland made for the Lord. And when he offered it to the Lord, the garland fell out as if showing the Lord's unacceptance of the offer. Then Kodhai brought the garland that she wore and told that Lord Krishna will like children and that she was playing with Lord Krishna, so he should accept the garland. Periazhwar offered it to the Lord in the temple and to his surprise the place was illuminated showing the acceptance.

Only then, he realised how blessed Kodhai was and adorned her with the name *"Soodi Kodutha Sudar Kodi"* meaning "The bright star like lady who gave the Lord the garland after wearing them". And as she ruled the Lord with her devotion, she was adorned with the name "Aandaal" meaning, the one who rules.

From then on she had an unwavering devotion to Lord Vishnu and when she reached the age to get married, she was stubborn that she will marry only Lord Ranganathar at Srirangam, which made Periazhwar baffle as to how it was humanly possible. Later Periazhwar felt the vision of the Lord at Srirangam to bring his daughter in full bridal adornment to Srirangam. When they went to Srirangam, Aandaal merged with Lord Ranganather completely at that point.

Aandaal is held in high respect and exalted to the level of Azhwar because of her unwavering and sincere devotion to Lord Vishnu. Her exemplary works, Thiruppavai and Naachiyaar Thirumozhi stand as a proof to her devotion. Not only she showed her sincere devotion, she also made the other girls of the country to follow that and started off a ritual called the Paavai Nonbu which she elaborates in her work – Thiruppavai. The songs in both Thiruppavai and Naachiyaar Thirumozhi express the grandeur and eloquence of Aandaal's thoughts about Lord Vishnu. This Paavai Nonbu is being followed during the month of Maargazhi even today, and the songs from Thiruppavai are sung each day during that month. It is in correlation to what Lord Krishna said in the Bhagavad Gita; of all the months, He is the month of Maargazhi. It is so auspicious that in all the Vaishnavite temples Maargazhi is celebrated widely to get the blessing of the Lord.

She has sung 143 songs in two separate collections – Thiruppavai and Naachiyar Thirumozhi. Vedantha Desikar has praised very highly of Aandaal's songs

*****

பாதகங்கள் தீர்க்கும் பரமனடி காட்டும்
வேதமனைத்துக்கும் வித்தாகும் - கோதைதமிழ்
ஐயைந்தும் மைந்தும் அறியாத மானிடரை
வையம் சுமப்பதும் வம்பு.

*****

Paadhagangal Theerkkum Paramanadi Kaatum
Vedham Anaithukkum viththaagum Kodhai Thamizh
Aiaindhum Aindhum Ariyadha Maanidarai
Vaiyyam Sumappadhu Vambu

*****

Meaning – (Thiruppavai) will remove your sins. It will show the divine lotus feet of the Supreme Lord Vishnu. It is the seed for the Vedas in entirety. It is a burden for the earth to bear all those who have not learnt the 30 songs (Five Fives and a Five) of the Thiruppavai

Now let's look at the very first song that expresses the strong devotion and splendour of Aandaal's expression. The song goes like this

* * * * *

மார்கழித் திங்கள் மதி நிறைந்த நன்னாளால்
நீராடப் போதுவீர் போதுமினோ நேரிழையீர்
சீர் மல்கும் ஆய்ப்பாடிச் செல்வச் சிறுமீர்காள்
கூர்வேல் கொடுந்தொழிலன் நந்தகோபன் குமரன்
ஏராந்த கண்ணி யசோதை இளம் சிங்கம்
கார் மேனி செங்கண் கதிர் மதியம் போல்
முகத்தான்
நாராயணனே நமக்கே பறை தருவான்
பாரோர் புகழப் படிந்தேலோர் எம்பாவாய்

* * * * *

Maargazhi Thingal Madhi Niraindha Nannaalal
Neeraada Podhuveer Podhumeeno Naerilazhaiyeer
Seer Malgum Aayippaadi Selva Sirumeergaal
Koorvael Kondunthozhilan Nandhagopan Kumaran
Yaeraarndha Kanni Yasodhai Ilam Singam
Kaarmaeni Sengann Kadhir Madhiyam Pol Mugathaan
Narayananae Nammakku Parai Tharuvaan
Paaror Pugazha Padindhaelor Empaavaai

* * * * *

Meaning –Oh! the wealthily adorned girls of Aaryarpadi, on the auspicious full moon lit month of Maargazhi, let us go and bathe and perform the paavai nonbu, because the Lord is the son of the Nandhagopan, who guards the country by giving pain to his enemies with his long spear. The young lion of the beautiful eyed Yasodha. He has the body coloured like the dark rainy clouds. His eyes are bright and are pleasant like the rays of the vivid full

226

moon. He is none other than Lord Narayanan who would bless us. So, let us observe the penance praised by the world – The Paavai Nonbu – by immersing ourselves in the water first.

We can see the literary eloquence and her power of faith in making the people perform a ritual to get the blessings of the Lord, which is an exemplary feat.

The verses following from Naachiyaar Thirumozhi express her glorious thoughts and imagination. In the following songs, she narrates to her friend about the dream that she had in the previous nights. She dreams about marriage ceremony between Her and Lord Narayanan. The magnificence and richness of thought can be seen throughout the verses

*****

வாரண மாயிரம் சூழவ லம்செய்து,
நாரண நம்பி நடக்கின்றா னென்றெதிர்,
பூரண பொற்குடம் வைத்துப் புறமெங்கும்,
தோரணம் நாட்டக் கனாக்கண்டேன் தோழீநான்

*****

Vaaranamaayiram Soola Valam Seidhu
Naarana Nambi Nadakindraan Endru Edhir
Poorana Porr Kudam Vaithu Puram Engum
Thoranam Naata Kanaa Kandaen Thozhi Naan

*****

She explains the dream that she had. The situation of this song is during the Maapillai Azhaippu ritual, where the groom (here the Lord himself) is invited and walked till the marriage hall. The meaning of the song – With a thousand elephants surrounded, Lord Narayanan walks majestically to the marriage hall. Because the Lord arrives and in order to receive him, Poorana Kumbham -

227

the pot usually made of gold is kept and in the place surrounded with decorative festoons and banners.

Each of these verses is adorned with the richness that explains the magnitude at which the occasion is being conducted. In the other verses she narrates about the people who attended the dream wedding. The people are all the Gods, including the head of the Devars – Indran and many others who make the marriage ceremony a grand one. The narration of dream shows the undiverted devotion She had to Lord Narayana.

Aandaal is just considered to be woman with an ardent devotional faith, which is unquestionable, but her wisdom is not just limited to faith alone. Her knowledge expands to other fields as well. Her songs show that she possessed a lot of knowledge in science and astronomy. She had the knowledge of tracking planetary movements just with bare eyes, the science behind rainfall.

*****

புள்ளின் வாய் கீண்டானைப் பொல்லா அரக்கனைக்
    கிள்ளிக் களைந்தானைக் கீர்த்தி மை பாடிப்
போய்ப்
பிள்ளைகள் எல்லாரும் பாவைக் களம்புக்கார்
    வெள்ளி எழுந்து வியாழம் உறங்கிற்று
புள்ளும் சிலம்பின காண் போதரிக் கண்ணினாய்
    குள்ளக் குளிரக் குடைந்து நீராடாதே
பள்ளிக் கிடத்தியோ. பாவாய். நீ நன் நாளால்
    கள்ளம் தவிர்ந்து கலந்தேலோர் எம்பாவாய்.

*****

Pullin Vaai Keendaanai Pollaa Arakkanai
Killi Kalaindhaanai Keerthimai Padippoi
Pillaigal Ellarum Pavai Kalampukkaar
Velli Ezhundhu Vyalam Urangitru

228

Pullum Silambinakaan Pothari Kanninaai
Kulla Kulira Kudaindhu Neeradadhae
Palli Kidaththiyo Paavai Nee Nannaalal
Kallam Thavirththu Kalandhaelor Empaavai

*****

Meaning – "The One" who decimated the asura who took the form of a stork and the One who nipped the cruel demon king is being praised by the Paavai songs by the girls who have already reached the spot where the Paavai Nonbu is being observed. Even the Venus (The morning star – Vidivelli) has risen and Jupiter (Vyazhan) has set down. The birds have risen and started chirping, and you my girl with beautiful eyes, instead of happily bathing in the cold waters, you are still lying down fast asleep. Don't ever think about you going alone and worshipping the Lord Vishnu and getting his blessings but get along with the others who also are observing the Paavai Nonbu.

Here the reference to Venus and Jupiter is where she has registered the fact that it was quite common to have the knowledge of planetary movements those days and Aandaal possessed that knowledge as well.

*****

ஆழி மழைக் கண்ணா ஒன்று நீ கை கரவேல்
ஆழி உள் புக்கு முகந்து கொடு ஆர்த்து ஏறி
ஊழி முதல்வன் உருவம் போல் மெய் கறுத்துப்
பாழிய் அம் தோளுடைப் பற்பனாபன் கையில்
ஆழி போல் மின்னி வலம்புரி போல் நின்று அதிர்ந்து
தாழாதே சார்ங்க முதைத்த சர மழை போல்
வாழ உலகினில் பெய்திடாய் நாங்களும்
மார்கழி நீராட மகிழ்ந்தேலோர் எம்பாவாய்

*****

229

Aazhi Mazhai Kanna Ondru Nee Kai Karavel
Azhiyul Pukku Mugandhu Kodu Aartheri
Oozhi Mudhalvan Uruvam Pol Mei Karuthu
Paazhiyam Thozhudai Padhmanaban Kayil
Aazhi Pol Minni Valaburi Pol Nindradhirndhu
Thaazhadhae Saarngam Udhaitha Saramazhai Pol
Vaazha Ulaginil Peidhidaa Naangalum
Maargazhi Neerada Magizhdhelor Empaavai

*****

Meaning – Lord Krishna the bestower of rainfall, do us a favour. Fetch enough water from the oceans, climb the mountains. Become the dark clouds in the colour of Lord Vishnu. Flood the lightning bolt as bright as the Sudharasan Chakra adorning the right side of the shoulders of Lord Padmanabhan that are as beautiful as bamboo and rumble heavily as thunder that matches the sound of the valamburi conch (Paanchachaniyam) that adorns His left shoulder. Pour down as rain that is like the deluge of arrows from the bow called Saarangam. That rain rejuvenates life on earth and we will happily get drenched in the rain in the month of Maargazhi.

This song illustrates her knowledge of how rainfall occurs, the process of convection, precipitation and the moist clouds that bring water from the evaporated oceans.

And it is with all this information in the songs that M. Raghava Iyengar, in his book Azhwargal Kaala Nilai, was able to trace the time she had lived– the 8th century between 710 CE – 735 CE

- Maargazhi Thingal – Thiruppavai 1

- Aazhimazhai Kanna – Thiruppavai 4

- Pullinvaai keendaanai – Thiruppavai 12

She is believed to have spent her later part of her life in Thirumaliruncholai – Azhagarmalai – after being married to Lord Ranganathar at Srirangam and references to this Thirumaliruncholai is filled in her Naachiyar Thirumozhi.

The Srivilliputhur Aandaal temple adds the name Aandaal to its crown showing the divinity of Aandaal. Being so divine and Godly has made Aandaal a unique Azhwar and her works and the Paavai Nonbu has earned a special name for her and will be remembered forever.

40. Priceless Padhartha Guna Chinthamani

Paati Vaidhiyam (Grandma's therapy) is the ancestral knowledge of food habits and medicinal practices with the herbs and food items that are available in the part of the country. It is used to cure many common ailments. It is also being followed in some homes even today. The practice of Paati Vaidhiyam has been passed on from one generation to another for many generations that people with that knowledge are able to understand the problem of an ailment or disease, diagnose it and cure it correctly. They are able to do it because; they knew the characteristics of the diseases and, most importantly, the characteristics of the medicines that were used to cure them. Medicines, in the sense, are nothing but herbs and other eatables that are used in the day to day life.

These substances with medicinal value are not only used on the incidence of an ailment, rather it was used regularly that prevented the incidence of that ailment, leading to a healthy and properous life. Nowadays, only some homes are gifted with the people with the knowledge of Paati Vaidhiyam, but the rest are not, because there is no one to tell the medicinal characteristics of the things that we used and consume in our day to day life. And such treasures get lost from that generation onwards and once lost, it is lost forever. Only a few people take some effort to make a note of these so that it gets propagated into the future. The advantage of Paati Vaidhiyam is that it diagnoses and cures the ailment perfectly and without any side-effects

Our siddhars have taken the pains to analyse the cause and treatment of the diseases and they have mentioned preparations to cure many diseases completely without any side-effects. The classification of the diseases and the treatment itself forms a great reference in the field of Medicine. Not all such references can be used by the common man, because it requires some background in medicine. However, there is one such great reference that can be used even by the common man. It is a rare treasure named "Padhartha Guna Chintamani" (Padhartham – Eatables, Gunam – Characteristic, Chintamani – The one that bestows all good things). It is one comprehensive reference that explains the medical characteristics about the food items and the utensils used to prepare those food items. It explains the medical characteristics of over 1000 items. The author of this masterpiece is a Siddhar named, Theraiyar. Theraiyar is the disciple and student of Agathiar. He is also known to be best student and has written many medical texts of which some perished and some remain.

Many legends exist about Theraiyar; let us see a few of them. The name Theraiyar is because when King had a severe chronic pain in his head, he treated it by opening the king's skull and removing the tadpole from the King's head. It is believed that when the King was bathing in a pond, the egg of a toad in the water went into the nostrils and up to his brain where it hatched and developed as a tadpole. Therai means Toad in Tamil. As he removed the toad from the King's head, he is named after that Theraiyar. It is also said that Avaiyar met Agathiar and asked him to take Theraiyar as his student. Theraiyar was the most illustrious student of Agathiar, that there is a legend that he turned a mountain into gold using herbs and got the praise of Agathiar.

Theraiyar's work, the Padhartha Guna Chintamani, is one of the masterpieces that exist even today. It is great collection and a central reference about the medicinal characteristics of the things that humans normally use or consume in their day to day life and the ones that are not normally consumed. It describes the characteristics of both vegetarian and non-vegetarian diets. It not only describes about the items that are eaten. It also describes the characteristics of the utensils used to prepare and serve the items consumed, for example, the medicinal characteristics of stone utensils used to prepare food or medicines is described.

Let us see some of the songs from that text. I have tried to give exact meanings for these songs, but in some cases, due to the medical nature, given approximately correct meanings. The following song describes about the characteristics of the various parts of the plantain tree.

*****

நற்கதலிக் கந்தம்அனல் நல்குந்த்தண் டோாகுடலிற்
சிக்குமயிர் தோல்நஞ்சிந் தீர்த்திடுங்காண் தொக்குறுபூ
மேகமொழிக் கும்பிஞ்சால் வெங்கடுப்பேகுங் காயால்
தேகமுழுக் கக்காலந் தேர்

*****

Narrkadhalikku Andham Anall Nalgum Thando Kudalil
Sikkum Mayir Thol Nanjum Theerthidumkaan Thokkuru Poo
Megam Ozhikkum Pinjaal Venkaduppu Yaegum Kaayaal
Dhegam Muzhukka Kaalam Thaer

*****

Meaning – the tuber of the plantain increases the body's internal heat, the stem cures ailments in the stomach and intestines, the flower cures skin disorders, the tender fruit cures ailments due to increase in body heat. Unripe fruit cause Vaadham (The proportion of air that exists in the human body) to accumulate causing bodyaches etc.

The following songs illustrates the properties of ginger

*****

இஞ்சிக் கிழங்குக் கிருமல்ஜயம் ஒக்காளம்
வஞ்சிக்குஞ் சந்நிசுரம் வன்பேதி விஞ்சுகின்ற
சூலையறும் வாதம்போந் தூண்டாத தீபனமாம்
வேலையுருங் கண்ணாய் விளம்பு

*****

Injikilangukku Irumal Aiyam Okkaalam
Vanjikkum Sanni Juram Vann Baedhi Vinjukindra
Soolai Arum Vaadham Pom Thoondadha Theebanamaam
Velaiarum Kannaai Vilambu

*****

Meaning – the ginger cures the following Cough, Cold, Dense Phlegm in the chest, delirious fever, Diarrhoea, Skin disease and Vaadham. It also makes one feel hungrier

The book even tells the properties of the boiled water boiled to different levels. Water that is 100% boiled, 75%, 50% and 25% boiled. The following songs explain those

*****

நெஞ்செரிப்பு நெற்றிவலி நீங்காப் புளியேப்பம்
வஞ்சமுற வந்த வயிற்றினோய் விஞ்சியே
வீழாமக் கட்டோடு வெப்பிருமற் சுட்டநீர்
ஆழாக்குட் கொள்ளவறும்

*****

Nenjerrippu Netrivali Neengaa Puliyaeppam
Vanjamura Vandha Vayitri Noi Vinjiyae
Veezhamal Kattodu Veppirumal Suttaneer
Azhaakku Uttkolla Arum

*****

Meaning – Heartburn, the burning sensation in the chest due to acidity, continuing sour belch, stomach ailments and dry cough will get cured when an Azhaakku – 1/8th of padi (A utensil used to measure liquid quantities) – of boiled hot water is taken.

This song tells the properties of water that is boiled 25% and 50%

*****

காற்கூறு காய்நீராற் காரிகையே பித்தம்போ
மேற்கூறு பாதிசுட்ட வெந்நீரான் மேற்கூறும்
வாதமொடு பித்தம்போம் வைத்தொருநாட்
சென்றுண்கு
ரோதம்போ மோடி யொளித்து

*****

Kaalkooru Kaaineeraai Kaarigaiyae Piththampom
Maelkooru Paadhi Sutta Venniraal Maelkoorum
Vaadhamodu Piththampom Vaithu Oru Naal Sendru Unn
Urodham Pom Odi Olithu

*****

Meaning – the water that is 25% boiled cures the (Piththam) body heat, and the water that is 50% boiled cures Vaadham and Piththam. If that water is taken a day after boiling then the diseases will run away and hide.

The next song is about the most hated of vegetables, but more medicinal in value, the Sundakkai. The Sundakkai is hated because of its bitter taste. But it is dried in the sun after soaking in curd to make the sundakkai vaththal, that is fried and eaten as such or to prepare a mouth watering kulambu variety called vaththal kulambu. The property of the Sundakkai is

*****

நெஞ்சின் கபம்போம் நிறைகிருமி நோயும்போம்
விஞ்சுவா தத்தின் விளைவுபோம் வஞ்சியரே
வாயை கசப்பிக்கும் மாமலையில் உள்ளசுண்டைக்
காயைச் சுவைப்பார்க்குக் காண்

*****

Nenjin Kabam Pom Niraikirumi Noiyum Pom
Vinju Vaadhathin Vilaivu Pom Vanjiyarae
Vaayai Kasapikkum Maamaliyil Ulla Sundai
Kaayai Suvaipaarukku Kaan

*****

Meaning – Sundakkai that grows in the mountains and tastes bitter, cures dense phlegm in the chest, diseases caused by bacteria, and the effects of Vaadham

The more amazing thing about Padhartha Guna Chintamani is that, it not only explains the characteristics of the food items we eat, but it also explains the characteristics of the metal and stone utensils in which food and medicines are prepared. The following songs tell that

*****

கருங்கற்கல் வுத்தவுழ்தங் காணில்உடற் கின்பாம்
நெருங்கிரத்தக் கல்தோசம் நீக்கும் ஒருங்குவெள்ளைக்
கன்மருந்தோ வீரமொடு காரமும்இல் மஞ்சள் அம்மி
யின்மருந்தோ நோயவிலக்கா எண்

*****

Karungarrkal Vuthavuzhtham Kaanil Udalkku Inbaam
Nerukiratha Kall Dhosham Neekkum Orungu Vellai
Kall Marundho Veeramodu Kaaramum Ill Manjal Ammiyin
Marundho Noi Vilakka Enn

*****

Meaning – black stones (Ammi, Aattukall) used to prepare food and medicine is really good for health. Red stones cure ailments. White stones reduce the impact of spicyness and potence of the food. But the yellow stone does not have any medicinal value.

*****

தெங்கின் குடுக்கை திகிரிதந்தப் பாத்திரத்தார்
நன்கிராப் புன்மருந்தும் தன்மருந்தாம் வெண்கலத்தால்
மையிருப்பால் கட்டைகளால் மார்க்கொம்பால்
பாத்திரங்கள்
செய்யினிரண் டாம்பட்சம் செப்பு

*****

Thengin Kudukkai Thigirithandha Paathirathaar
Nankiraa Punmarundhum Thanmarundhaam– Venkalathaal
Mai Yiruppaal Kattaikalaal Maarkombaal Paathirangal
Seiyyin Irandaam Patcham Seppu

*****

Meaning – the shell of the coconut, the utensils of bamboo are good for storing medicines. But utensils out of bronze, iron, wood, horns of animals stand second to them.

Let us conclude by digging further into this treasure with one last song about Vilaambalam. One great fruit with a hard shell usually mixed with Khandsari Sugar (Vellam). The taste is really out of this world. The speciality of this fruit is that the lump of fruit inside has no contact with the outer shell. If shaken, we can hear the fruit lump rolling in. It is believed that elephants like this fruit very much and are able to absorb the fruit within without breaking the outer shell, mysterious as it may sound, but it is the fact that I have heard about elephants and this fruit.

*****

எப்போதும் மெயக்கிதமாம் ஈளைஇரு மல்கபமும்
வெப்பாருந் தாகமும்போம் மெய்ப்பசியாம்
இப்புவியில்
என்றகிளுங்கனிமேல் இச்சைவைத்துத்தின்ன
வெண்ணித்
தின்றால் விளாங்கனியைத் தின்

*****

Eppodhum Meikidhamaam Eelai Irumal Kabamum
Veppaarum Thaagamum Pom Meipasiyaam Ippuviyil
Endrakilum Kanimael Ichchai Vaithu Thinna Enni
Thindral Vilaankaniyai Thinn

*****

Meaning – The Vilaambalam is always good for health. It cures severe cold, cough, dense phlegm, and thirst during summer. It also induces digestion. If you intend and desire to eat any fruit on this earth, then eat this Vilambalam

The book is completely amazing, because the collection and classification of so many plants, vessels and meat of animals is a herculean one. And that too prepared hundreds of years ago, when the people in most countries at that time wouldn't have even imagined of such research. We should really admire and praise Theraiyar for such an invaluable text.

This one text proves, how advanced the Tamil culture was and how knowledgeable our ancestors were thousands of years ago. But the sad part of it is that, masterpieces like these are slowly disappearing because our people really don't take care about it or are in the oblivion that these texts even exist.

Also, this knowledge is years of experimenting and researching done painstakingly for the benefit of humanity. Books like these are not only a great medical references, but they stand to add to our pride of our ancestral knowledge that they had the far-fetched thought of compiling a great book like this and propagating the great amount of knowledge for generations to come.

41. Dasavatharam – Its message to Humanity

Dasavatharam meaning The Ten Incarnations. The legend is about the 10 incarnations of Lord Vishnu to save the life and humanity on earth, from the monstrous demons and ruthless giants. This might sound like something that is for the persons interested in mythology. But to me, these avatarams or avatars are not just legends; they carry a message that is so in-depth and subtle. The subtlety of the message is that it might superfically seem to convey that God is here to save people in trouble, but actually, it contains the message about the origin and the evolution of life on the planet that lead to the humans. The avatarams are not just incarnations but has to be construed as transformations that life forms took in the planet over time. The avatarams are

- Macha Avataram
- Koorma Avataram
- Varaaga Avataram
- Narshima Avataram
- Vamaana Avataram
- Parasurama Avataram
- Rama Avataram
- Balarama Avataram
- Krishna Avataram
- Kalki Avataram

The Macha Avataram is the Fish Avataram, Macha means fish. So, life on the planet starts from aquatic creatures like fish and so on, which live solely on water. This also means that life existed in the planet even before fish took form, so the major transformation is a complex living being that had a skeleton and a spine that formed the basis of evolution, Vertebrae and Invertebrae.

The Koorma Avataram means The Turtle Avataram, Koorma means turtle. The next transformation is of course the amphibian that was able to live in both land and water. This was a great change that became the beginning of diverse life forms on earth

The Varaaga Avataram mean The Boar Avataram, Varaaga means boar. This evolution is about the beings that got totally transformed into land living creatures, so that their aquatic past got erased completely from their creation. These are the primitive herbivores that lived on eating plants.

The Narashima Avataram means the Human Lion. This is about the species that is a hybrid from of the previous evolution, but that which created the Predator–Prey relationships. These creatures started hunting other creatures for their living

The Vaamana Avataram means a short human Avataram. This was a missing link in the evolution chain. They were mythological creatures, until scientists found the Hobbits that form part of the early human ancestry. Scientist have found skeletal remains of such species not more than 3 feet tall and lived about 18,000 years ago, in the Indonesian regions.

The Parasurama Avataram is the avataram depicted as a man carrying an axe to take revenge of demon ancestry. This avataram indicates the early primitive humans using primitive tools like axe, spears. Rather the Old Stone Age and the New Stone Age.

The Rama Avataram depicts a more civilised human with better tools like bow and the arrow and other mechanical tools to make life easy. This is the beginning of the societal nature of living of humans that has the social welfare of their groups and clans as the prime motive.

PRABHU R

The Balarama Avataram is the next avataram, depicted as a human carrying a plough. This indicates that advancement of humans into cultivating their own food for their living. Until then humans had been hunting and eating fruits from trees until this transformation, where the humans learnt how to cultivate their own food.

The Krishna Avataram is the avataram that is more concentrated over diplomacy, art of war, conquests and where humans started to use their brains to invade and conquer territories. More of industrial and organised growth was in this transformation.

The Kalki Avataram, the most modern of Avataram. People say that this avataram is yet to happen. And this avataram is where humanity is heading towards. The avataram is depicted as a human on a horse with a sword and other costumes of war that is considered to be more modern. We do not know how that form is going to be in reality. Time has to tell the answers.

All these avatarams have a legend behind them, when Lord Vishnu saves the world. The motive of the aforesaid explanations is not to dispute that those legends are false. But to explain that they contain a hidden message along with all the virtues that the legends about the Dasavatarams have. I believe that those legends have happend and there are proofs that exist even today about the happenings mentioned in the legend like the bridge to Sri Lanka (The Rama Avataram), the Kurukshetra war (Krishna Avataram).

Our ancestors have been so intelligent enough that they were able to include the message about the evolution of life, in the form of legends. The rigorous statements and discoveries might fade away over time because all might not be able to understand what those discoveries state. But these legends and fables will convey this hidden message and the legend for generations to come without any change and will not fade away over time.

42. Venerated Vasuki

Vasuki – the name that stands from the days of the legend till date. Vasuki refers to two identities; one is the five-headed snake that was used as a rope, tied around Mount Meru to churn the ocean of milk to get the Amirdham, the sacred potion that would give immortality. The other identity is the female icon that is eulogised as an epitome of chastity and the devotion to her husband has elevated her in the minds of the Tamil people and also considered virtuous. She is considered an equal to Kannagi, Savithiri, Nalaayini and other women whose devotion to their husband exalted them a level above among the people.

Devotion to the husband does not mean that the wife is a slave, and nobody in the legend and real life treat them that way. Devotion means the understanding, the belief and the faith they had in their spouse. This devotion also applies to men. And Lord Rama stands as an example of a devout husband by being an "Eka Pathini Viradhan" meaning, a devout husband to one and only wife.

Vasuki Ammaiyar was a devout wife of the great Thiruvalluvar, who wrote the 1330 couplets of the Thirukkural. Her exaltation was due to the fact of her devotion to her husband and the great respect she had in him. Also Thiruvalluvar had very great respect for her, on seeing her devotion and respect for him. He knew that she has the power to do anything because she was a "Pathiviradhai" – meaning a devout wife (Pathi means husband, Viradhai means woman devotee). When he went to ask her father to have Vasuki in marriage, he tested her by giving her a bag of sand and asked her to cook delicious food. She accepted and her undiverted thoughts made the sand into a great meal.

The reason that Vasuki is so enlivened, as a devout wife, is a series of events that showed her power to the world because of the devotion she had. The events described below are a few of them. These legends have been passed on for generations since Vasuki's time.

Once, she was drawing water from the well that was in the backside of their house. And then Thiruvalluvar called for her. On hearing her husband calling, she left the rope that she was pulling and ran to address him. The pot that she was pulling out of the well while drawing the water, was in mid air. And when Vasuki ran to address her husband's call, the pot did not fall into the water from mid-air. Instead it hung as Vasuki left it. It did not fall back into the well. People believe it is because of the devotion she had in her husband that all the things in the world came into her control without any question.

Another event in her life is that, Valluvar used to have his meal in the plantain leaf. One day, he told Vasuki that she should keep a bowl of water and a thorn nearby the plantain leaf, whenever she serves food for him. She did not question, why Valluvar asked her to do so. However after every meal, she noticed that Valluvar used neither the bowl of water nor the thorn. She was puzzled; however, she did not ask a question and start an argument, but thought that there could be some reason. And during her death, when she was was in her deathbed, Valluvar asked if she wanted him to do anything for her. She told that she was very much blessed to live a life with Valluvar, but she wanted to know the reason why he asked her to keep the bowl of water and thorn during every meal in spite of not using them. Valluvar replied that each grain of rice is a farmer's effort and that should not go wasted. So while serving food if any grain of rice spilled out of the plantain leaf into the sand, he could prick it with the thorn and then wash it in the bowl of water and then eat it. But Vasuki's way of serving was so careful and gentler that he did not have the need to use it. She was proud and happy when she died, that her husband had high regards and respect in her and she has fulfilled her part as a wife to the great man whom the world reveres.

There is one more incident that really proves her virtuousness. There was a Siddhar named Kongani Siddhar also called Konganavar. When Konganavar was meditating deeply as a penance, a stork that flew above dropped its excrement on him. He came out of his meditation in anger and furiously looked at the stork and the stork was burnt alive. This incident made him to take pride of the powers he obtained out of his penance. And one day, he went to Thiruvalluvar's home to ask food. At that time, Thiruvalluvar was having his meal and Vasuki was serving him. She said that she will address Konganavar in a bit and asked him to wait. Konganavar could wait no longer, looked furiously at her. Nothing happened! Konganavar looked puzzled. Vasuki on seeing him puzzled uttered the following

*****

கொக்கென்றெண்ணினையேயோ கொங்கணவா?

*****

Kokku Endru Enninayo Konganavaa?

*****

Meaning – did you think that I am the same stork that you burnt earlier.

Kokku – Stork

Endru Enninayo – Think (Enni) that way (Endru)

Konganavaa – Kongani Siddhar.

Now, Konganavar was baffled even more. He was puzzled how Vasuki knew that he burnt a stork alive just by looking furiously at it. And then realised that it was Vasuki's virtuousness that enabled her to visualise what had happened. He felt ashamed and apologised to Vasuki for his mistake and went away.

Vasuki's virtuousness was the reason that Thiruvalluvar sang a complete Adhikaaram (Chapter) called Vaazhkai Thunai Nalam, meaning welfare of the spouse in which the following couplet appears.

*****

தெய்வம் தொழாஅள் கொழுநன் தொழுதெழுவாள்
பெய்யெனப் பெய்யும் மழை

*****

Dheivam Thozhaal Kozhunan Thozhudhezhuvaal
Peyena Peyyum Mazhai

*****

Meaning – a woman who is devout to her husband need not worship any God. And she is comparable to the rains that pour when in great need, so virtuous and inevitable. There is even another interpretation, which means, the rains will pour when a wife, who is devout to her husband, orders the rains to do so. It symbolises that the even Nature will heed to the virtuous women.

Dheivam Thozhaal – Woman who does not worship God (Dheivam). Thozhudhal indicated worship

Kozhunan – Husband, Head of the family

Thozhudhu – Worship

Ezhuvaal – Rise after worship

Peyena – Order the rains to pour

Peyyum – The act of rains pouring

Mazhai – Rain

Vasuki and Thiruvalluvar's virtuousness is an example for all of us on how to live a life that will bring happiness to all. The trust and the faith that the spouses have in each other exalts them in the way they live their life on the planet. The Tamil culture revered virtuous woman as equivalent to God and the legends about Vasuki still prevailing after 2000 years stand as an example on how modesty and virtuousness are praised and famed.

43. Subtle Senses

Senses are the subtle instincts that guide the living being throughout its entire life. Many have attempted to classify the senses of various living beings especially humans. Though Thirumoolar has classified the senses of human beings to be 10, as we have seen in earlier chapters, the widely accepted fact is the human are six-sensed beings. It is interesting to know that this classification of beings based on the numbers of senses they predominantly use, has been done way back by the Tamil people.

The classification of the senses and the specifying of beings that fall under this classification is found in the oldest surviving work on Tamil Grammar – The Thollkaappiyam. Thollkaappiyam is a combination of the words Thonmai (very old, ancient) + Kaappiyam (Literature). The name Thollkaappiyam stood because the actual time when this piece of literature was written is not known, some say it is over 2000 years old and some say it was written between 1st CE and 10th CE. Also some say that the name of the author, Thollkaappiyar, is a generic name derived from the name of the work, as the exact details of the person who wrote it is not known. And some strongly believe that Thollkaappiyar was a disciple of Agathiar, the first and foremost of Siddhars and Thollkaappiyar wrote his work based on Agathiar's work Agathiam. However, Thollkaappiyam is a masterpiece and the oldest surviving work on literature on any language. Well, lets get back to the classification.

Thollkaappiyar, classifies the beings based on the senses they use predominantly, in the section called Marabiyal (Marabu – generally accepted practices since old days, culture, tradition; Iyal – Research work, Science). The poems in each called Suthirams

(Formulae) describe about various aspects of grammar, habitat, etc. The song that we intend to read goes like this

*****

ஒன்று அறிவதுவே உற்று அறிவதுவே
இரண்டு அறிவதுவே அதனொடு நாவே
மூன்று அறிவதுவே அவற்றொடு மூக்கே
நான்கு அறிவதுவே அவற்றொடு கண்ணே
ஐந்து அறிவதுவே அவற்றொடு செவியே
ஆறு அறிவதுவே அவற்றொடு மனனே
நேரிதின் உணர்ந்தோர் நெறிப்படுத்தினரே.

*****

Ondru Arivadhuvae Uttru Arivadhuvae
Irandu Arivadhuvae Adhanodu Naavae
Mondru Arivadhuvae Avattrodu Mookae
Naangu Arivadhuvae Avattrodu Kannae
Aindhu Arivadhuvae Avattrodu Seviyae
Aaru Arivadhuvae Avattrodu Mananae
Naeridhin Unarrndhor Neripaduthinarae

*****

Meaning, beings with one sense are those that have the sense of TOUCH. Beings with two senses are those that have the sense of TASTE along with the above. Beings with three senses, have sense of SMELL in addition. Beings with four senses, have sense of SIGHT, along with the above. Beings with five senses, have sense of HEARING, in addition. The beings with six senses, have a MIND, along with the above. The people who have realised this truth have classified and organised it appropriately

Ondru, Irandu, Moondru, Naangu, Aindhu, Aaru – 1, 2, 3, 4, 5, 6 respectively

Arivadhu – Know, feel, realise, sense

Uttru – Touch, come into contact

Athanodu – Along with some other thing (usually when the number of objects is two)

Avattrodu – Along with some other things (usually when the number of objects is more than two)

Naavu – Tongue, in this context, taste

Mooku – Nose (for sense Smell)

Kann – Eye (Sight)

Sevi – Ear (Hearing)

Manam – Mind

Naer Idhu – This truth (the above mentioned classification)

Unarrndhor – People who realised this truth

Neripaduthinarae – Classified and organised the truth

Thollkaappiyar, does not stop with this classification alone, he also gives examples of beings in each of these classifications. The poems go like below

*****

புல்லும் மரனும் ஓர் அறிவினவே
பிறவும் உளவே அக் கிளைப் பிறப்பே

*****

Pullum Maranum Ore Arivinavae
Piravum Ulavae Akkilai Pirappae

*****

Meaning – Grass (Pull) and Trees (Maram) have single sense, that is, the sense of touch. Similar beings also form part of this branch.

*****

நந்தும் முரளும் ஈர் அறிவினவே
பிறவும் உளவே அக்கிளைப் பிறப்பே.

*****

Nandhum Muralum Eer Arivinavae
Piravum Ulavae Akkilai Pirappae

*****

Meaning – Snails (Nandhu) and Oysters or Molluscs (Mural) have two senses; the sense of touch and taste. Similar beings also form part of this branch.

*****

சிதலும் எறும்பும் மூ அறிவினவே
பிறவும் உளவே அக் கிளைப் பிறப்பே.

*****

Sidhalum Erumbum Moo Arivinavae
Piravum Ulavae Akkilai Pirappae

*****

Meaning –Termites (Sidhal) and Ants (Erumbu) have three senses, the sense of touch, taste and smell. Similar beings also form part of this branch.

*****

நண்டும் தும்பியும் நான்கு அறிவினவே
பிறவும் உளவே அக் கிளைப் பிறப்பே.

*****

Nandum Thumbiyum Naangu Arivinavae
Piravum Ulavae Akkilai Pirappae

*****

Meaning – Crabs or Crustaceans (Nandu) and Dragonfly or Beetles (Thumbi) have four senses, the sense of touch, taste, smell and vision. Similar beings also form part of this branch.

*****

மாவும் மாக்களும் ஐ அறிவினவே
பிறவும் உளவே அக் கிளைப் பிறப்பே.

*****

Maavum Maakkalum Aindhu Arivinavae
Piravum Ulavae Akkilai Pirappae

*****

Meaning – Horses, Elephants, Pigs (Maa) and other similar animals and birds (Maakkal) have five senses, the sense of touch, taste, smell, vision and hearing. Similar beings also form part of this branch.

*****

மக்கள்தாமே ஆறு அறிவு உயிரே
பிறவும் உளவே அக் கிளைப் பிறப்பே.

*****

Makkalthamae Aaru Arivu Uyirae
Piravum Ulavae Akkilai Pirappae

*****

Meaning – Only humans have six senses, the sense of touch, taste, smell, vision, hearing and mind. Similar beings also form part of this branch.

Truly amazing classification, though these classifications are based on what the beings predominantly use for their survival. For e.g. though the ants have eyes, they predominantly use the three senses mentioned above. This proves that Thollkaappiyar is not only an expert in literature and grammar, but also a multifaceted human having expertise in animal and plant life and other sciences too. It is no surprise that the Tamil Culture having an ancient history that spans over thousands of years to have made this classification and much more. His work in our hands is what we need to be proud of and we can proclaim it to the world for generations to come that our culture, tradition and civilisation has a long standing history that only a very few cultures have in this world.

44. Elusive Expressions

Expressions are realisations or reflexes of the humans under different situations of their life. These reflexes or realities are quite elusive that they stay for just a small time. Just imagine how many expressions you remember having made for yourself. And how many of us know about how many expressions we express in various situations. Classifying expressions has been a subject on its own and that is what today's movie makers capitalize when they make any great hits. These expressions form the essence of who we are. Tamil literature has a mastermind who has classified these expressions; he is none other than the famous Thollkaappiyar. He classifies the expressions in eight categories, grouping four in each category. The song in the section Meipaatiyal, in his work Thollkaapiyam, goes like this. Also, I have tried to get the closest or correct English words for the each of the terms below. Pardon me if I am wrong in any of those.

*****

நகையே அழுகை இளிவரல் மருட்கை
அச்சம் பெருமிதம் வெகுளி உவகை என்று
அப் பால் எட்டே மெய்ப்பாடு என்ப.

*****

Nagaiyae Azhugai Ilivaral Marutkai
Achcham Perumidham Veguli Uvagai Endru
Appaal Ettae Meipaadu Enba

*****

Meaning – Laughter (Nagai), Crying (Azhugai), Weakness (Ilivaral), Astonishment (Marutkai), Fear (Achcham), Pride (Perumidham), Anger (Veguli), Happiness (Uvagai), are the eight different expression categories.

Each of these eight categories mentioned above have four different expressions in them. The following songs enlist what they are

For Laughter

*****

எள்ளல் இளமை பேதைமை மடன் என்று
உள்ளப்பட்ட நகை நான்கு என்ப

*****

Ellal Ilamai Paedhamai Madan Endru
Ullappatta Nagai Naangu Enba

*****

Meaning – Snicker (Ellal), Ilamai (Laughter when young or immature or Innocent laughter), Paedhamai (Laughter out of foolishness), Madan (Laughter for Ignorance) are the four laughters that come from one's heart

For Crying

*****

இளிவே இழவே அசைவே வறுமை என
விளிவு இல் கொள்கை அழுகை நான்கே.

*****

"Ilivae Izhavae Asaivae Varumai Ena
Vilivu Ill Kollkai Azhugai Naangae"

*****

Meaning – Ilivae (Insult, Defamation), Izhavae (Death, loss), Asaivae (Restlessness, Tension), Varumai (Poverty) are the four different aspects of crying

For Weakness

*****

மூப்பே பிணியே வருத்தம் மென்மையொடு
யாப்புற வந்த இளிவரல் நான்கே

*****

Moopae Piniyae Varutham Menmaiyodu
Yaapura Vandha Ilivaral Naangae

*****

Meaning – Moopae (Senility), Piniyae (Disease), Varutham (Sorrow), Menmaiyodu (Feebleness) indicate weakness.

For Astonishments

*****

புதுமை பெருமை சிறுமை ஆக்கமொடு
மதிமை சாலா மருட்கை நான்கே.

*****

Pudhumai Perumai Sirumai Aakkamodu
Madhimai Saala Marutkai Naangae

*****

Meaning –Pudhumai (Being latest and new), Perumai (Pride), Sirumai (Being very simple), Aakkamodu (Being powerful) are the various astonishments that man expresses

For Fear

*****

அணங்கே விலங்கே கள்வர் தம் இறை எனப்
பிணங்கல் சாலா அச்சம் நான்கே.

*****

Anangae Vilangae Kalvar Tham Irai Enba
Pinangal Saala Achcham Naangae

*****

Meaning – Anangae (Fear of Devils, Intimidating Goddesses like Kaali), Vilangae (Fear of Animals), Kalvar (Thieves), Tham Irai Enba (One's Gods) are tracts of fear.

For Pride

*****

கல்வி தறுகண் புகழ்மை கொடை எனச்
சொல்லப்பட்ட பெருமிதம் நான்கே.

*****

Kalvi Tharukan Pugazhmai Kodai Ena
Sollappatta Perumidham Naangae

*****

Meaning – Kalvi (Education) Tharukan (Bravery), Pugazhmai (Fame) Kodai (Donation, Benefaction) are the facets of Pride.

For Anger

*****

உறுப்பறை குடிகோள் அலை கொலை என்ற
வெறுப்பின் வந்த வெகுளி நான்கே

*****

258

Urupparai Kudikole Alai Kolai Endra
Veruppin Vandha Veguli Naangae

*****

Meaning – Urupparai (Dissection), Kudikole (Treason), Alai (Torture), Kolai (Murder) are the four different expressions of Anger.

For Happiness

*****

செல்வம் புலனே புணர்வு விளையாட்டு என்று
அல்லல் நீத்த உவகை நான்கே

*****

Selvam Pulanae Punarvu Vilayaatu Endru
Allal Neetha Uvagai Naangae

*****

Meaning – Selvam (Wealth), Pulanae (feelings), Punarvu (Intimacy), Vilayaatu (Play) are expressions of happiness

We will have to go through the complex and subtle classifications carefully to be able to understand the difference in each of them. Thollkaapiyar should have been a great person in analysing human behavior, emotions and, of course, psychology to such a great extent to classify the subtleties of the elusive human expressions. What human relations experts do now and psychologists analyse about human behaviour has been done by a genius thousands of years ago. And that genius was a part of the awesome Tamil civilization.

45. Power of Curse

We would have seen the Power of Aram in a previous chapter, that is primarily the power to prove that truth always wins. There can be a remedy to the consequences caused by the power of Aram (Truth), but curse in most cases is not remediable. The person has to undergo the trials and tribulations of a curse. Curse can come by the way of the victim cursing the criminal/defaulter verbally and by the way of one's own action. The latter has more impact and bad effect than the former. We would have heard about the famous Curse of King Tutankhamun. Though that one is disputable if it is actually a curse or not, the ones that Thirumoolar points, in his masterpiece – Thirumandhiram – are definitely the list of curses, especially, the curse due to one's action of insulting or hurting his/her Guru, who showed them the way to enlightenment and knowledge.

The curses Thirumoolar explains are songs so strong and potent, that we can realise why such acts carry with them, effects so strong and powerful. It does not need to be that the Guru will utter the curse; the act itself carries with it such a curse. Now let us see those songs that are really mindblowing and awe-inspiring. In fact, the acts that we should not do or allow our younger generations to do.

*****

ஒரெழுத்து ஒருபொருள் உணரக் கூறிய
சீரெழுத் தாளரைச் சிதையச் செப்பினோர்
ஊரிடைச் சுணங்கனாய்ப் பிறந்தங் குழர்உகம்
பாரிடைக் கிருமியாய் மாய்வர் மண்ணிலே

*****

"Ore Ezhuthu Ore Porul Unara Kooriya
Seer Ezhuthaalarai Sidhaiya Seppinor
Ooridai Sunanganaai Pirandhu Angorugam
Paaridai Kirumiyaai Maaivar Mannilae"

*****

Meaning – The person who insults/hurts the heart of the Guru, who taught or gave the meaning and knowledge about the one lettered universal Mantra – OM – and the universal being – The Brahmam, by vituperating about the Guru will be born as a dog that wanders aimlessly in the country and then as parasitic creatures for a Yugam and then perish in this earth.

Ore Ezhuthu – One letter, in this context, the Mantra OM

Ore Porul – One thing, in this context, The universal being

Unara – Realise

Kooriya – Explain, utter

Seer Ezhuthaalar – refer the Guru (Teacher)

Sidhaiya – Destroy, hurt badly

Seppinor – Utter

Ooridai – in the country, place

Sunganan – Dog

Pirandhu – Being born

Angu Ore Ugam – There for for Yugam

Paar – Earth

Kirumi – Bacteria, Parasitic Creatures

Maaivar – Perish

Mannilae – In the soil or sand or earth

261

If this song appears harsh, the next one is even harsher, it goes like this

*****

பத்தினி பத்தர்கள் தத்துவ ஞானிகள்
சித்தங் கலங்கச் சிதைவுகள் செய்தவர்
அத்தமும் ஆவியும் ஆண்டொன்றில் மாண்டிடும்
சத்தியம் ஈது சதாநந்தி ஆணையே

*****

Pathini Paththargal Thathuva Gnanigal
Siththam Kalanga Sidhaivugal Seidhavar
Aththamum Aaviyum Aandondril Maaindhidum
Sathiyam Eedhu Sadhanandhi Aanaiyae

*****

Meaning – Those who hurt the feelings of the noble family persons and the persons considered as knowledgable nobles/divines making them worry, will have their wealth and their life wiped out within a year. And promising on Lord Shiva, it is the real truth.

Pathini Paththar – People who lead a noble family life

Thathuvam – Great Thought

Gnani – Wise man, Holy person

Siththam – Mind

Kalanga – Disturb

Sidhaivu – Destruction

Seidhavar – Person who does something

Aththam – Wealth

Aavi – Life, the soul

262

Aandu Ondru – One Year

Maandu – Die

Sathiyam – Truth

Sadhanandhi – other name for Lord Shiva

Aanai – Promise, rule

The next one song applies not only to a person but to a country, the king and his subjects

*****

ஈசன் அடியார் இதயம் கலங்கிடத்
தேசமும் நாடும் சிறப்பும் அழிந்திடும்
வாசவன் பீடமும் மாமன்னர் பீடமும்
நாசமது ஆகுமே நம்நந்தி ஆணையே.

*****

Easan Adiyaar Idhayam Kalangida
Dhesamum Naadum Sirappum Azhidhidum
Vaasavan Peedamum Maamannar Peedamum
Naasamadhu Aagumae Nann Nandhi Aanaiyae

*****

Meaning – if the minds of the devotees of Lord Shiva are hurt, then the country, its state and its fame will be destroyed completely. Even Lord Indran's throne and the thrones of the great emperors will be destroyed. These are the truths that could be promised on Lord Shiva.

Easan Adiyaar – Lord Shiva (Easan), Devotees (Adiyaar)

Idhayam – Heart

Kalangida – Disturb

Dhesamum – Country

Naadu – State, also refers to country and used synonymously with Dhesam

Sirappu – Fame, Popularity

Azhindhidum – Destroy

Vaasavan – Lord Indran

Peedam – Throne

Maamannar – Emperor

Naasam – Destruction

Aagum – Happen

Nann Nandhi – Divine Nandhi (Lord Shiva)

The next song is stricter in a sense that it describes about what happens if one lies to his Guru.

*****

சன்மார்க்க சற்குருச் சந்நிதி பொய்வரின்
நன்மார்க்க மும்குன்றி ஞானமும் தங்காது
தொன்மார்க்க மாய துறையும் மறந்திட்டுப்
பன்மார்க்க மும்கெட்டுப் பஞ்சமும் ஆமே.

*****

Sanmaarga Sarrguru Sannidhi Poivarin
Nanmaargamum Kundri Gnanamum Thangaadhu
Thonmaarga Maaya Thuraiyum Marandhittu
Panmaaragamum Kettu Panjamum Aamae

*****

Meaning – if one utters a lie to the great guru who inculcated great virtues and righteousness, then his righteousness will decline, along with his knowledge. Also, he will forget the traditional values and virtues. Then all his ways for livelihood will get destroyed and will result in misery for life

264

Sanmaargam, Nanmaaragam – Virtue, Righteousness

Sarrguru – Great Guru

Sannidhi – Sanctum

Poi – Lie

Varin – coming

Kundri – decline

Thangaadhu – Negation Thangum which means staying or remaining

Thonmaarga – Traditional Virtues

Thurai – Area of study, department, etc

Marandhittu – Forgetting

Panmaargamum – Others ways of virtuous life and livelihood

Kettu – Spoil

Panjam – Misery, Famine

The songs that Thirumoolar has given us intimidates at the outset, but those songs are not to intimidate but to realise the fact the people who should be held in high regards should not be denigrated or insulted. If so, the result of such insult will automatically be attributed to the person insulting. Those consequences are really bad putting people in difficulty for a long period of time. And through songs like these, Thirumoolar inculcates righteousness that has to be followed in everyone's life. The songs are a forerunner to the realisations of truth, because those consequences put the defaulter into oblivion that he/she will not have a chance to know the reason for the suffering. This righteousness is simple and easy to follow that keeps us out of trouble forever.

46. Literary Treasure – Thandialangaram – Part 1

Tamil literature is so rich with its works on Grammar with Tholkaapiyam (தொல்காப்பியம்) by Tholkaapiyar (தொல்காப்பியர்) being the oldest work on Tamil Grammar. There were other great works on Tamil Grammar during different periods of time that includes Nannool (நன்னூல்), Yapparum Kalakaarigai (யாப்பருங்கலக்காரிகை), Veera Chozhiyam (வீரசோழியம்), and Maaran Alangaaram (மாறனலங்காரம்). – I would like to provide some fascinating aspects of a great work in Tamil Grammar that I came across – Thandialangaram (தண்டியலங்காரம்). Actually, it is a book on Ani Ilakkanam (அணி இலக்கணம்), the Grammar on Poetical Decorations.

Before I begin getting deeper into this, I would like to mention that I am not a scholar in Tamil nor am I an expert in Tamil Literature, so I would request the readers to bear with me if there are any mistakes or errors.

Thandialangaram is written by Thandiyaasiriyar, however not much is known about this person. Some scholars say that he was the son of Ambikapathi, son of the great poet, Kavichakravarthi Kambar making Thandiyaasiriyar, the grandson of Kambar. They quote the following song as a supporting evidence of that information

*****

'வடதிசை யிருந்து தென்மலைக் கேகி
மதிதவழ் குடுமிப் பொதிய மால்வரை

இருந்தவன் தன்பால் அருந்தமிழ் உணர்ந்த
பன்னிரு புலவரின் முன்னவன் பகர்ந்த
தொல்காப் பியநெறி பல்காப் பியத்தும்
அணிபெறு மிலக்கணம் அரிதினில் தெரிந்து
வடநூல் வழிமுறை மரபினின் வழா அது
ஈரிரன் டெல்லையின் இகவா மும்மைப்
பாரத விலக்கணம் பண்புறத் தமீஇத்
திருந்திய மணிமுடிச் செம்பியன் அவையயத்து
அரும்பொருள் யாப்பி னமைவுற வகுத்தனன்
ஆடக மன்றத்து நாடக நவிற்றும்
வடநூ லுணர்ந்த தமிழ்நூற் புலவன்
பூவிரி தண்பொழிற் காவிரி நாட்டு
*வம்பவிழ் தெரியல் **அம்பி காபதி***
மேவருந் தவத்தினிற் பயந்த
*தாவருஞ் சீர்த்தித் **தண்டி**யென் பவனே.'*

*****

However some other scholars say that is a different person who lived in a period earlier than Kambar. Most people agree that he lived during the period of Kulothunga Cholan II of the 12th century

Thandialangaram consists of 3 parts

1. பொதுவியல் – Describes the general rules/grammar about poetic decorations

2. பொருளணியியல் – Describes the different types of expression/meaning

3. சொல்லணியியல் – Describes the various forms of word usage

When one reads the Thandialangaram, they not only see the grammatical rules of the languages but also appreciate the beauty of the language, as to how flexible and creative it can be. The following song illustrates such a beauty of the Tamil language

*****

ஓங்க லிடைவந் துயர்ந்தோர் தொழவிளங்கி
ஏங்கொலிநீர் ஞாலத் திருளகற்றும் ஆங்கவற்றுள்
மின்னேர் தனியாழி வெங்கதிரோன் றேனையது
தன்னே ரிலாத தமிழ்

*****

Ongal Idai Vandhu Uyarndhor Thozha Vilangi
Yaengoli Neer Gnalathu Irul Agatrum Aangavatrul
Minnaer Thannazhi Ven Kadhiron Yaenayadhu
Thannaeriladha Thamizh

*****

Meaning – The ones that rise from the mountains and worshipped by all great men, illuminate and enlighten this world covered by the high seas; One is the electrifying and the bright Sun, the other is the language Tamil. The analogy here is that the Sun rises above the mountains and removes out the darkness from the world, likewise, Tamil, which originated from the Kudagu Mountains removes the darkness of ignorance and enlightens the mind.

Thandialangaram is so dense and vast that it has figures of speech, poetic decorations which can be discussed at length and there are many books written with the explanation for its contents. However, in this chapter, we will get on to the more interesting bits first.

Tamil poetry primarily has four forms – Aasu Kavi (ஆசுகவி), Madhura Kavi (மதுரகவி), Chithira Kavi (சித்திரக்கவி), and Viththaara Kavi (வித்தாரக்கவி). Aasu Kavi is spontaneous overflow where the poet sings the song on the spot complying with the grammatical rules; these songs can be one of the other three forms as well. Madhura Kavi is a song that has a good rhyme. Chithira Kavi is the poem that can be represented in a drawing. Viththaara Kavi is the form that has a song within a song, for example, if the odd letters are gathered, it forms one poem and if the even letters are gathered it gives another poem, as a whole the song itself is one poem – there are many such permutations which we will see in the next part of the book.

One of the sections that Thandialangaram describes is the Chithira Kavi, a poetic form that can be represented as a drawing. Such forms of poetry are classified as Rathabandham, Thani naaga bandham, Irattai Naaga Bandham, Komoothri Bandham, Murasu bandham, Chakkara Bandham etc. We have already seen the Rathabandham or the Chithira Thaer in an earlier chapter; we will see the rest in this chapter

KOMOOTHRI BANDHAM

This is an interesting form of Chithira Kavi where the poem can be read in different ways yet we read the same poem

*****

பருவ மாகவி தோகன மாலையே
பொருவி லாவுழை மேவன கானமே
மருவு மாசைவி டாகன மாலையே
வெருவ லாயிழை பூவணி காலமே

*****

Paruvam Aaga Idho Ganam Maalaiyae
Poruvila Uzhai Meivana Kaanamae
Maruvum Aasai Vidaa Ganam Maalaiyae
Veruvu Alaa Aayizhai Poovani Kaalamae

*****

Meaning – the friend of the lady in the song is consoling her because her husband/lover has gone away on some business and has not returned yet. The season that the lady's husband said he he will return has started; the signs of which are showing up, the clouds of rain have gathered; the deer in the forest are seen and so, not to worry. Her husband will soon be there to adorn her with the garlands

The poem above is drawn as shown in the following diagram, the first two lines are written in the top row and the second two lines are written in the bottom row.

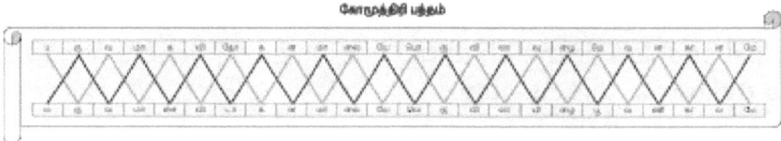

Komoothri Bandham

There is another way to read this poem. For the first two-lines follow the orange line and for the second two-lines follow the blue line in the diagram.

Ko – Ox, Cow, Moothri – Urine. Meaning when the ox urinates while walking, the urine's path will be zigzag. Likewise the drawing to interpret the song resembles the zigzag pattern of the urine and hence the name

MAALAI MAATRU (PALINDROMES)

Tamil language has its own share of Palindromes at least a thousand years ago. A Palindrome is a textual construct that reads the same even in the reverse

*****

நீவாத மாதவா தாமோக ராகமோ
தாவாத மாதவா நீ'

*****

Neevaadha Maa Dhava Thaa Moga Raagamo
Thaavadha A Maadhu Ava Nee

*****

Meaning – You are a great person with an undisturbed meditation, however you will have to bestow on the wishes of the lady who is thinking about you

*****

வாயாயா நீகாவா யாதாமா தாமாதா
யாவாகா நீயாயா வா'

*****

Vaaya Yaa Nee Kaava Yaadhu Aam Maadhu Aam Maa Thaa
Yaa Aagaa Nee Aayaa Vaa

*****

Meaning – What is there that we would not get when you guard us. If you don't bless us, she will become very sad. So, please come to us Lord Krishna, the cow herdsman.

Thirugnanasambandhar has done all forms of these poetry here is one from his Thevaram called the Seergaazhi Thirupathigam. Each verse in this pathigam is a palindrome

*****

சீகாழி – திருமாலைமாற்று

யாமாமாநீ யாமாமா யாழீகாமா காணாகா
காணாகாமா காழீயா மாமாயாநீ மாமாயா.

யாகாயாழீ காயாகா தாயாராரா தாயாயா
யாயாதாரா ராயாதா காயாகாழீ யாகாயா

தாவாமுவா தாசாகா ழீநாதாநீ யாமாமா
மாமாயாநீ தாநாழீ காசாதாவா மூவாதா

நீவாவாயா காயாழீ காவாவானோ வாராமே
மேராவானோ வாவாகா ழீயாகாயா வாவாநீ

யாகாலாமே யாகாழீ யாமேதாவீ தாயாவீ
வீயாதாவீ தாமேயா ழீகாயாமே லாகாயா

மேலேபோகா மேதேழீ காலாலேகா லாணாயே
யேனாலாகா லேலாகா ழீதேமேகா போலேமே

நீயாமாநீ யேயாமா தாவேழீகா நீதானே
நேதாநீகா ழீவேதா மாயாயேநீ மாயாநீண

நேணவராவிழ யாசைழியே வேகதளேரிய ளாயுழிகா
காழியுளாயரி ளேதகவே யேழிசையாழவி ராவணனே

காலேமேலே காணீகா ழீகாலேமா லேமேபூ
பூமேலேமா லேகாழீ காணீகாலே மேலேகா

வேரியுமேணவ காழியொயே யேனை நிணேமட
ளோகரதே

தேரகளோடம ணேநினையே யேயொழிகாவண
மேயுரிவே

நேரகழாமித யாசழிதா யேனனியேனனி ளாயுழிகா
காழியுளானின யேனினயே தாழிசயாதமி ழாகரனே.
- திருஞானசம்பந்தர்

*****

Likewise, Ramalinga Adigalar also known as Vallalaar has also written a thirupathigam where each verse is a palindrome.

*****

வள்ளலார் மாலைமாற்றுத் திருப்பதிகம்

திருஅருமரு தூராகாரா வாடாகரு ணாசாகா
காசாணாரு கடாவாரா காராதூரு மருஅருதி *(1)*

தாபாதா தாமருத ராலூடவ மேதவமே
மேதவமே வடலூரா தருமதா தாபாதா *(2)*

யாரிது காளாவ டுகூகையோ கியோ
யோகி யோகைகூடு வளாகா துரியா *(3)*

யாகாஆகாங் லிமராயா காயமாமாய
யமாமாய காசயாரா மலிங்கா ஆகாயா *(4)*

யாபாசனஞானா மதாதீதா ஓதாநாதா சாதாகாசா
சாகாதாசா தாநாதாஓதா தீதாமனா ஞானசபாயா *(5)*

யாதிஜோதியா ராவாராக சீவசாதீயா மசனாபோ
போனாசமயாதீசா வசீகரா வாராயாதி ஜோதியா *(6)*

யாசாயாமா சாபூதைவாதே காமலாலீ காமுறுஆ

ஆறுமுகா லீலாமகா தேவாதைபூசா மாயாசாயா *(7)*

காலபாதீ சோகாடபாப தீதாாஈரானீ யாடிமுடிய
யடிமுடியா நீராாஈதா தீபபாடகா சோதீபாலகா *(8)*

ராகாவியா விகாடாமடு கூவிலக திருகு
குருதிகலவி கூடுமடா காவியா விகாரா *(9)*

யகழ்வா களையா கருணீகா சமரசா
சாரமச காணீருக யாளைக வாழ்கய *(10)*

***** *

NAGABANDHAM

This is one of the complex forms of poetry, in which letters of the poem are represented along the body of a snake from head to tail; the shape of snake is convoluted to form a symmetric Kolam. Kolam is art form in Southern parts of India, where women clean the front side of their house during sunrise with water and draw artistic figures using rice flour/coloured powder, usually. This is done to welcome the goodness into their homes daily and also to feed the small forms of life like the ants. These kolams are not permanent but erased and drawn daily. Coming back to the poem, when you trace the letters from the head to tail of the snake, you get the poem. There are many variants in the Nagabandham

- Ottrai Nagabandham – Poem written on 1 snake

- Irattai Nagabandham – Poem written on 2 snakes

- Naangu Nagabandham – Poem written on 4 snakes

- Ashta Nagabandham – Poem written on 8 snakes

First let us look at the Ottrai naagabandham. The following image is the representation of the Ottrai naagabandham, if we trace the letters from the head of the snake to its tail we get the song mentioned below.

OTTRAI / THANINAAGA BANDHAM
(ஒற்றை/தனி நாகபந்தம்)

Thani Naagabandham

The beauty of this form of poetry is the convoluted shape is what we call the "Kolam" and with colours added becomes Rangoli. The complexity is that shape is symmetrical and the cells at the intersections of the path have the same letter

*****

வந்தறந் தோய்ந்தி வையழமுய தந்தநம் வாமிசுதன்
தந்திரஞ்சேர் மதமார்வார் முன் சாய்ந்தவபோதனுசன்
சந்ததம் சீர்த்திவதிதுதி மாதவர் தந்தன்புசெய்
செந்தில்
வந்தந்த நந்தந்தமிழார் நஞ்சிதாசிவனே

*****

Vandhu Aram Thoindhu Ivvaiyam Uyya Thandha Namm
Vaami Sudhan
Thandhiram Saer Madham Aarvaar Munn Saai Thava
Podhanusan
Sandhadham Seerthi Vadhi Thudhi Maadhavar Thandha
Anbu Sei Senthil
Vandhandha Nandham Thamizhaar Nanjidha Sivanae

275

Meaning – For the salvation of this world, Lord Murugan came with all the noble characters. Those with evil minds would fall at His feet. The devotees who worship Him are bestowed with goodness. We praise Lord Shiva who begot him for us Tamil people

IRATTAI / THUVI NAAGA BANDHAM
(இரட்டை/துவி நாகபந்தம்)

The next form is the Irattai Naaga Bandham; where there are two snakes are involved, still the shape is symmetrical. Here in this there are two songs, one that runs on the body of one snake and the second song on the other

*****

அருளின் நிருவுருவே யம்பலதா யும்பர்
தெருளின் மருவாசீர்ச் சீரே பொருவிலா
வொன்றே யுமையா ஞூடனே யுருத்தரு
குன்றே தெருள வருள்

*****

Arulin Thiru Uruvae Amabalatha Umbar
Therulin Maruva Seer Seerae Poruvlia
Ondrae Umaiyaal Udanae Uruththaru
Kundrae Therula Arul

*****

Meaning – You are the manifestation of grace, the One who has the Thiruchitrambalam Stage. The One who cannot be perceived even by the Devars; The One who is a flawless Universal Being; The One who stands like a mountain with Umayaal (Goddess Parvathi). Enlighten our minds to understand/perceive "You".

*****

276

மருவி னவருளத்தே வாழ்சுடரே நஞ்சு
பெருகொளியான் றேயபெருஞ் சோதித் திருநிலா
வானஞ் சுருங்கு மிகுசுடரே சித்த
மயரு மளவை யொழி

*****

Maruvinavar Ullathae Vaazh Sudaraee Nanju
Perugu Oliyaan Aeya Perum Jothi Thirunila
Vaanam Surungum Migu Sudarae Siththam
Ayarum Alavai Ozhi

*****

Meaning — Lord Shiva, You live as the light in the hearts of those who worship you. You have the great poison in Your neck, yet you shine in all brightness that dwarfs the brightness of the moon. Bestow me with the wish that my mind does not forget "You".

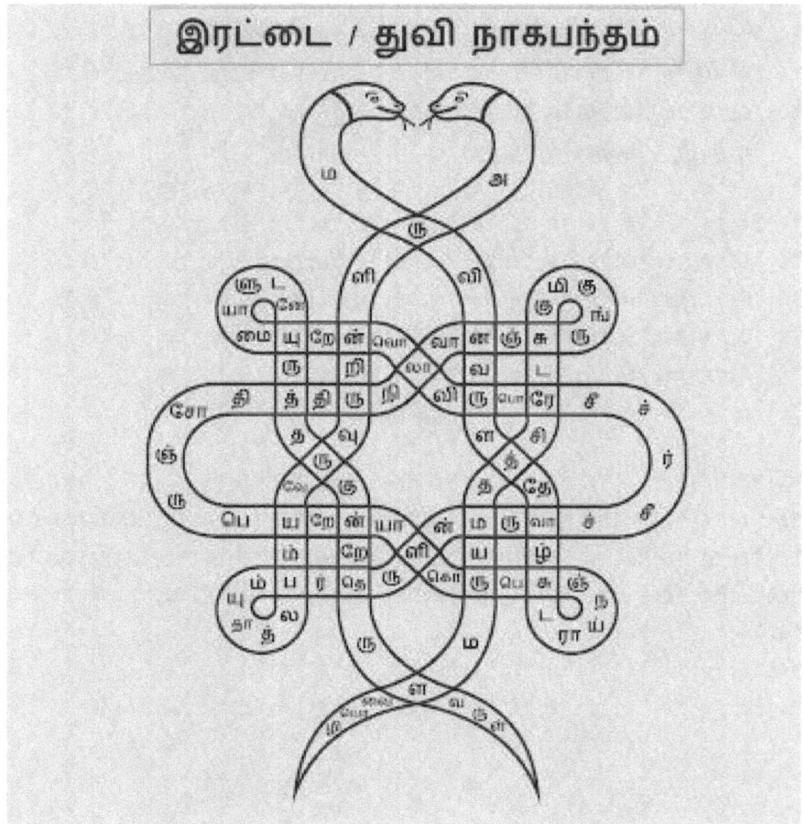

The following is another version of the Irattai Naagabandham, the only difference from the former is that there only one song that runs through the two snakes where the intersections share the letters. The first two lines run on one snake and the last two on the other.

*****

சேயா சேயாதே தேயா சேயாசே
மாயா மாயாவா வாயா மாயாமா
வாயா மாவாயா மாயா சேமாசே
யோயா நோயாவோ யாயே தேயாளே

278

*****

Seyaa Seyaadhae Theyaa Seyaase
Maayaa Maayaavaa Vaayaa Maayamaa
Vaayaa Maavaayaa Maayaa Semaase
Yoya Noi Aavoi Aayedhae Aayaalae

*****

The poem above is believed to cure any curse that relates to snakes. Kaalasarpadosham, etc and also to attain peace in life, if the poem is recited in front of Lord Muruga daily, it is believed to bring peace and betterment in one's life

Unfortunately, I am not able to successfully interpret and provide the meaning for this poem. I tried interpreting it, but it leads to multiple interpretations, so to avoid giving any wrong interpretation / meaning I have not written the meaning for the song. I request the reader to help me and I would be very grateful to anyone who provides the meaning. The song was sung by Pamban Swamigal who has also sung many such songs in praise of Lord Murugan. Those songs especially are of the Chithira Kavi form – Mayura Bandham, Kamala bandham etc.

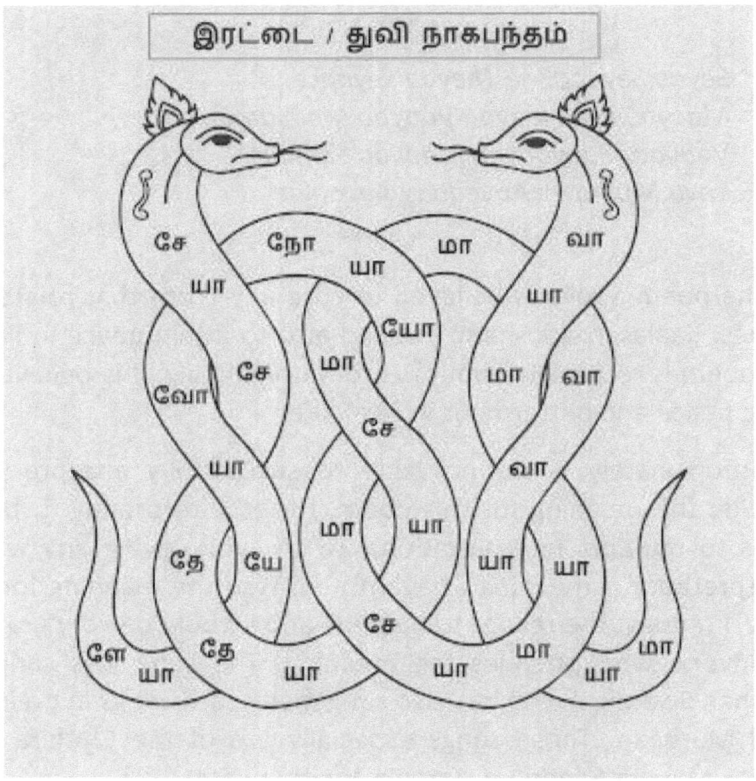

NAANGU / CHATHUR NAAGABANDHAM (நான்கு / சதுர் நாகபந்தம்(

The next naagabandham form is the Naangu or the Chathur Naagabandham, where there are 4 snakes and the verses of the poems run along the bodies of 4 snakes.

தன்னை யறிதல் தலைப்படுத்துங் கல்வியதாலெங்ங னறித லுலகியலை - முன்னுவந்துன்னை யறிக முதல்.

நீக்கு வினைநீக்கி நேர்மைவினைக் கின்னலையாதீங்குநீ நன்மனத்தால் நன்னயங்க ஞுன்ன வுடன்பெறு வாயுய் தலை

ஓங்குபனை போலுயர்ந் தென்னே பயனுன்னத்தீங்கு
தனைமனத்து எண்ணித்தீ நீக்காதார்தீங்கினைத் தீப்படுந்
தீ

உன்னை யறிதற் குனதூழ் தரப்பெற்றபொன்னைப்பெண்
மண்ணாசை போக்கலைக் காணாயேலென்னை பயக்குமோ
சொல்

*****

Thannai Aridhal Thalaipaduththum Kalvi Adhellam Enganam
Aridhal Ulagiyalai Munnu Vandhu Unnai Ariga Mudhal
Neeku Vinai Neeki Nermai Vinaikku Innalai Yaadheengu Nee
Nanmanaththaal Nann Nayangal Unnavudan Peruvaai
Uyidhalai
Ongu Panai Pol Uyarndhu Ennae Payanunna Theenguthanai
Manaththul Enni Thee Neekaadhaar Theenginai Thee
Padum Thee
Unnai Aridharkku Unadhoozh Tharapetra Ponnai Penn
Mannaasai Pokalai Kaanayael Ennai Payakkumo Sol

*****

Meaning – One's self realisation, Elevating Knowledge can be acquired when one reaches You realising your Supreme Beingness

The Supreme Being will eliminate one's past karmas, the ones that will occur in the future once you get to realise that He is the route to salvation

What is the use even if one is exalted to the height of a palm tree, if one cannot remove the evil thoughts from their mind, which in turn will cause evil back to them?

To attain self realisation, one will have to forgo the following even if it is the fate to have those – the wealth, the better half, the land, which is materialistic, If not what is the use in attaining self realisation.

281

In the image below, each of these verses run through each snake with the intersections having the same letters

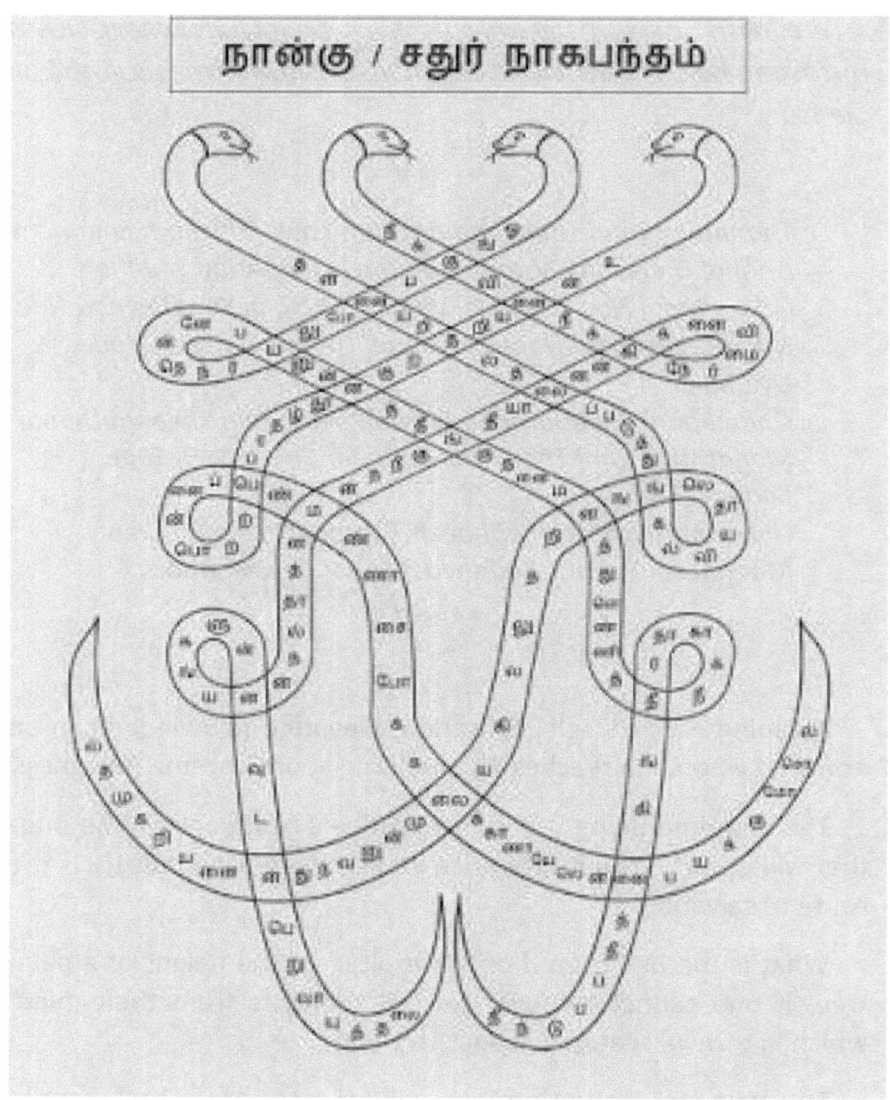

ASHTA NAAGABANDHAM (அஷ்ட நாகபந்தம்(

In this form there are 8 snakes, and each line/verse of the poem runs along each of the snakes. I was not able to find an illustrative song / drawing for this form. Any help from the readers would be much appreciated. However the following is the rule for an ashta naagabandham song

ஒருநான்கக் கரத்தொடுநாற் பத்தொன் றாமா
றுடனாற்பத் தைந்தாமெட் டுடனைந் நான்காம்
இருளறுபன் னிரண்டுடனே பதினெட் டாகும்
இருபத்தி ரண்டுடனே நாற்பத் தேழாம்
பரவுமிரு பத்துநான் குடன்முப் பத்தொன்
பானாமுப் பான்மூன்றோ டைம்பத் தொன்றாம்
அருமுப்பத் தேமுடனே நாற்பத் தொன்பா
னாமட்ட நாகபந்த மாஞ்செய் யுட்கே.

There are even more complex poetry forms, which we will see in the next volume of the book, no wonder there were people who carried the Anna Kavadi for more than 6 months to learn this masterpiece from a sanyasi

(Continued in Part 2)

REFERENCES

1. Abithana Chinthamani – Singaraveloo Mudhaliar (Seethai Pathipagam)
2. Padhartha Guna Chinthamani – Theraiyar (Thamarai Noolagam)
3. Kaalamegam Thanipaadalgal – Puliyur Kesigan (Mullai Nilayam)
4. Avvaiyar Thanipaadalgal – Puliyur Kesigan (Mullai Nilayam)
5. Sivavaakiyam (Thamarai Noolagam)
6. Thirumandhiram – G. Varadarajan (Palaniappa Brothers)
7. Naalayira Dhivya Prabandham - Dr. R.V. Kamalakannan (Vardhamanan Pathipagam)
8. Thandialangaram – Puliyur Kesigan (Saradha Pathipagam)
9. Thandialangaram – www.tamilvu.org
10. Arthamulla Hindu Matham – Kannadasan (Vanathi Pathipagam)
11. Kumaresa Sadhagam – Gurupaadha Daasar (Balaji Printers & Pathipagam)
12. Aasarakkovai – G. Manickkavasagan (Uma Pathipagam)
13. Tholkaapiyam – www.projectmadurai.org
14. Arappaleeswara Sadhagam – Ambalavana Kaviraayar (Dhanalakshmi Puthaga Nilayam)
15. Vivega Chinthamani - G. Manickkavasagan (Uma Pathipagam)
16. Abirami Andhadhi – Abirami Battar
17. Na. Kathiraiverpillai Thamizh Mozhi Agaradhi – P.V. Namachivayan (Saradha Pathipagam)
18. Thirukkural – (Manivaasaga Pathipagam)

APPENDIX

1. பிரபவ - PRABAVA

ஆதி பிலவத்தி லம்புவியின் மானுடர்க்குச்
சோதனையாய்ச் சாவுதுன்பந் தோன்றுமே
தருப்பொலியுந் ம:்கமிகுந் தண்மாரி யோங்கும்
பருத்தியுப்பு மாமணக்கும் பாழ்

விளக்கம்:

பிரபவ வருடத்தில் உலகில் மக்களுக்கு சோதனைகளாய்
சாவும் துன்பமும் தோன்றும். பழமரங்கள் நன்கு காய்க்கும்
யாகங்கள் மிகும் மழை நன்கு பொழியும். பருத்தி உப்பு
ஆமணக்கு பாழாகும்.

Aadhi Pilavathil Ambuviyil Maanidarkku
Sodhanaiyai Saavu thunbam Thonumae – Needhi
Tharu Poliyum Akkam Migum Thannmaari Ongum
Paruthiuppu aamanukku Paazh

During the first year Prabava, humans will see deaths, problems
and difficulties. The trees will be good amounts of fruit, yaagams
will be done. Rains will be good. Cotton, castor and Salt will get
destroyed.

2. விபவ - VIBAVA

செய்ய விபவதனிற் செய்புவனந் தான்விளையும்
பெய்யுமழை யெங்கும் பெருகுமே ஐயமின்றி
மிக்க சுகம்பெறுவர் மேதினியோர் வேந்தர்க்குத்
தக்கவபி மானமுண்டு தான்

விளக்கம்:

விபவ வருடத்தில் விளைச்சல் நன்றாக இருக்கும் மழை நன்றாக பெய்யும். மக்கள் பயம் நீங்கி இன்பமாக இருப்பர். அரசாள்பவர்க்கு நன்மதிப்பும் அபிமானமும் உண்டு

Seiyya Vibava Thannil Sei Bhuvanam Thaan Vilaiyum
Peiyyum Mazhai Engum Perugumae Ayyamindri
Mikka Sugam Peruvar Medhiniyor Vendharkku
Thakka Abimaanam Undu Thaan

In the year of Vibava harvests will be good, rains will inundate everywhere. People will live happily without fear. The rulers will be liked by everyone

3. சுக்கில - SUKKILA

நன்மைபெறுஞ் சுக்கிலத்தி நாடெங்கு மேசெழிக்கும்
புன்மைவினை நீங்கி பொருள்சேரும் நன்மை
இருக்கும் பசுகறக்கு மெங்குமமழை யோங்கும்
பருத்தியுப்புந் தான்குறையும் பார்

விளக்கம்:

சுக்கில ஆண்டில் நன்மைகள் நடக்கும் நாடெங்கும் செழிப்பாக இருக்கும் துன்பம் நீங்கி பொருளும் இன்பமும் சேரும். பசுக்கள் நன்கு கறப்பதனால் பால்வளம் மிகும், மழை நன்றாக பெய்யும். பருத்தியும் உப்பும் உற்பத்தியில் குறையும்

Nanmai Perum Sukkilathil Naadu Engumae Sezhikkum
Punmai Vinai Neengi Porul Saerum Nanmai
Irukkum Pasu Karakkum Engum Mazhai Ongum
Paruththi Uppum Thaan Kuraiyum Paar

In year Sukkila, things will prosper and every place in the country will flourish. The sorrows will go away and people will get possessions, Goodness will permeate, cows will produce lots of milk. Rainfall will be good. But, cotton and salt will reduce in production.

4. பிரமோதூத – PRAMOTHOODHA

வரும்பிரமோ தூத வருடமழை கொஞ்சங்
கரும்பு மிகப்பலிக்குங் கண்டாய் திரும்பப்
பயமுண்டு பூமி பலியாது வேந்தர்
நயமுண்ட தாயிருப்பர் நன்கு

விளக்கம்:

பிரமோதூத வருடம் மழை கொஞ்சமாக பெய்யும். கரும்பு விளைச்சல் நன்றாக இருக்கும் திரும்பிய திசை எங்கும் பயம் உண்டு. பூமி விளைவு எதிர்பார்த்த வகையில் அமையாது. அரசாள்பவர்கள் நற்பயன்களை தருவார்கள்

Varum Pramoothoodha Varudam Mazhai Konjam
Karumbu Miga Palikkum Kandaai Thirumba
Bayamundu Bhoomi Pailyaadhu Vendhar
Nayam Undathaai Iruppar Nangu

Pramothoodha year bestows lesser rainfall. Sugarcane will grow well. Fear will arise all around. Lands will not produce crops to the expected levels. Rulers will be beneficial to the people.

5. பிரசோற்பத்தி – PRAJORPATHTHI

துய்யபிர சோற்பதியிற் றோன்றுமே நற்காலம்
பெய்யு மழையதிகம் பேருழவாம் வையகத்தில்
உள்ளவகைச் சாதி யுயிர்தழைத்து வாழ்ந்திருப்பர்
கள்ளமில்லை யென்றேநீ காண்

விளக்கம்:

தூய்மையான பிரசோற்பத்தி நற்காலமான ஆண்டு மழை அதிகமாக பெய்யும் விவசாயம் தழைக்கும் உலகத்தில் அனைத்து மக்களும் செழிப்பாக வாழ்வார்கள். திருட்டுபயம் இருக்காது எனலாம்

Thuyya Prajorpaththiyil Thondrumae Narkaalam
Peyyum Mazhai Adhigam Paeruzhavaam Vaiyagaththil
Ullavagai Saadhi Uyir Thazhaiththu Vaazhdhiruppar
Kallamillai Yendrae Nee Kaan

In the pristine year of Prajorpaththi, good times will set it. Rainfall will be abundant; as a result agriculture will flourish and give a good yield. People at all levels in the country will prosper. Fear of robbery will not be there.

6. ஆங்கீரச – AANGEERASA

ஆங்கீ ரசவருட மான மழைமிகுத்து
நீங்காம னீரோடி நீள்புவனம் பாங்காய்
விளைவின்றிப் பஞ்ச மிகுமே யுயிர்கட்
களவின்றிச் செல்வ மறும்

விளக்கம்:

ஆங்கீரச வருடம் மழை மிகுதியாக பெய்து அனைத்துப்பக்கங்களிலும் நீர்வெள்ளம் ஓடி விளைச்சலை நாசம் செய்து பஞ்சம் உண்டாக்கும். மக்கள் அளவில்லாமல் சேர்த்த செல்வத்தினை இழப்பர்

Aangeerasa Varudam Aana Mazhaimiguththu
Neengamal Neerodi Neel Bhuvanam Paangaai
Vilaivindri Panjam Migumae Uyirgatku
Alavindri Selvam Arum

In the year Aangeerasa, rains will flood everywhere and will destroy the crops and scarcity of food will go on the rise. People will lose their wealth

7. ஸ்ரீமுக – SREEMUGA

தேடுநற் சீமுகத்திற் றேசந் தழைத்தோங்கும்
நாடியே முன்மழையோ நல்காது நீடியபின்
நானமழை யுண்டு நவதா னியம்பெருகுந்
தானோவு முண்டென்றே சாற்று

விளக்கம்:

ஸ்ரீமுக ஆண்டில் தேசம் தழைத்து ஓங்கும். ஆண்டின் முற்பகுதியில் மழை இருக்காது. பிற்பகுதியில் நல்ல மழை பெய்து நவதானியம் நன்கு விளையும். இந்த ஆண்டில் நோய்கள் பரவும் .

Thaedu Nall Seemugathil Desam Thalaithongum
Naadiyae Munn Mazhaiyo Nalgaadhu Neediya Pinnana
Mazhai Undu Navadhaaniyam Perugum Thaan
Novum Undu Endrae Saatru

In Sreemuga year, the country will prosper, the rains in the first half of the year will fail but the second half will see good rains. The nine cereal crops will give a good yield. Diseases will spread in the country.

8. பவ – BAVA

பவவருடந் தோன்றிற் பரிவார மோங்குந்
தவமிகுதி யாகுந் தளத்தில் நவமதிகம்
பெய்யுமழை தானதிகம் பிள்ளைபெறு மாதர்தாம்
ஐய மடிவ ரறி

விளக்கம்:

பவ வருடத்தில் படை பலம் பெருகும் தவச்செயல்கள் அதிகரிக்கும் புதியவைகள் உருவாகும் மழையும் அதிகமாக பெய்யும். பிள்ளைபெறும் பெண்கள் மடிவது உயரும்.

Bava Varudam Thondril Parivaaram Ongum
Thavam Migudhi Aagum Thalaththil Navam Adhigam
Peyyum Mazhai Thaan Adhigam Pillai Perum Maadhar
Thaam
Aiyya Madivar Ari

In the year Bava, the military will get strong. Worshipping will increase. New things will get into existence. Rainfall will be abundant. The death of women delivering babies will go on the rise.

9. யுவ – YUVA

யுவவருடம் பூவுலகி லுள்ளோர்க ணோயாற்
றவவருந்து வார் பசுமா தங்கும் நவமாக
வாழும் பரிவார மாரியுண்டு நெல்விளையுந்
தாழ்வான தொன்றுமில்லை தான்

விளக்கம்:

யுவ வருடத்தில் பூமியில் உள்ளோர் நோய்வாய்ப்பட்டு வருந்துவர் . பசுக்களும் மாமரமும் நன்கு பலன் தரும். படைகள் புதிய ஆயுதங்களுடன் பலமாக இருப்பர் நல்ல மழை பொழியும், நெல் நன்றாக விளையும் இவ்வருடத்தில் தாழ்சியாவதற்கு ஏதுமில்லை

Yuva Varudam Boovilagil Ullorgal Noiyaatra
Varundhuvaar Pasu Maa Thangum Navamaaga
Vaazhum Parivaaram Maari Undu Nell Vilaiyum
Thaazhvaanadhu Ondrum Illa Thaan

Yuva year will get people worries because of the onset of diseases. Cow (Cattle) and Mangoes will sustain good yield. Military will get stronger with modern weapons. Rainfall will be good; Rice will give a good yield. Things won't go low than they are now.

10. தாது – THAADHU

தாது வருடந் தராதலத்தோர் வாழ்ந்திருப்பர்
வேதனையு மில்லை விளைவுண்டு சீதமழை
பெய்யும் பரிவாரம் பேருடனே யெந்நாளும்
உய்யும் படியுலகி லுண்டு

விளக்கம்:

தாது வருடத்தில் உலகில் உள்ளோர் வாழ்வு நலமாக இருக்கும். வேதனைகள் இருக்காது விவசாயத்தில் நல்ல விளைவு இருக்கும். மழை அளவாக பெய்யும் படைகள் காப்பதினால் உலகம் (நாடு) பாதுகாப்பாக இருக்கும்.

Thaadhu Varudam Thaarathalaththor Vaazhndhu Iruppar
Vedhanaiyum Illai Vilaivundu Seedhamazhai
Peiyum Parivaaram Perudanae Ennaalum
Uyyumpadi Ulagil Undu

In the year Thaadhu, people will live safely. There won't be things that would worry them. Agricultural produce will be good. Rains will be adequate. The military defending the country will make the people live a safe life.

11. ஈஸ்வர – ESWARA

நக்க னெனுமீச் சுரவருட நாமமதில்
மிக்கபதி னெட்டுவகை வேளாண்மை தக்க
விளைவுண்டு மாரியுண்டு மேதனியின் மாக்கள்
தளர்வின்றி வாழ்வார் தழைத்து

விளக்கம்:

சிவனின் நாமம் கொண்டிருக்கும் ஈஸ்வர வருடத்தில் பதினெட்டு வகையான பயிர்களும் விளையும் நல்ல மழை உண்டு, மக்கள் நலமாக வாழ்வார்கள்

Nakkan Ennum Eswara Varuda Naamam Adhil
Mikka Padhinettu Vagai Velaanmai Thakka
Vilaivundu Maariyundu Maedhaniyil Maakkal
Thalarvindri Vaazhvaar Thazhaiththu

Eswara, the year that holds of the name of Lord Shiva, will bestow good yields for the 18 varieties of crops. Rains will be good and people will live a tireless life.

12. வெகுதானிய - VEGUDHANYA

வெகுதா னியவருட மேதினியி லெல்லாந்
தகுமாரி பின்பெய்யுந் தான்முன் முகில்சோர்ந்து
கொஞ்சமழை பெய்யுங் குலவு தழைதழைக்கும்
பஞ்சும் பருத்தியுப்புப் பாழ்

விளக்கம்:

வெகுதானிய வருடம் பூமியில் மழை வருட பிற்பகுதியில் பெய்யும், முற்பகுதியில் மேகக்கூட்டம் சோர்ந்து மழை குறைவாக பெய்யும். விவசாயம் தழைக்கும். பஞ்சு, பருத்தி, உப்பு பாழாகும்.

Vegudhanya Varuda Maedhaniyil Vellaam
Thagumari Peyyumthaan Munn – Mugil Soarndhu
Konja Mazhai Peyyum Kulavu Thazhai Thazhaikkum
Panjum Paruthi Uppu Paazh

In the year Vegudhanyam, rains will set a record though during the early part of the year rains will be less. Agricultural yields will be good, but wool, cotton and salt would be destroyed.

13. பிரமாதி - PRAMADHI

வெய்யபிர மாதியினில் வேந்தர் கொடுமையுறும்
ஐயகேள் பஞ்ச மடுக்குமே செய்ய
பசுக்கள் மெலியுமே பாரிற் குடிகள்
சிசுக்க ளுடனலைவார் தேர்

விளக்கம்:

பிரமாதி வருடத்தில் வேந்தர்கள் கொடுமை அனுபவிப்பார்கள். பஞ்சம் தலைவிரித்து ஆடும், பசுக்கள் உணவின்றி மெலியும். குடிமக்கள் தத்தம் பிள்ளைகளோடு பஞ்சம் பிழைக்க ஊர் ஊராக திரிவர்

Veyya Pramadhiyil Vendhar Kodumaiyilum
Ayyakael Panjamadukkumae – Seyya
Pasukkal Meliyum Paarir Kudigal
Sisukaludan Alaivaar Thaer

During Pramadhi, even the kings will be in a torment, and heed with fear that famine will strike. As a result, all the cattle would starve, and the people of the world would make an exodus with their children.

14. விக்கிரம - VIKRAMA

விக்கிரம வாண்டதனின் மேவியநன் மாரிகொஞ்சம்
அக்க ணுயிர்க எழியுமே தொக்க
பயிர்தீயும் நோயும் பழியுயுமாம் பின்பு
செயிர்தீர்ந்த வோர்மழையாஞ் செப்பு

விளக்கம்:

விக்கிரம வருடத்தில் மழை கொஞ்சமாக பெய்யும் உயிர்கள் அழியும் பயிர்கள் நாசமுறும் நோய் பரவும், பழியும் சேரும் ஆண்டின் பிற்பகுதியில் ஆதரவாக சிறிது மழை பெய்யும்

Vikrama Aandathanil Meviya Nannmaari Konjam
Akkanuyirkal Azhiyumae – Thokka
Payirtheeyum Noyum Pazhiyumamaam Pinbu
Seyirtheerndha Mazhaiyaam Seppu

Vikrama year will bring lesser rains, crops will perish, diseases and curses will spread, and later in the year the rains would be remedial to the past effects

15. விஷு - VISHU

பாரில் விஷுவருடம் பாலர்க்குப் பீடையுண்டாம்
கார்பொழிவ தில்லைமுற் காலத்தில் ஏரி
பெருகாது பிற்காலம் பெய்யுமே மாரி
இருகால முஞ்சமன்னெ றென்

விளக்கம்:

விஷு வருடத்தில் உலகில் உள்ள குழந்தைகளுக்கு கெடுதல் உண்டாம். வருட முற்பகுதியில் மழை பெய்யாது ஏரிகள் நிறையாது, வருட பிற்பகுதியில் நல்ல மழை பெய்யும். மொத்தத்தில் சராசரியான ஆண்டு.

Paaril Vishu Varudam Paalarkku Peedaiundaam
Kaarpozhivadhillai Murkaalathil – Yeri
Perugadhu Pirrkaalam Peyyumae Maari
Irukaalamum Samannedru Enn

In the year Vishu, children will have a bad time, rains will fail during the early part of the year and water sources like lakes, reservoirs would not have their water levels increased. In the later part of the year rains will be good and consider the two parts of the year to be equal in giving benefits

16. சித்திரபானு - CHITIRABANU

சித்திர பானு சிறக்க மழைமிகுத்து
வித்துள்ள வெல்லாம் விளையுமே எத்திசையும்
பார்ப்பாருக் காகாது பார்வேந்தர்க் கேநலமாந்
தீர்ப்பாகப் பூமிபயஞ் செப்பு

விளக்கம்:

சித்திரபானு வருடத்தில் மழை சிறப்பாகப் பெய்யும். அதனால் விதைத்தது எல்லாம் நன்கு விளையும். பிராமணர்களுக்கு அனைத்து திசைகளிலிருந்தும் தீமை விளையும். ஆட்சி செய்பவர்களுக்கு நன்மை உண்டாகும். பூமி சார்ந்த பயம் இருக்கும் (நிலநடுக்கம், எல்லை சண்டை போன்றவை)

Chitirabanu Sirakka Mazhai Miguththu
Vithulla Vellaam Vilayumae – Ethisaiyum
Parparukku Aagadhu Paarvendharkkae Nalamaam
Theerpaga Bhoomi Bayam Seppu

In the year Chitirabanu, rains will be good and adequate resulting in good agricultural yield. Kings will benefit in this year however those involved in divine activities may have a bad time. Territorial disputes/natural land disasters/threats/fears will exist.

17. சுபானு - SUBANU

*சொன்னேன் சுபானுதனிற் றோன்றுமழை
கொஞ்சமாம்
மின்னே விளைவு பெருகாது மன்னேதுன்
மத்திமக்கோ ஞண்டா மடியுநாற் காற்சீவன்
சற்றுஞ் சுகமில்லைத் தான்*

விளக்கம்:

சுபானு வருடத்தில் மழை தோன்றுவது குறையும். அதனால் விளைச்சல் இருக்காது. கோள்களின் நிலை மத்திம பலன் கொடுப்பதாகவே அமையும். கால்நடைகள் மடியும்.. சற்றும் சுகமில்லாத வருடம்.

*Sonnaen Subanuthanil Thodrum Mazhaikonjamam
Minnae Vilaivu Perugathu Mannethun
Mathima Kolundaam Madiyum Naarkaal Jeevan
Sattrum Sugam Illai Than*

In the year Subanu, rainfall will dwindle, and as a result crops would not yield. Moderate benefits during the middle of the year. Cattle would die in large proportions. Overall, it is not a good year for the world.

18. தாரண - DHAARANA

தாரணத்தின் மாரியறுந் தாரணியிற் கேடுமல்கும்
ஒரிலுயிர் வரக்கமவை யுய்யாவாற் பார்ப்பிணியால்
ஐய மடியுமே ய:கங் குறையுமே
வெய்யர் பயமே மிகும்

விளக்கம்:

தாரண வருடத்தில் மழை குறையும். இயற்கை சீற்றம் முதலிய கேடு பல விளையும். உயிர்கள் உய்யாது நோய் பிணியால் மடியும். யாகங்கள் குறையும். பகைவர் பயமே மிகுதியாகும்.

Dhaaranathil Maari Arum Dharaniyil Kaedummalgum
Oriluyir Vargamavai Uyyavaam Paarpiniyaal
Ayyamadiyumae Yakkam Kuraiyumae
Veiyar Bayamae Migum

In the year Dhaarana, rains will fail, catastrophe and bad events would occur. The beings on earth would not attain comfort or salvation. The world would die of difficulties etc., divine activities like yaagams etc., will reduce. Terrorist / Inimical threats would increase.

19. பார்த்திப - PARTHIBA

தேச மிசைபார்த் திபவருடஞ் சிங்களத்தார்
தேசங் கேடுமனந்த தேசத்து ராசர்
அநியாயஞ் செய்வா ரதமேறு மாரி
இனிதாம் விளைவுமுள தாம்

விளக்கம்:

பார்த்திப ஆண்டில் இலங்கை தேசத்தவர்களுக்கு தீமை
உண்டாம். மற்றைய தேசத்து அரசர்கள் அநியாயம்
செய்வர். மழை நன்றாக பெய்யும். விவசாய விளைச்சலும்
நன்றாக இருக்கும்.

Desamisai Parthiba Varudam Singalathar
Desam Kedum Ananda Desathu – Rasar
Aniyayam Seivar Radham Yerum Maari
Inidhaam Vilaivum Ulavaam

During the year Parthiba, the Srilankans would have a bad time,
having their internal and external relations spoiled. Kings and
Rulers of other countries would do blatant injustice. Rains will
batter the world. The yield on crops would be very good.

20. விய - VIYA

வியவருட மாரி விளைவுண்டாஞ் சீனம்
சுயவாழ் வுடனே சுகமாம் உயர்வாம்
பதினெட்டு வித்தும் பதிவாய்ப் பலிக்குஞ்
சதிர்பெறுநல் ல:ஃகமிகுந் தான்

விளக்கம்:

விய வருடத்தில் மழை நன்றாக பெய்யும் பதினெட்டு வகையான பயிர்களும் நன்கு விளையும். மக்கள் மகிழ்வுடன் இருப்பர். சீனதேசம் உயர்வு பெறும். யாகங்கள் மிகும்.

Viyavarudam Maari Vilaivundaam Cheenam
Suya Vaazvudanae Sugamaam Uyarvaam
Pathinettu Viththum Pathivaai Palikkum
Sathir Peru Nallakkam Migumthaan

In the Viya year there will very good rainfall and all the 18 major crops will grow well. China will grow to be self–sufficient. And good deeds and yaagams will rise on this planet.

21. சர்வசித்து - SARVASITHU

சருவசித்து தன்னிற் நலத்திற் பலவும்
ஒருபதி னெட்டுவித்து மோங்கும் பெருமையுடன்
மிக்கவிளை வுண்டாகு மேன்மேலு மரியுண்டாந்
தக்க சுகம்பெருகுந் தான்

விளக்கம்:

சருவசித்து வருடத்தில் பதினெட்டு வகையான
பயிர்களும் நன்கு செழித்து விளையும் மேன்மேலும் மழை
பொழியும். மக்கள் யாவரும் மகிழ்ச்சியாக இருப்பர்

Sarvasithu Thannil Avathil Palavum
Ore Pathinettu Vithuthum Ongum Perumaiyudan
Mikka Vilaivindaam Menmaelum Maariyundaam
Thakka Sugam Perugum Thaan

During Sarvasithu all the 18 crops will have good yield. Rains will pour continuously in quantities more than required. All happiness and comfort will last throughout the year.

22. சர்வதாரி - SARAVADHAARI

நற்சருவ தாரிதனி நல்லமழை யுண்டாகும்
அற்பவித் தனவெல்லா மாகாது சொற்பெரிய
ஐந்து வகைவிளைவு மாகுஞ் சுகமுடனே
மைந்தரெல்லாம் வாழ்ந்திருப்பர் மற்று

விளக்கம்:

நல்ல சருவதாரி ஆண்டில் நல்ல மழை உண்டாகும். ஐந்து முக்கிய பயிர்களை தவிர மற்றை எல்லாம் விளையாது. மக்கள் மகிழ்வுடனே வாழ்ந்து இருப்பர்

Narr Sarvadhaarin Nalla Mazhai Undaam
Arppa Vithaanadhellam Aagadhu Sorrperiya
Aindhu Vagai Vilaivum Aagum Sugamudanae
Maindhar Ellam Vaazhndhiruppar Matru

During Sarvadhaari rains will be good, but only the 5 major crops will have a good yield, the rest would not. And people will live a comfortable life.

23. விரோதி - VIRODHI

நீடு விரோதி நிலத்தின் மழைமிகுதி
மேடுகா டெல்லாம் விளைவுண்டாம் நீடும்
அரசர்போ ராலே யழியு முலகந்
திரமிகுநோய் சேருமெனச் செப்பு

விளக்கம்:

விரோதி வருடத்தில் காடு மேடென அனைத்து இடங்களிலும் மழை மிகுதியாக பெய்து நல்ல விளைச்சலை தரும். அரசர்கள் போர் செய்து பழிச்சொல் பெறுவார். உலகத்தில் கொடிய நோய் பெருகும்.

Needu Virodhi Nilathin Mazhai Migudhi
Medu Kaadellam Vilaivundaam Needum
Arasar Peraalae Azhiyum Ulagam
Thiramigu Noi Saerumena Seppu

During Virodhi rains will pour everywhere, and hence there will be good growth of crops everywhere, be it plains or hills. Rulers and Kings (can be interpreted as countries) will fight with each other and cause devastation and destruction. Contagious and diseases will be on the rise.

24. விகிர்தி - VIKRUDHI

வையந் தனில்விகிர்தி மாரி விளைவதிகஞ்
செய்ய வளங்கள் சிறக்குமே ஐயகேள்
மாடு கழுதை வயப்பரி நோய்மிக்குச்
சட மெலியுமே தான்

விளக்கம்:

விகிர்தி வருடம் மழை நன்றாக பெய்யும் விளைவு அதிகம். வளங்கள் அனைத்தும் நன்கு சிறக்கும். மாடு, கழுதை போன்ற கால்நடைகள் நோய்வாய்ப்பட்டு மெலியும் அல்லது மடியும்.

Vaiyam Thanil Vikrudhi Maari Vilaivadhigam
Seiyya Valangal Sirakkumae Aiyya Kael
Maadu Kazhudhai Vayapari Noi Mikku
Saada Meliyumae Thaan

During Vikrudhi, rains and crop harvest will be good. All the resources will be abundant, but cows and donkeys (to be interpreted as cattle) will catch disease and die in large numbers

25. கர - KARA

கரவருட மாரிபெய்யுங் காசினியு மூய்யும்
உரமிகுத்து வெல்லமெங்கு மோடும் நிரைமிகுத்து
நாலுகாற் சீவ னலியுநோ யான்மடியும்
பாலுநெய்யு மேசுருங்கும் பார்

விளக்கம்:

கர வருடம் மழை நன்கு பெய்யும் மக்களும் நன்கு வாழ்வர். நீர்வெள்ளம் அனைத்து இடங்களையும் ஓடி நிரப்பும் . மாடு முதலிய நாலுகால் சீவன்கள் நோய் வாய்ப்பட்டு மடியும். பால் நெய் உற்பத்தி குறையும்.

Kara Varudam Maari Peiyum Kaasiniyum Uyiyum
Uramigundha Vella Engum Odum Nirai Migundhu
Naalukaal Seevan Azhiyum Noiyaal Madiyum
Paal Neiyumae Surungum Paar

During Kara year, rains will be good and the people in the world will attain bliss and salvation, but floods will inundate everywhere and four legged cattle will die in large numbers because of diseases. And hence, milk and ghee will go scarce.

26. நந்தன - NANDHANA

நந்தனத்தின் மாரியறு நாடெங்கும் பஞ்சமிகும்
நந்துமுயிர் நோயா நலியுமே அந்தரத்தின்
மீனுதிருந் தூமமேழும் மிக்க கெடுதியுண்டாம்
கோன்மடிவ னென்றேநீ கூறு

விளக்கம்:

நந்தன வருடம் மழை பொய்க்கும் நாடெங்கும் பஞ்சம்
வரும். உயிர்கள் நோய்வாய்ப்படும். வால்நட்சத்திரம்
தோன்றும் அரச பதவில் உள்ளோர்கள் மடிவார்கள்.

Nandhanathin Maariyarum Naadengum Panjam Migum
Nandhumuyir Noyaal Naliyumae Andharathin
Meenu Thirundhu Thooman Ezhum Mikka Keduthi Undaam
Kone Madivan Endrae Nee Kooru

During Nandhana year, rains will fail and famine will strike throughout the world. Beings will die as a result of diseases. Comet will appear indicating a bad omen. Kings and Rulers will die in this year.

27. விஜய - VIJAYA

மண்ணில் விசய வருட மழைமிகுதி
எண்ணுசிறு தானியங்க எங்குமே நண்ணும்
பயம்பெருகி நொந்து பரிவார மெல்லாம்
நயங்களின்றி வாடுமென நாட்டு

விளக்கம்:

விசய வருடம் மழை நன்கு பெய்யும். சிறுதானியங்கள் எல்லாம் நன்கு விளையும். நாட்டில் பயம் பெருகுவதால் படைகளும் மக்களும் வருந்தி நல்லவை நடைபெறாது வாடுவார்கள்.

Mannil Vijaya Varudam Mazhai Migudhi
Ennum Siru Dhaniyangal Engum Nannnum
Bayam Perugi Nondhu Parivaaram Ellam
Nayangalindri Vaadum Ena Naatu

In the Vijaya year, rainfall will be abundant. Pulses (Crops) will grow well. Fear will mount, and as a result, the army and people will become unhappy and weak.

28. ஜெய - JEYA

செயவருடந் தன்னிலே செய்புலங்க எல்லாம்
வியனுறவே பைங்கூழ் விளையும் நயமுடனே
அஃகம் பெரிதா மளவில் சுகம்பெருகும்
வெஃகுவார் மண்ணிறை மேல்

விளக்கம்:

ஜெய வருடத்தில் அனைத்து நிலங்களிலும் விளைவு நன்றாக இருக்கும். யாகங்கள் பெருகும் மக்கள் மகிழ்வுடன் இருப்பர். அரசர்கள் பேராசை கொண்டு அதற்கேற்றார்போல் செயல்கள் செய்வர்.

Jeya Varudam Thannilae Sei Pulangal Ellam
Viyanuravae Painkoozh Vilayum Nayamudanae
Akkam Peridhaam Alavil Sugam Perugum
Vekkuvaar Mannirai Mael

During the Jeya year, crops will yield a good harvest in both the Nanjai and Punjai lands. Divine activities like Yaagams and Poojas will be on the rise. Everyone will be happy and comfortable. The rulers will become greedy and proud.

29. மன்மத - MANMADHA

மன்மததின் மாரியுண்டு வாழுமுயி ரெல்லாமே
நன்மைமிகும் பல்பொருளு நண்ணுமே
மன்னவரால்
சீனத்தில் சண்டை உண்டு தென்திசையிற் காற்று
மிகுங்
கானப் பொருள்குறையுங் கான்

விளக்கம்:

மன்மத ஆண்டில் மழை நன்கு பெய்யும் உயிர்கள்
அனைத்தும் நன்மை பெரும் பொருள் சேரும். மன்னவர்கள்
சீன தேசத்தோடு போர் புரிவர் தென்திசையில் காற்று
மிகும். கானக பொருட்கள் வரத்து குறையும்.

Manmadhathin Maariyundu Vaazhum Uyirellamae
Nanmai Migu Palporulum Nannumae Mannavaraal
Seenathil Sandai Undu Then Disayil Kaatru Migudhi
Kaanapporul Kuraiyum Kaan

In the year Manmadha, rains will be good. People will live well
and be bestowed with good things. Because of the decisions made
by the rulers, China will have to face war. The southern regions of
India will have more winds. As a result, items obtained from the
forests will get reduced.

30. துர்முகி - DHUNMUGI

மிக்கான துர்முகியில் வேளாண்மை யேறுமே
தொக்கமழை பின்னே சொரியுமே மிக்கான
குச்சர தேசத்திற் குறைதீர வேவிளையும்
அச்சமில்லை வெள்ளையரி தாம்

விளக்கம்:

துர்முகி ஆண்டில் விவசாய விளைச்சல் ஏற்றம் பெரும். மழை வருட பிற்பகுதியில் பொழியும் குஜராத் தேசம் நல்ல முன்னேற்றம் காணும். மக்கள் அச்சமின்றி வாழ்வர். வெள்ளை பொருட்களான உப்பு, பஞ்சு, பால், தயிர் போன்றவை குறையும்.

Mikkaana Dhunmugiyil Velanmai Yaerumae
Thokka Mazhai Pinnae Soriyumae Mikkaana
Kuchara Desathil Kurai Theeravae Vilayum
Achamillai Vellai Aridhaam

In the year Dhunmugi, agriculture will flourish, good amount rains will fall in the later part of the year. Gujarat will see good harvest. There is nothing to fear in this year, but products that are white – milk, salt, cotton etc. will become scarce.

31. ஹேவிளம்பி - HEYVILAMBI

ஹேவிளம்பி மாறியற்ப மெங்கும்
விலைகுறைவாம்
பூவில் விளைவரிதாம் போர்மிகுதி சாவதிகம்
ஆகுமே வேந்த ரநியாய மேபுரிவர்
வேகுமே மேதணிதீ மேல்

விளக்கம்:

ஹேவிளம்பி வருடம் அற்பமான மழை பொழியும். விவசாய விளைச்சல் குறையும். விற்கும் பொருள் லாபம் தராது விலை குறையும். போர் மிகும் சாவு அதிகரிக்கும். ஆட்சி புரிவோர் அநியாயம் புரிவர். தீயில் வேகுவதுபோல் மக்கள் துன்பமுறுவர்

Heyvilambi Maari Arpam Engum Vilai Kuraiyumae
Poovil Vilaivaridhaam Pormigudhi Saavadhigam
Aagumae Vendhar Aniyayamae Purivar
Vegumae Maedhani Thee Mael

During Heyvilambi, rains will fail and harvests will fall. Countries will wage war against each other. Rulers will begin to do blatant injustice; as a result, people will go through torment as if the world burns on fire.

32. விளம்பி - VILAMBI

விளம்பி வருடம் விளைவுகொஞ்ச மாரி
அளந்து பொழியு மரசர் களங்கமுடன்
நோவான் மெலிவரே நோக்கரிதா குங்கொடுமை
ஆவா புகலரி தாம்

விளக்கம்:

விளம்பி வருடம் மழை அளந்து பெய்யும், விளைச்சல்
கொஞ்சமாக இருக்கும். ஆட்சி பொறுப்பில் இருப்போர்
கடுமையாக இருப்பர் அதனால் மக்கள் அவதியும்
கவலையுமுறுவர். கொடுமை மிகும் சிறப்பில்ல வருடம்.

Vilambi Varudam Vilaivu Konjam Maari
Alandhu Pozhiyum Arasar Kalangmudan
Novaan Melivarae Nokkaridhaagum Kodumai
Aava Pugalaridhaam

Vilambi year will see less harvests, rainfall will be just sufficient. Rulers will commit blatant injustice, torture and tyranny. Successful happenings will become scarce.

33. விகாரி – VIKARI

பார் விகாரிதனிற் பாரணநீ ருங்குறையும்
மாரியில்லை வேளாண்மை மத்திமமாம் சோரர்
பயமதிக முண்டாம் பழையோர்கள் சம்பாத்
தியவுடைமை விற்றுண்பார் தேர்

விளக்கம்:

விகாரி ஆண்டில் மழைநீர் குறையும், குடிநீர் தட்டுபாடு வரும். விவசாய விளைச்சல் சராசரி அளவாக இருக்கும். திருடர்கள் பயம் அதிகம் உண்டாகும். மக்கள் சேர்த்த சொத்தினை விற்று உண்ணும் அவலநிலை உண்டாகும்

Paar Vigarithanil Paarana Neerum Kuraiyum
Maariyillai Velaanmai Maththimamaam Sorar
Bayam Adhigam Undam Pazhaiyorgal Sambaathiya
Udaimai Vitrunbaar Thaer

During Vigari rains will fail, there will be shortage or potable water. Agricultural yield will be average. Thievery and robbery will rise. People will sell their belongings to make a living.

34. சார்வரி – SAARVARI

சாருவரி யாண்டதனிற் சாதிபதி னெட்டுமே
தீரமறு நோயாற் றிரிவார்கள் மாரியில்லை
பூமிவிளை வில்லாமற் புத்திரரு மற்றவரும்
ஏமமின்றிச் சாவா ரியம்பு

விளக்கம்:

சாருவரி ஆண்டில் அனைத்து தரப்பு மக்களும் நோயுற்று திரிவார்கள். மழை பெய்யாது. விவசாயம் பொய்த்து விளைச்சல் குன்றும் உணவு இல்லாமையினால் பிள்ளைகளும் மற்றோரும் மடிவர்.

Saruvari Andathanil Saadhi Pathinettumae
Theeramaru Noyaal Thirivaargal Maari Illai
Boomi Vilaivillaamal Puththirarum Matravarum
Yaemam Indri Saavaar Iyambu

In the year Saarvari, people across the country will be hit by epidemics. Rain and crops will fail. People and their progeny will die out of food scarcity.

35. பிலவ – PILAVA

பிலவத்தின் மாரிகொஞ்சம் பீடைமிகும் ராசர்
சலமிகுதி துன்பந் தருக்கும் நலமில்லை
நாலுகாற் சீவனெல்லா நாசமாம் வேளாண்மை
பாலுமின்றிச் செயபுவனம் பாழ்

விளக்கம்:

பிலவ ஆண்டில் மழை கொஞ்சமாக பெய்யும் அரசாள்பவர் கோபம் அதிகம் கொள்வர் கொடுமைகள் புரிவர் மக்களுக்கு நலமில்லை. கால்நடைகள் பெருத்த அளவில் மடியும். விவசாயம் பொய்க்கும். பாலும் உணவும் இன்றி உலகம் பாழாகும்

Pilavathin Maarikonjam Peedai Migum Raasar
Salam Migudhi Thunbam Tharukkum Nalamillai
Naalukaal Seevan Ellaam Naasamaam Velaanmai
Paalum Indri Sei Puvanam Paazh

In the Pilava year, rains will be scanty, sorrows will mount. Rulers will be angry and will cause harm to the subjects of the country. Cattle will die in large numbers as a result, crops will fail and milk production will go down. People will suffer because of the scarcity.

36. சுபகிருது – SUBAKRIDHU

சுபகிருது தன்னிலே சோழதே சம்பாழ்
அவமாம் விலைகுறையு மான்சாம் சுபமாகும்
நாடெங்கு மாரிமிகு நல்லவிளை வுண்டாகுங்
கேடெங்கு மில்லையதிற் கேள்

விளக்கம்:

சுபகிருது ஆண்டில் சோழநாட்டிலே பொருட்கள் வீணாகி அந்நாடு பாழாகும். மணப்பண்டங்களின் விலை குறையும். மழை நன்கு பெய்து விளைச்சல் உண்டாகும். மழையினால் வேறு எந்த கேடும் இல்லை இவ்வாண்டில்.

Subakridhu Thannilae Chola Desam Paazh
Avamaam Vilai Kuraiyum Maansaam Subamaagum
Naadengum Maarimigum Nalla Vilaivu Undaagum
Kaedengum Illayadhil Kael

In the year Subakridhu, Chola kingdom will be devastated and things there will go of waste. Aromatic consumables will go down in price. Rains will be very good and will bestow good harvest but the rainfall will not do any damage to the country.

37. சோபகிருது – SOBAKRIDHU

சோப கிருதுதன்னிற் றொல்லுலகெல்
லாஞ்செழிக்குங்
கோப மகன்று குணம்பெருகுஞ் சோபனங்கள்
உண்டாகு மாரி யொழியாமற் பெய்யும்மெல்லாம்
உண்டாகு மென்றே யுரை

விளக்கம்:

சோபகிருது ஆண்டில் உலகில் எல்லாம் செழிப்பாக
இருக்கும். மக்களிடையே கோபகுணம் அகன்று நல்ல
எண்ணங்கள் பெருகும். நற்செயல்கள் பெருகும் மழை
நன்றாக பெய்யும் எல்லா வித்துக்களும் விளையும்
நன்மைகள் உண்டாகும்.

Sobakridhu Thannil Tholulagellaam Sezhikkum
Kobam Agandru Kunam Perugum Sobanangal
Undaagum Maari Ozhiyaamal Peyyum Ellam
Udaagum Endru Urai

In the year Sobakridhu, The whole world will flourish. People's
thoughts and actions will be good. Good deeds will increase. Rains
will be abundant and agricultural harvests will be good. All the
goodness will happen.

38. குரோதி – KURODHI

கோரக் குரோதிதனிற் கொல்லைமிகுங் கள்ளரினாற்
பாரிற் சனங்கள் பயமடைவார் கார்மிக்க
அற்ப மழைபெய்யு மஃகம் குறையுமே
சொர்ப்பவிளை உண்டெனவே சொல்

விளக்கம்:

குரோதி வருடம் கோரம் மிகுந்ததாக இருக்கும். கொலைகள் அதிகமாக நடக்கும். திருடர்களினால் மக்கள் மிகுந்த அச்சம் கொள்வர். மழை குறைவாக பெய்யும் யாகங்கள் குறையும். விளைச்சல் குன்றும்.

Gorakurodhi Thannil Kolaigal Migum Kallarinaal
Paaril Sanangal Bayamadaivaar Kaarmikka
Arppa Mazhai Peyyum Akkam Kuraiyumae
Sorppa Vilaivu Unndenavae Sol

In the ruthless year Kurodhi, Mass killings will be on the rise. Thieves doing robbery will make people scared. Rainfall will become scarce. Yaagams will reduce. Agricultural produce will go down.

39. விசுவாவசு – VISUVAVASU

விசுவா வசுவருடம் வேளாண்மை யேறும்
பசுமாடு மாடும் பலிக்குஞ் சிசுநாசம்
மற்றையரோ வாழ்வார்கண் மாதவங்கண் மீறுமே
யுற்றுலகி னல்லமழை யுண்டு

விளக்கம்:

விசுவாவசு ஆண்டில் விவசாயம் பெருகும். பசுமாடும் ஆடும் நல்ல பலன் தரும். குழந்தைகளுக்கு கெடுதல் உண்டாகும். மற்ற மக்கள் நலமாக வாழ்வர். தவங்கள் பெருகும். மழை நன்கு பெய்யும்.

Visuvaavasu Varudam Velaanmai Yaerum
Pasumaadum Aadum Palikkum Sisunaasam
Matraiyor Vaazhvaarkaan Maadhavangal Meerumae
Uttra Ulagil Nalla Mazhai Undu

In the year, Visuvaavasu, agricultural yields will go on the rise. Cows and goats will give good benefits. Kids and Children will have a bad time. The rest of the people will be good. Good deeds will increase and the rains will be good.

40. பராபவ – PARAABAVA

மிக்க பராபவத்தின் மேதினியிற் பின்மழையாந்
தக்க பசுக்க டழைக்குமே இக்குப்
பலிக்காது நான்குவகைப் பல்லுயிர்க்கு மின்பங்
கலிக்கா தெனவே கருது

விளக்கம்:

பராபவ வருடத்தில் உலகில் வருட பிற்பகுதியில் மழை பெய்யும். பசுக்கள் நல்ல பலன் அளிக்கும். கரும்பு விளைச்சல் நன்றாக இருக்காது. பலதரப்பட்ட மக்களுக்கு இன்பம் இருக்காது.

Mikka Paraabavathin Maethiniyil Pinn Mazhaiyaam
Thakka Pasukkal Thazhaikkumae Ikku
Palikkaadhu Naangu Vagai Palluyirkkum Inbam
Kalikkaadhu Envae Karudhu

In the year Paraabava, Rainfall will be in the later part of the year. Cows and cattle will provide good benefits. Sugarcane yield will go down. Overall people from all sects and levels will not be happy.

41. பிலவங்க – PILAVANGA

பிலவங்க வாண்டதனிற் பேதகங்கண் மிஞ்சிப்
பலவந்த மாமடிவார் பாரில் நலமுந்து
வேளாண்மை மெத்த விளையுமே ய:கமோ
கேளா யதிகமதி கம்

விளக்கம்:

பிலவங்க ஆண்டில் கருத்து வேறுபாடுகளினால் கலவரங்கள் மிகுந்து மக்கள் மடிவர். விவசாயம் செழிக்கும் யாகங்கள் அதிகமாக நடத்தப்படும்

Pilavanka Aandathanil Pethagankal Minji
Palavantama Madivar Paaril Nalamundhu
Veḷaanmai Meththa Viḷaiyumae Yaagamo
Kelaai Adhigam Adhigam

In the year Pilavanga, disputes and riots will arise and will result in many deaths. Agriculture will give a good yield. Yaagams will be performed in abundance.

42. கீலக – KEELAGA

கீலகத்தின் மாரிமிகுங் கெம்பீர மெத்தவனு
கூலமுறு மானிடர்க்குக் கொண்டாட்டம் ஞாலமதில்
நல்விளைவுண் டாகுமே நாடெங்கு மேசெழிக்கும்
பல்வளமு மொங்குமெங்கும் பார்

விளக்கம்:

கீலக ஆண்டில் மழை நன்கு பொழியும். வீரசெயல் புரிவோர் அனுகூலம் பெறுவர். மக்கள் மகிழ்வோடு கொண்டாட்டம் கொள்வர். விவசாய விளைச்சல் நன்றாக இருக்கும். அனைத்து வளங்களும் பெற்று நாடு செழிப்பாக இருக்கும்.

Keelakathin Maarimikum Kambira Meththavan
Anukoolamuru Maanidarkku Kondaatam Gnalamadhil
Nall Vilaivundakumae Naadengumae Selikkum
Pall Valamum Ongum Engum Paar

In the year Keelaga, rains will be abundant; people doing heroic acts will be rewarded. People will be happy and celebrate their happiness. Agriculture will have a good yield. The entire nation will flourish and all resources will be abundant.

43. செளமிய – SOWMIYA

செய்ய சவுமியத்திற் றேசத்திற் பல்லுயிரும்
உய்யு மழைமிகுதி யுண்டாகும் வெய்ய
வினையகலும் பூமி விளைவீனுஞ் செல்வம்
மனையகலா தென்றே மதி

விளக்கம்:

செளமிய ஆண்டில் தேசத்தில் உள்ள எல்லா உயிர்களும் சிறப்பாக வாழும். மழை நன்கு பெய்யும். தீமைகள் அகலும். நிலம் நல்ல விளைச்சலை தரும் வீடுகளில் செல்வம் தங்கும்.

Seyya Sowmiyaththin Desathil Pall Uyirum
Uyyum Mazhai Migudhi Undaagum Veyya
Vinaiagalum Boomi Vilaivu Eenum Selvam
Manai Agalaadhu Endrae Madhi

In the year Sowmiya, all life will flourish, rains will be abundant. Bad things will disappear. The land will bestow good yields. People will become wealthier.

44. சாதாரண – SAADHARANA

சாதா ரணவருடந் தானியங்க ளோங்குமே
ஆதார மாமமழைபின் னாகுமே தீதாக
இல்லையெனும் பஞ்ச மிலாடத்திற் றோன்றுமென்றே
சொல்லுப்பு வெள்ளைசுருங் கும்

விளக்கம்:

சாதாரண வருடத்தில் தானிய விளைச்சல் நன்கு இருக்கும். பெரும் மழை வருட பிற்பகுதியில் இருக்கும் அதனால் தீமை ஒன்றும் விளையாது. இலாட நாடு (வங்கதேசம் சேர்ந்த பகுதிகள்) பஞ்சம் தோன்றும். உப்பு மற்றும் வெள்ளை பொருட்கள் அரிதாகும்.

Saadharana Varudam Dhaaniyangal Ongum
Aadhaara Maamazhai Pinnaagumae Theedhaga
Illai Enum Panjam Ilaadathil Thondrum Endrae
Sollu Uppu Vellai Surungum

In the year Saadharana, crops will give a good harvest. Rainfall will be good in the later part of the year. Famine will strike in the regions of Bengal. Salt, milk, cotton and similar things that are white in nature will dwindle in produce.

45. விரோதிகிருது – VIRODHIKRIDHU

மிக்க விரோதிகிர்த் மாரி விளைவுண்டு
தக்க சிறப்புந் தனமுண்டு இக்குண்டு
உப்பு பருத்தி யுலகத்தி லேகுறையுந்
துப்புமிகு மாமணக்காஞ் சொல்

விளக்கம்:

விரோதிகிருது வருடம் மழை நன்கு பெய்து விளைச்சல் நன்றாக இருக்கும். மக்களிடம் செல்வமும் சிறப்பும் சேரும். கரும்பு நன்றாக விளையும் ஆனால் உப்பு பருத்தி உற்பத்தி குறையும். ஆமணக்கு நன்றாக விளையும்

Mikka Virodhikridhu Maari Vilaivundu
Thakka Sirappum Thanam Undu Ikkundu
Uppu Paruththi Ulagathilae Kuraiyum
Thuppumigum Aamanakkam Sol

In the year Virodhikridhu rains will be good as a result crops will give good yield. People's wellbeing will be good and become wealthy. Sugarcane produce will be good. However, salt, cotton will dwindle in yield. Castor produce will be good.

46. பரிதாவி – PARIDHAVI

சொன்னபரி தாவிதனிற் றொல்லுலகின்
மாரிகொஞ்சம்
பொன்னே விளைவுளதாம் பூதலத்திற் பன்னும்
பருத்தியுப்போ டாமணக்குப் பாரிற் குறையும்
வருத்தமற வேயுயிர்வா ழும்

விளக்கம்:

பரிதாவி ஆண்டில் உலகில் மழை குறைவாக பெய்யும். சித்திரை போக வேளாண்மை அளவாக பயன் தரும். பருத்தி, உப்பு, ஆமணக்கு விளைச்சல் குறையும். மக்கள் வருத்தத்தோடு உயிர் வாழ்வார்கள்

Sonna Paridhavi Thannil Tholulagil Maari Konjam
Ponnae Vilaivulathaam Poothalaththil Pannum
Paruthi Uppodu Aamanakku Paaril Kuraiyum
Varutham Aravae Uyir Vaalum

In the year Paridhavi, rains will be scanty. The agriculture done during the month of Chithirai will give adequate yield. Cotton, Salt and Castor will go down in yield. People will live their lives in worry.

47. பிரமாதீச – PRAMADHEESA

நற்பிரமா தீசத்தி னாட்டிலே சாவதிகம்
சொற்பெரிய மாரிமிகத் தோன்றுமே மற்பிடித்து
மல்லிட்டு மாண்டிடுவர் வாளினா லேயறுவர்
கொல்லும் வறுமையெனக் கூறு

விளக்கம்:

பிரமாதீச ஆண்டில் நாட்டில் மக்கள் அதிகமாக மடிவர். மழை மிக அதிகமாக பெய்யும். மக்கள் பகைகொண்டு ஒருவரையொருவர் வெட்டிக்கொண்டு மடிவர். மேலும் மக்கள் கடும் வறுமையில் வாடுவர்

Nar Pramadheesaththil Naatilae Saavu Adhigam
Sorperiya Maari Miga Thondrumae Marpidithu
Mallitu Maandiduvar Vaalinaalae Aruvar
Kollum Varumaiyena Kooru

In the year Pramadheesa, the country will see many deaths. Rains will batter all over the country. People will grow enmity and fight with weapons like swords and kill one another. People will struggle with poverty.

48. ஆனந்த – ANANDHA

ஆனந்த வாண்டதனி லாகாத தொன்றுமில்லை
வானம் பொழியும் வரிவிளையுந் தேனே
கரும்புண்டா மாமணக்குக் காணாது காயில்
வருந்தானி யங்குறைவாம் வந்து

விளக்கம்:

ஆனந்த வருடத்தில் கெடுதல்கள் ஏதும் ஏற்படாது. மழை நன்கு பொழியும். நெல், கரும்பு நன்கு விளையும். ஆமணக்கு விளையாது. மொச்சை, தட்டை போன்ற காய் தானியங்கள் குறைவாக விளையும்.

Anandha Aandathanil Aagaadhadhu Ondrum Illai
Vaanam Pozhiyum Varivilayum Thaenae
Karumbu Undam Aamanakku Kaanaadhu Kaayil
Varum Dhaaniyam Kuraivaam Vandhu

In the year Anandha, bad things won't happen. Rains will be good. Rice and Sugarcane will give a good yield. Castor will not give a good yield. Cereals will have low produce.

49. இராக்ஷஸ – RAKSHASHA

ராட்சதத்தில் மாரியறு மின்வானிற் றூமமெழும்
தாட்சியொடு தேயந் தயங்குமே சூட்சியுடன்
மன்னர் பயமிகுதி மாதே யுலகினிலே
யன்னமறு மென்றுணரு வாய்

விளக்கம்:

இராக்ஷஸ வருடத்தில் மழை பொய்க்கும் கேட்டிற்கு அறிகுறியான வால்நட்சத்திரம் தோன்றும். நாட்டின் வளர்ச்சி தாழ்ந்து பற்றாக்குறை அதிகரிக்கும். சூழ்ச்சியினால் அரச பொறுப்பில் இருப்போருக்கு பயம் அதிகமாகும். உணவு பற்றாக்குறை அதிகமாகும்.

Raatchadhathil Maari Arum Minvaanil Thoomam Ezhum
Thaatchiyodu Theyam Thayangumae Sootchiyudan
Mannar Bayam Migudhi Maadhae Ulagaginil
Annam Arum Endru Unaruvaai

In the year Rakshasa, rains will fail. Comets will appear indicating a bad omen. Country's growth will decline and will have shortages everywhere. Rulers will fear connivance and betrayal. Food will scarcity will be on the rise.

50. நள – NALA

சீர்தீர் நளவருடஞ் சேர்வடக்கி லேகலகம்
பாரோர் மடிவர் படையெழுச்சி காரோ
பொழியா திரத்தப் புணரி பெருகும்
அழியு மரசர் படை

விளக்கம்:

நள வருடத்தில் வடதேசத்தில் கலகம் தோன்றி மக்கள் மடிவர். படையெடுப்பு நிகழும் போர்மூழும் இரத்தம் கடல் போல பெருகும் அரசர் படை அழியும். மழை பொய்க்கும்.

Seer Theer Nala Varudam Saer Vadakkil Kalagam
Paaror Madivar Padai Ezhuchi Kaaro
Pozhiyaadhu Raththa Punari Perugum
Azhiyum Arasar Padai

In the year Nala, the countries in the northern region will have confusions and riots and as a result many will die. Army incursion will happen, war will begin, and blood will be all over the place like sea. The ruler's army will be defeated. Rains will fail.

51. பிங்கள – PINGALA

பிங்களத்திற் காவேரி யாறு பெருகியே
கொங்கவள நாட்டிற் குடியழிக்கும் மங்களமாய்த்
தென்பூமி தான்விளையுஞ் சேரும் பொருளோடு
மன்கேட தாம்வடக்கின் மற்று

விளக்கம்:

பிங்கள வருடம் காவேரி ஆற்றில் வெள்ளம் பெருகி கொங்கு தேசத்து மக்களை அழிக்கும். தெற்கு பகுதியில் நல்ல விளைச்சல் மற்றும் பொருள் சேரும். வடதேசத்தில் அரசால்வோருக்கும் மக்களுக்கும் கேடு விளையும்.

Pingalathil Kaveri Aaru Perugiyae
Kongavala Naatil Kudi Azhikkum Mangalamaai
Then Boomi Thaan Vilayum Saerum Porulodu
Mannkedu Adhaam Vadakkin Matru

In the year Pingala, the river Kaveri will overflow and destroy the people in the Kongu region. The southern regions will flourish with good harvest and richness. The rulers in the northern region and its people will suffer badly.

52. காளயுக்தி – KALAYUKTHI

காளயுத்தி யாண்டதனிற் காஞ்சியிலே பஞ்சமிகும்
காலமழை பெய்யாது காசினியில் மேலுந்
தெலுங்கத்திற் கொஞ்சமழை தென்றிசையி லின்ப
நலங்காணு மென்றே நவில்

விளக்கம்:

காளயுக்தி ஆண்டில் காஞ்சியில் பஞ்சம் உண்டாகும். காலத்தில் மழை பொழியாது. தெலுங்கு தேசத்தில் குறைவாக மழை பெய்யும். தெற்கு பகுதிகளில் நல்ல செழிப்பும் நலமுன் உண்டாகும்.

Kaalayukthi Aandathanil Kaanjiyilae Panjam Migum
Kaala Mazhai Peyyadhu Kaasiniyil Maelum
Thelungaththil Konjam Mazhai Then Disaiyil Inba
Nalam Kaanum Endrae Navil

During Kaalayukthi year, Kanchipuram region will suffer from famine. Rainfall will not be there in the right time. Telugu regions will receive some rainfall. However the southern regions will flourish and will be prosperous

53. சித்தார்த்தி – SIDDHARTHI

ஆனசித் தார்த்திதனி லற்பமழை யுண்டாகும்
ஏனல்கம் பிராச்சியத்தி லேமிகுதி ஊனமுடன்
வெட்டிமடி வாரரசர் வேற்றரசர் நாடாகும்
நட்டி வடக்கிலென்றே நாட்டு

விளக்கம்:

சித்தார்த்தி ஆண்டில் மழை மிக குறைவாக பெய்யும். நாட்டில் திணை, மற்றும் கம்பு மட்டுமே விளையும். அரசாள்பவர் ஒருவருக்கு ஒருவர் சண்டையிட்டு வெட்டி ஊனமுடன் மடிவர். வேற்று நாட்டு அரசன் இங்கு அரசாள்வான். வடக்கு பகுதியிலே பெரும் இழப்பு ஏற்படும்.

Aana Siddharthi Thanil Arpa Mazhai Undaagum
Yaenal Kambu Raajiyathilae Migudhi Oonamudan
Vetti Madivar Arasar Vetru Arasar Naadaagum
Natti Vadikilendrae Naatu

During Siddharthi year, rains will be scanty. Only millets and bajra will give good yield. The rulers will fight with each other causing injury and damage to each other and eventually die. The country will fall in the hands of the King of another state/country. The northern regions will suffer heavy damages.

54. ரௌத்திரி – ROWTHRI

மிக்க ரௌத்திரியில் வேளாண்மை யற்பமாம்
மக்கணோ யான்மடிவர் வான்பொருள்போந் தொக்க
மனக்கவலை யுற்றுழல்வர் மாதர் வடக்கிற்
கனக்க வறுமைவருங் காண்

விளக்கம்:

ரௌத்திரி ஆண்டில் வேளாண்மை பொய்க்கும் அற்ப விளைச்சலே உண்டாகும். மக்கள் நோயுற்று மடிவர். மக்களுக்கு பெருத்த பொருள் நட்டம் உண்டாகும். பெண்களுக்கு கவலை சூழும். வடநாட்டில் பெரும் வறுமை உண்டாகும்.

Mikka Rowthriyil Velaanmai Arppamaam
Makkal Noyaal Madivar Vaan Porul Pom Thokka
Manakkavalai Uttru Uzhalvar Maadhar Vadakkil
Ganakka Varumai Varum Kaan

In the year Rowthri, agriculture will have a poor yield. People will die of diseases. There will be heavy loss to property. Women will become gloomy and sad. The northern part of the country will see a huge scarcity of resources.

55. துன்மதி – DHUNMADHI

துன்மதியின் மாரியற்பஞ் சோகமுறுங் கீழ்சாதி
நன்மையில்லை மத்தியநன் னாடுதனில்
உண்மையாக்
கொண்டுதுங்க பத்ரிமுதற் கோதா விரியளவும்
விண்டுபஞ்ச மாகி விடும்

விளக்கம்:

துன்மதி ஆண்டில் மழை சொற்பமாகப் பெய்யும். கீழ்
சாதியை சேர்ந்தோர் சோகம் அடைவர். மத்திய
நன்னாட்டிலே நன்மை உண்டாகாது. துங்கபத்ரை நதி
முதல் கோதாவிரி நதி வரை பஞ்சம் தலைவிரித்து ஆடும்.

Dhunmadhiyil Maari Arpam Sogamurum Keezh Saadhi
Nanmai Illai Madhya Nannaadu Thanil Unmaiyaak
Kondu Thungbadhri Mudhal Godaviri Alavum
Vindu Panjamaagi Vidum

In the year Dhunmadhi, rains will be scanty. The lower caste will become worried. There won't be goodness happening in the middle region of the country. Especially, the region from River Thungabadra to River Godavari will experience a worse famine.

56. துந்துபி – DHUNDHUBHI

துந்துபியின் மிக்கசுப சோபனமுண் டாம்புவியில்
சந்ததமும் வாசமலர்த் தாமரைமேல் இந்திரையும்
செல்வ மிகக்கொடுப்பாள் செந்நெல்விளை
வுண்டாகுமே
நல்லமழை யுண்டு நவில்

விளக்கம்:

துந்துபி ஆண்டில் உலகில் நிறைய நற்செயல்களும் நன்மைகளும் சேரும். வருடம் முழுதும் திருமகள் அருளால் செல்வம் மிகுதியாக கிடைக்கும். நெல் நன்கு விளையும் நல்ல மழையும் பெய்யும்

Dhundhubhiyil Mikka Sobanam Undam Puviyil
Sandhadhamum Vaasamalar Thaamaraimel Indhiraiyum
Selvam Miga Koduppaal Sennell Vilaivu Undaagumae
Nalla Mazhai Undu Navil

In the year Dhundhubhi, everything will be very good for the whole world. The Goddess of Wealth (Lakshmi) will bestow all the wealth. Rice will grow well and rainfall will be abundant.

57. ருத்ரோத்காரி – RUDRODHKAARI

ஆருத் திரோற்காரி ய:கங் குறையுமே
மாறியற்பஞ் சோரபய மாகுமே பாரிற்
கடைமாரி பெய்யுங் கனவித்து நன்றாய்த்
தடையறவே யுண்டாகுந் தான்

விளக்கம்:

ருத்ரோத்காரி வருடம் யாகங்கள் குறையும். வருட
முற்பகுதியில் மழை குறைவாக பெய்யும். திருடர் பயம்
அதிகமாகும். வருட பிற்பகுதியில் மழை நன்கு பெய்யும்.
கரும்பு முதலிய கனமான வித்துக்கள் நல்ல விளைச்சல்
தரும்.

Rudhrodhkaari Yaagam Kuraiyumae
Maari Arpaam Sora Bayamaagumae Paaril
Kadaimaari Peyyum Ganaviththu Nandraai
Thadaiyaravae Undaagum Thaan

In the year Rudhrodhkaari, spiritual activities like yaagams will be on the decline. The earlier part of the year will not receive good rainfall. People will fear thievery and thieves. The later part of the year will see good rains and thick crops like sugarcane will give a good yield

58. ரத்தாக்ஷி – RATHTHAAKSHI

ரத்தாக்ஷி யாண்டதனி னாற்சாதிக்கும் பயமாம்
மெத்தமழை யுண்டு விளைவுண்டு இத்தரையில்
வேந்தர் பகைத்திடுவார் வெய்யதெற்கு வாரிதியிற்
சார்ந்தபஞ்ச மாய்விடுமே தான்

விளக்கம்:

ரத்தாக்ஷி ஆண்டில் அனைத்து சாதி மக்களும் பயம் கொள்ளுமாறு சூழ்நிலைகள் அமையும். மழையும் விளைவும் நன்கு இருக்கும். அரசாள்பவர் பகை கொள்வர். தேசத்தின் தெற்கு கடலோர பகுதிகளில் பஞ்சம் வரும்

Raththaakshi Aandathanil Naal Saadhikkum Bayamaam
Meththa Mazhai Undu Vilaivundu Iththaraiyil
Vendhar Pagaithidhuvar Veyya Therkku Vaaridhiyil
Saarndha Panjamaaividum

In the year Raththaakshi, all the people irrespective of caste, creed and status will have a fearful life. Rains and agricultural harvest will be good. Rulers will show enmity. The southern coastal regions will suffer from famine and scarcity.

59. குரோதன – KURODHANA

குரோதனத்திற் பஞ்சமாங் கூர்ச்சரதே சத்தில்
விரோதத்தால் வேந்தர் மெலிவர் உரோருகத்து
மானேதென் பூமி மகிழுந் திடமுடனே
தானே விளைவுமுண்டு தான்

விளக்கம்:

குரோதன ஆண்டில் குஜராத்தில் பஞ்சம் வரும். அரசாள்பவர் விரோதம் கொண்டு பலம் இழப்பர். தெற்குப்பகுதி நன்கு செழிப்பாகவும் நல்ல விளைச்சளுடனும் இருக்கும் அப்பகுதி மக்கள் மகிழ்வுடன் இருப்பர்.

Kurodhanaththil Panjamaam Koorchara Desaththil
Virodhaththaal Vendhar Melivar Urorugaththu
Maanae Thenn Boomi Magizhum Dhidamudanae
Thaanae Vilaivum Undu Thaan

In the year Kurodhana, Gujarat will face famine and scarcity. Rulers will become powerful because of the animosity and the fights. The southern regions will be fertile with good harvests and people will be happy.

60. அக்ஷய – AKSHAYA

மானேகே எஷயத்தின் மாரியற்ப மானாலுந்
தானே நலமுண்டு தாரணியில் வானூருங்
கார்பொழியும் வேளாண்மை கானமெங்குந்
தோன்றுமே
சீர்பொழிய வோங்கும் திரு

விளக்கம்:

அக்ஷய ஆண்டில் முற்பகுதியில் மழை குறைவாக
பெய்தாலும் நலம்பயக்கும். வருடபிற்பகுதியில் நல்ல
மழை பெய்யும் விவசாயம் தழைக்கும். காடுகள்
செழிப்புறும். மொத்தத்தில் செல்வம் கொழிக்கும் ஆண்டு

Maanae Kael Akshayathil Maari Arpam Aanaalum
Thaanae Nalamundu Thaaraniyil Vaanoorum
Kaar Pozhiyum Velaanmai Kaanam Engum Thondrumae
Seer Pozhiya Ongum Thiru

In the year Akshaya, though the rains will be inadequate, the benefits will be derived. In the later part of the year, rains will be abundant and as a result agriculture will give a good yield, forests will flourish and things will be progressive in this year.

www.ingramcontent.com/pod-product-compliance
Lightning Source LLC
Chambersburg PA
CBHW051342280526
45784CB00007B/2775